Fraud in Education: Beyond the Wrong Answer

FRAUD IN EDUCATION:
BEYOND THE WRONG ANSWER

Tonya J. Mead, MBA, MA

Certified Fraud Examiner, Compliance Agent, Private Investigator

ISBN: 1539301842
ISBN 13: 9781539301844

EXECUTIVE SUMMARY

"Grand jury votes second superseding indictment charging five with conspiracy to murder overseas" is a recent headline based upon a FBI investigation where one defendant attempted to use $5,000 in student financial aid to fund travel overseas [47, para 1]. The purpose of the trip was to commit murder on behalf of the Islamic State of Iraq and the Levant [47, para 3]. While education aid and grant money obtained by fraud to commit violent crime and support terrorism may not be the norm, researchers are beginning to find that "white-collar criminals do display violent tendencies and, contrary to popular belief, can become dangerous individuals" [48, para 3].

How can we protect ourselves, and more importantly our children? By learning more about the existence of white collar and related crime in the education sector. This book serves to do just that. The U.S. Department of Education defines fraud as deceit or trickery involving U.S. Department of Education funds or programs [1]. Fraud and misuse of federal and state funds can implicate employees, grant recipients, pre-k, elementary, secondary, post- secondary, career and technical education, vendors, contractors, collection agencies, loan servicers and lending institutions.

The educational system comprising pre-school, k-12, and post-secondary schools, colleges, and universities is one of the largest industries in the United States. Collectively, "the 50 states and the District of Columbia reported $603.7 billion in funding collected for public elementary and secondary education" [2, para 8]. State and local governments generally provide "91 percent of all funding" for education [2, para 8], leaving the remaining 9 percent of discretionary spending approximating $70 billion provided by the federal government in the form of Title I, Title IV and IDEA grants [3]. For an idea of the largest of the education system, in the fall 2014, about 75.2 million people were enrolled in 100,000 American schools and 7,200 colleges and universities taught by 4.6 million teachers and faculty. They are in turn supported by 5.3 million administrators and staff [4].

The threat of fraud increases as the perception grows of easy money flowing into and out of the coffers of education. Students have filed up to $40 million in lawsuits alleging the payment of tuition for classes that were never held and the falsification of records to "enroll them and keep them enrolled so that government grant and loan dollars would keep flowing "[5][6][7]. Harvard University conducted an inquiry in 2010 of scientific misconduct concerning problems of "data acquisition, data analysis, data retention and the reporting of research methodologies, and results" [8]. The Chair, Afro-American Studies at the University of North Carolina-Chapel Hill faced fraud charges for teaching 200 "no show" classes over a 15-year period [9]. An El Paso Superintendent was sentenced for contract fraud and data manipulation [10]. An Ohio Auditor charged Columbus City Schools District Superintendent for presiding over a culture of data manipulation which alleged changing grades, deleting absences and falsifying the number of dropouts. The allegations escalated to FBI investigations of possible fraud and misappropriation of federal funds [11]. Auditors in Washington, DC found that schools failed to maintain internal controls over graduation requirements [12] and special education [13]; Detroit, for vendor fraud [14] and Miami Dade County for theft and scholarship fraud [15]. Data tampering extends to scientific research with estimates up to 65% of retractions "due to misconduct" [16]. The failure of universities to control data led to "$222 million in overpayments to more than 42,000 distance education students who did not earn any credits during the payment period" [17]. In 2012, a former El Paso district superintendent was sentenced to four years imprisonment, $56,600 in fines, and $180,000 in restitution for contract fraud and data manipulation. Secondary educators were indicted for racketeering and sentenced for up to 11 years imprisonment in a landmark case of educator cheating on standardized tests.

As mentioned, fraud in education can even threaten national security. Immigration and student visa fraud have been directly implicated in the 9/11 bombings. To date, ICE officers have reported that "approximately 36 convicted terrorists cams to the country using various forms of student visas" [169, p. 11].

These headlines, prison convictions, and terrorist cells posing as students sound alarms in the staid education community. They have implications for: (a) teacher certification programs as they prepare educator entrants for this new landscape; (b) education administrators as they conduct job-embedded training programs for ethics and integrity; (c) policy-makers and regulators as they refine policy guidance and regulations to address the harsh realities; (d) information technology companies and specialists as they work to design, manage, and maintain data systems while safeguarding confidential data; and (e) investigators in search of motive, intent, and means to build sound theories for cases leading to prosecution and resolution.

Keywords: educator fraud, assessment, teacher preparation, visa and immigration fraud, false claims, fraudulent, misrepresentations, data tampering, test security, fraud prism, fraud triangle, misconduct, corruption, white collar crime, fraud diamond, ethics.

Occupational Fraud

Occupational fraud occurs "when an employee abuses the trust placed in him or her by an employer for personal gain" [18, p.6]. Why does it occur? It largely results from a response to pressures to do "whatever it takes to meet goals, to seek personal gain." Criminals rationalize that the act is not illegal and victimless [19, p.6]. However, in a "legal sense, victimless crimes do not exist because crimes are acts that injure society, organizations, and/or individuals" [20].

Regulators in education have yet to broaden or define educator fraud and cheating with specificity such that the risks are fully explored. There were futile attempts in the early 2000s to present an expos of corruption occurring in education by Segal [21] and Fusco [22] but failed to take hold.

Criminologists have yet to create a formalized occupational fraud category for educators industry-wide to address the individual actor and organizational dysfunction leading to corruption or to present an educator fraud paradigm to researchers, academia and educators. Nor have scientists examined the precipitating factors underpinning an organizational environment present in victim schools and colleges making them ripe targets for criminals to assail.

The Fraud Diamond

Image 1. The Fraud Diamond

Criminal behavior is learned [23] in association with others who have criminal attitudes and values. How are these attitudes developed? For white collar crime [24], the literature draws upon the "Fraud Diamond" showing four factors: rationalization, incentive, opportunity, and capability. Wolfe coined the term "The Fraud Diamond" [25] to summarize perpetrator rationalizations that the act is not illegal or that "everyone is doing it;" [26, p. 30-31]. An incentive presents a motive, a perceived opportunity; and capability, the potential criminal's assessment as to whether he/she has the skills to commit the crime without being noticed [27].

While the Fraud Diamond [28], the Fraud Triangle [29] and the Fraud Scale [30] are universally accepted concepts for describing the motives for fraud, as the concept has evolved [31], they are insufficient for analyzing fraud perpetrated by educators. They are inadequate for evaluating why schools and universities are targets for white collar criminals. Therefore, the Fraud Prism [32] has been developed to address these deficiencies. The Fraud Prism is three dimensional and is viewed through an enforcement risk lens (composite discovery, enforcement, and prosecution) which has the power to bend one's perception of rationalization, incentive, opportunity, and capability. All are discussed in greater in Chapter 3 of this book.

Insider or Internal Fraud

Insider, internal or occupational fraud can be perpetrated by a malicious insider with authorized and/or unauthorized access to an organization's network, system, or data. The inside access or knowledge about internal systems and processes within an organization is then intentionally exceeded or misused. The misuse, mismanagement of information negatively affects the confidentiality, integrity, or availability of the organization's information or information systems. Information obtained maliciously by an insider can be used for financial gain or sabotage [33].

In the business, non-profit, and private sectors, typical schemes for conducting occupational fraud have been categorized into three main areas: misappropriation of assets; corruption by way of misuse of influence for personal gain; and financial statement misrepresentation [34].

Collusion

Collusion occurs when two or more people agree in secret to defraud someone or to take something illegally. The Association of Certified Fraud Examiners [35] estimates that about 80% of financial losses from insider fraud involve collusion, even though collusion cases represented 45% of all fraud cases reported.

Educational Institutions as Victims (Outsider or External Fraud)

Schools, colleges and universities are ripe targets for white collar criminals and fraudsters. The Association of Chief Police Officers in the United Kingdom define external fraud as actions "perpetrated by individuals outside of the organization and covers activities such as theft, deception and computer hacking." Outsider fraud perpetrated against individuals or organization is "the result of inadequate safeguards" [36].

Purpose and Introduction

This book is divided into four parts. Part One focuses on fraud in education. Part Two emphasizes the negligent handling of data. Part Three offers a new paradigm called the *Fraud Prism*™ used to explain fraud, manipulation of data, and negligent disclosure of confidential data. Part Four presents solutions for deterring, detecting, investigating, and resolving fraud, computer and data-related crime.

There are numerous societal factors associated with increased fraud, computer, and data-related crime in the education sector. Even so, criminologists have yet to create a model to explain this phenomenon. For instance, teacher preparation programs are ill-equipped to prepare future educators, education administrators lack ethics and integrity training, and educational institutions lack the commitment to establish policies, procedures and systems to combat fraud and computer-related crimes.

Criminologists have not yet formulated an occupational fraud category unique to the education sector for addressing individual and organizational dysfunction that leads to corruption. Nor have scientists examined the precipitating factors existing in the organizational environment that make victim schools ripe targets to assail. For two years, the education industry has ranked fifth in the top 10 list [37] [38].

Industry	2012	2010	Growth Rate
Banking and Financial Services	16.7	16.6	6%
Government and Public Administration	10.3	9.8	11%
Manufacturing	10.1	10.7	9%
Health Care	6.7	5.9	19%
Education	6.4	5.0	26%

Table 2. Top 5 Industries of Reported Fraud Cases: 2010 and 2012
Source: Association of Certified Fraud Examiners, Global Fraud, 2010 and 2012

Fraud Research by Academia

Researchers and scholars are beginning to take notice of the heightened threat of education fraud as exhibited by the frequency of citations appearing in Google Scholar. This author utilized internet word searches in two popular search engines, "Google Web/URL" and "Google Scholar." The words "education fraud" ranked twelfth in the general interest search engine "Google Web/URL." The same phrase, however, considerably higher (fourth rank) in "Google Scholar." Google Scholar is becoming a viable method for sourcing research materials. When Google Scholar and Thomson ISI Web of Science were analyzed for the generation of citations and scholarly contributions the output of the two sources were comparable. [39]. Another study found that Google Scholar search results were more comprehensive than Thompson Institute for Scientific Information for computer and social science disciplines [40].

Rank	Industry	Google URL	Rank	Industry	Google Scholar
1	Financial Fraud	237,000,000	1	Financial Fraud	801,000
2	Government Fraud	236,000,000	2	Government Fraud	770,000
3	Contract Fraud	180,000,000	3	Bank Fraud	484,000
4	Health Care Fraud	159,000,000	4	Education Fraud	414,000
5	Nonprofit Fraud	22,000,000	5	Contract Fraud	339,000
6	Insurance Fraud	20,700,000	6	Insurance Fraud	290,000
7	Retail Fraud	19,200,000	7	Tax Fraud	288,000
8	Consumer Fraud	16,600,000	8	Health Care Fraud	280,000
9	Bank Fraud	14,500,000	9	Consumer Fraud	228,000
10	Tax Fraud	14,400,000	10	Securities Fraud	138,000
10	Securities Fraud	14,400,000	11	Retail Fraud	76,800
11	Mortgage Fraud	12,700,000	12	Mortgage Fraud	51,700
12	Education Fraud	11,300,000	13	Nonprofit Fraud	34,400

Table 3. Google Word and Citation Searches: Fraud by Industry
Source: Google URL/Web and Google Scholar Searches conducted 8/16/2015

Threat to National Security

The United States Government Accountability Office conducted a review of the Student and Exchange Visitor Program (SEVP) which authorizes 850,000 active foreign students to enroll in over 10,000 certified schools in the US and determined that SEVP

"(1) does not evaluate program data on prior and suspected instances of school fraud and noncompliance, and (2) does not obtain and assess information from the Counterterrorism and Criminal Exploitation Unit (CTCEU) and ICE (U.S. Immigration Custom's Enforcement) field school investigations and outreach events" [174, p.2].

Immigration and student visa fraud has been directly linked to the 9/11 bombings. To date, ICE officers have reported that "approximately 36 convicted terrorists came to the country using various forms of student visas" [165, p. 11].

Accountability Systems

Taxpayers have become frustrated with the lack of stringent accountability systems to thwart the mismanagement, waste, and abuse of publicly-financed institutions. So much so that reformists and educational advocates are pushing for the application of fiduciary duties to extend beyond the business managers in pre-k to 12 schools and chief financial officers employed by universities to "school boards, administrators, teachers, staff, policy-makers, and laypersons to varying degrees; that is anyone who comes in contact with school resources in some manner" [41, p. 112].

Detrimental Effects on Student Outcomes

Regardless of the continent or country in which fraud and corruption occurs, it has detrimental effects on student outcomes. For instance, Segal [42] notes that the "consequences of fraud and waste on learning can be devastating." Based upon her research, Segal concluded that "the most academically beleaguered school systems tend to be the ones with the longest, most serious, most systematic investigative records." The same is true globally.

Ferraz et. al [43] examined federal education misappropriation data from Brazil's local governments and determined that fund leakages impacted educational attainment. Student data from 56 countries participating in the Program for International Student Assessment (PISA) showed that reductions in educational resources resulting from funding misappropriations also reduced educational quality. "There was a strong negative association between a country's corruption level and its performance on the international standardized exams" [44].

Lifelong Threat from Identity Theft

A review of the literature illustrates the numerous societal factors associated with increased occurrences of fraud, data breaches, computer and data-related crime in the education sector. Even so, criminologists have yet to create a model to explain this phenomenon. The primary purpose of this presentation is to present a new paradigm called the *Fraud Prism*™ to explain fraud, data, and computer-related crime in the education sector and their underlying causes, deterrence methods leading to better investigations, and prevention measures.

Registration and financial aid subsidies in pre-school, elementary, secondary and post-secondary levels require the submission of confidential student and family information. The potential for severe harm is considerable. As such, criminals may "purposely target children because of the often lengthy time between the fraudulent use of the child's information and the discovery of the crime" [45, p.1] (ITRC Fact Sheet 120, 2015, p.1).

The threat of child identity theft is so severe that the Federal Trade Commission (FTC) provided information stating that, "a child's social security number can be used by identity thieves to apply for government benefits, open bank and credit card accounts, apply for a loan or utility service, or rent a place to live..." [50]. The FTC urges consumers to take **immediate action** if their child's information is being misused.

PART ONE

FRAUD IN EDUCATION

Fraud in Education Represents a Global Problem

Daniel Guhr, an expert cited by Elizabeth Redden, *Inside Higher Education* has remarked, "fraud in international higher education is a $1.5 billion to $2.5 billion business" [47]. Fraud schemes in higher education include aggravated identity theft, forged academic documents, plagiarism, proxy testing on standardized exams, fraudulently- obtained visas, purchased credentials, and bribery.

After analyzing enrollment, admissions fraud, document forgery, and diploma mills, Tobenkin asserted that the "United States is the nexus of fraudulent activity" [48, p. 35]. Criminals residing in Nigeria and China, for instance, use the United States to perpetrate fraud. This unenviable position as the number one hotbed for fraud is attributed to weak regulations and lenient enforcement of current laws.

Ferraz et. al [49] examined federal education misappropriation data from Brazil's local government and determined that fund leakages and kickbacks impacted educational attainment. Student data from 56 countries participating in the Program for International Student Assessment (PISA) showed that reductions in educational resources resulting from funding misappropriations also reduced educational quality. "There was a strong negative association between a country's corruption level and its performance on the international standardized exams" [50].

To further illustrate how factors in international corruption are applicable to education, Klitgaard [51, p.4] developed the following formula,

Corruption (C) = (M) Monopoly Power + (D) Discretion by officials − (A) Accountability

"Lubrication payments are not subject to the going rate. They are usually determined by what the traffic will bear" [52]. Research appearing in the Journal of Education for

International Development estimated that "leakage of funds from ministries of education to schools represent more than **80% of the total sums** allocated (non-salary expenditures) in some countries... **the problems posted by corruption in education have been neglected for too long**" [53][54].

Global fraud and corruption impact American taxpayers. After a number of years in decline, in 2005, the State Department announced an annual commitment of $15 billion in education allocations [55, p. 107]. U.S. federal government spending for foreign aid to fund education scholarships alone was estimated at $1 billion in 2005 [56, p. 108].

Anti-fraud and corruption internal controls are needed to prevent foreign aid leakages. "International development agencies need to strengthen the access of developing countries to data on education and health. Currently, the collection and quality-control mechanisms are deeply flawed" [57]. Hallak and Poisson issued this concluding statement, "It is clear that the fight against corruption in the specific sphere of education should be regarded as a **major priority** as it affects not only the volume of educational services, including their quality and efficiency, but also equity in education and public confidence in educational systems"[58] [59].

Fiscal Irresponsibility in Education on the Rise in the United States

Fund leakages, fiscal irresponsibility, and poor management are not confined to entities operating in countries in need of U.S. financial aid to support education. Internally, organizations obtaining U.S. funds and operating in the United States experience similar symptoms fostering an environment where fraud festers. "As of December 1, 540 colleges or universities were facing the extra scrutiny known as heightened cash monitoring, up from 499 in September, when the department last reported the figures" [169, para. 2]. Seventy-seven new institutions were added to the list, representing an overall 10% increase from the previous quarter. This occurred even after 35 colleges were removed due to improved performance. While a clear majority of the institutions listed were domestic, 8 of the institutions listed in the original March 2015, list were based in the United Kingdom [170].

"Collectively, the institutions on the monitoring list received nearly $8 billion in student loans and grants from the federal government last year alone, an Inside Higher Ed analysis of federal records found" [169, para 4].

The list was not publically disclosed until March 2015. The U.S. Department of Education citing 'substantial competitive injury' ultimately relented after receiving several requests from American taxpayers, investigative journalists and media outlets such as Inside Higher Education [171, para 10]. For a complete list prepared by the U.S.

Department of Education, visit Appendix A for Table of Institutions on Heightened Monitoring List as of 6-1-2016 [172].

The inflation of administrative staff as a portion of the number of students and faculty is another component of fiscal irresponsibility. The New England Center for Investigative Reporting analyzed staffing data from 1987 to 2011 and determined that "universities and colleges collectively added 517,636 administrators and professional employees, or an average of 87 every working day" [173, para 3]. For percentage changes in staffing changes by university, visit Appendix B, Table of US College Staffing Changes [173].

Institutions of higher learning are not the only entities with problems related to fiscal irresponsibility, poor management, and porous internal control systems. During the course of routine A-133 audits, independent auditors examined the internal records of primary and secondary schools as grantees of the U.S. Department of Education (cfda 84.0). During the August 2014 to December 2015 reporting period, a number of entities (26) were cited for significant deficiencies and material weaknesses. For a complete list, visit Appendix C for Table of Schools and Districts with Significant Deficiencies and Material Weaknesses as of 12-31-2015 [174].

Fraud in Education: A Growing Problem in the United States

Fraud is defined as a white collar crime involving: a misrepresentation of a material fact, made knowingly with the intent to deceive. The victim relied upon the misrepresentation ultimately resulting in injury or damage. "Weak internal controls, poor management oversight, and/or the use of one's position and authority" present opportunities to commit fraud [175, p. 2].

The perpetrator's deceptive intentions are often the hardest element to prove, even for criminologists. A further complication is academia's proclivity to debate the abstract ad infinitum. To compound the problem, "few statistics are kept, including by national associations, and many numbers floated tend to be guesstimates" [60, p. 36].

There were only 6 cases reported to the U.S. Department of Education Office of Inspector General in 1999 [61]. By 2013, the number of suspected cases increased **tenfold** to 65 leading to the successful prosecution of 96 defendants and attempted recovery of $94 million [62]. By 2014, the number of cases dropped precipitously to 37, though the number of defendants held steady at 85. Interestingly, the amount of potential losses for recovery totaled $163.6 million, a 70% increase. The number of actual cases prosecuted as a result of fraud crimes in education excludes many more that were investigated though not brought to trial.

For instance, the Office of Inspector General opened just 16 investigations into suspected student loan fraud in 2005. By 2012, the figure increased substantially to 119 [63]. Further, the tally excludes the $219.3 million in false claims settlements brought by the US Securities and Exchange Commission, and other state and local enforcement agencies as referenced in Image 30 in a succeeding chapter of this book. For these reasons, the number may appear low. The Center for Popular Democracy tallied $203 million in waste, fraud, and abuse in the charter schools alone [64]. This represented more than a 40% increase from the previous year. Cases of mismanagement, fraud, and abuse in education often go unreported as alluded to by Tobenkin [65]. Educator fraud cases often resulted in disciplinary actions; reprimands, suspensions, loss of license and job [66].

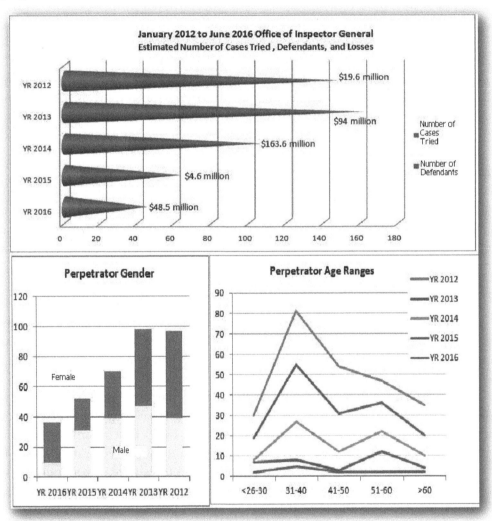

Image 4. Estimated Fraud Cases, Defendant Demographics and Losses in Education 2012-2016 [67]
Source: Office of Inspector General, U.S. Department of Education: 1999-2016

While the tables and charts above are perhaps the most definitive compilation and analysis of fraud crimes in the education sector, there are limitations to the data. Of the 157 cases brought to trial and tallied, 16 cases lacked a complete listing of defendant gender, age, or employee status. This made it difficult to cross reference the data through the years and reconcile for quality. Further in some instances, an investigation in one year could yield several individual cases that were independently tried in subsequent years. Added complications centered on plea- bargain agreements before cases were brought to trial.

Perpetrator Threats
An in-depth analysis of the Investigation Reports published during the periods of January 2012 to June 2016, U.S. Department of Education, Office of the Inspector General revealed that 63% of the cases were perpetrated by insider threats and 36% were from outsiders [67].

Insider Demographics
The Association of Certified Fraud Examiners defines internal, or insider, fraud as "the use of one's occupation for personal enrichment through the deliberate misuse or misapplication of the employing organization's resources or assets" [68 p. 1]. In evaluating the January 2012 to June 2016 insider threats for fraud in education, 72% of the crimes were committed by C-Suite executives such as chief executive officers, district superintendents of traditional schools, educational testing services, career academies, tutoring companies, and charter schools. Twenty-one percent of the insider fraud crimes were committed by mid-level managers and technical experts such as contracting officers, district accountants, financial aid advisors, and teachers. In seven percent of the insider cases, fraud crimes were committed by lower-level employees, such as tutors and temporaries. Regarding losses, the estimated dollar amount fraudulently obtained during this period was $330,582,986 million [69].

The table below provides a listing of the types of insider cases by charges for the January 2012 to June 2016 period. The charts illustrate insider demographics. These images exclude cases of filing false claims and for making material misstatements settled by the US Justice Department and the US Securities and Exchange Commission. Kaplan settled with the Justice Department to refund $1 million in tuition to 289 students [71]. ATI Enterprises, a chain of schools agreed to a $3.7 million payout for filing false claims [72]. The Securities and Exchange Commission charged ITT [73] and Corinthian College [74] for making material misstatements in their disclosures to investors and auditors. References to larger false claims settlements can be found on Image 30.

All Insider Charges	Count
Conspiracy to commit Program Fraud (7) to commit Mail Fraud (6) to Launder Money (4) to conspire to Defraud (3) to commit Bribery, accept Kickbacks and/or Rig bids (3) to Steal government funds (2) to commit Mail and Wire Fraud (2) to commit Financial Aid Fraud (2) to commit an Offense against the US (1) to Embezzle (1) to commit Wire Fraud (1) to commit Tax Fraud (1)	33
Theft	22
Tax charges, Tax Evasion, Corporate Tax Evasion, Filing a False Tax Return	16
Mail Fraud	13
Embezzlement	12
Accepting/paying Bribery, accepting/offering Kickbacks, making Corrupt payments	11
Submitting False Claims (False claims act)	11
Fraud	8
Obstruction of justice, obstruction of federal audit	8
Wire Fraud	7
False Statements	7
Student Financial Aid Fraud	6
Federal Program/Grant Fraud	5
False Certification, falsified corporate books and student records	5
Forgery	3
Money Laundering	3
Bank Fraud	2
Stealing and/or Mishandling	2
Bank Fraud	2
Stealing and/or Mishandling	2
Unlawful Conversion of school funds	2
Witness Tampering	2
Cashing of checks to fictitious vendors	1
Illegally accepting benefits	1
Cheating on state exam	1

Conflict of interest	1
Deprivation of Honest Services	1
Engaging in monetary transaction in property derived from unlawful activity	1
Enrollment Fraud	1
Failure to return federal funds	1
Felony Ethics	1
Felony Fraud	1
Foreign Student Visa Fraud	1
Larceny	1
Misprision of a felony	1
Operating and participating in a criminal enterprise	1

7 Lower Level Employees
20 Mid-Level Managers
69 C- Suite Executives

OIG Fraud Cases Demographics January 2012 to June 216

Insiders 61%
Outsiders 39%

Table 4. Types of Insider Cases: By Charges 2012- 2016 [70]
Source: Office of Inspector General, U.S. Department of Education, 2012- 2016

Public's Perception of Educators

The historical public perception of the educators has been exceptionally high, making the detection and prosecution of crimes committed by educators difficult. In 2013, Gallup conducted a random sample poll of 1,031 adults to determine the public's perception of honesty and ethical integrity across professions [76]. Seventy percent of the respondents, when asked to rate the ethical standards of people in different fields using a 5 point Likert scale, rated nurses at the top of the list. Tying in second place were grade school educators and pharmacists.

2013 Rank	%	Profession	2014 Rank	%	Profession
1	82	Nurses	1	80	Nurses
2	70	Pharmacists	2	65	Medical Doctors
2	70	Grade School Teachers	2	65	Pharmacists
3	69	Medical Doctors	3	48	Police Officers
4	69	Military Officers	4	46	Clergy
4	54	Police Officers	5	23	Bankers
5	47	Clergy	6	21	Lawyers
6	46	Day care providers	7	17	Business executives
7	45	Judges	8	10	Advertising practitioners
8	32	Nursing home operators	9	8	Car salespeople
9	29	Auto mechanics	10	7	Members of Congress
10	27	Bankers			
11	23	Local officeholders			
12	22	Business executives			
13	21	Newspaper reporters			
14	20	Lawyers			
15	20	TV reporters			
16	14	Advertising practitioners			
17	11	State officeholders			
18	9	Car salespeople			
19	8	Members of Congress			
20	6	Lobbyists			

Table 5. 2013 and 2014 Gallup Poll of Honesty in Professions: A Comparison [77]
Source: T. Mead (2015). Longitudinal Comparison of Gallup Poll for
Honesty in Professions. Unpublished Manuscript.

A comparison of the 2014 Gallup Poll [78] results with its predecessor brings about a striking difference. As public outcries of fraud in education, standardized exam cheating, and "no show classes" abound, the education profession fell from the top ten.

Education Industry Susceptible to Criminals

The way in which humans act in a given setting, the underlying trigger, cause, and the meanings inferred have been of considerable interest to researchers. The relationship among variables and categories of attributes within social systems are highly complex. Causality is difficult to determine in the study of organizational behavior [79]. Moreover, Barnes [80, p.20] discerned, "fraud is not a random event." Outsider and insider criminals, target their victim organizations based upon the industry sector, size, and type. In fact, Wortley [81] and Cornish and Clarke [82] argue that situations not only make the commission of a crime easier, but they can even precipitate, or cause crime to occur. As cited by Wortley,

> "The first stage of the model involves situational forces that precipitate criminal conduct. Behavior may be entirely avoided if relevant situational precipitators are adequately controlled. In the event that behavior is initiated, then, in the second state of the model, performance of that behavior is subject to consideration of the costs and benefits that are likely to follow" [83, p.46].

A few of the environmental conditions such as industry upheaval and collusion are discussed in this chapter. For an extensive review of situational factors, please refer to chapter two and three.

Constant Change and Upheaval

An insider may carry out a fraud scam in an environment where, "unbridled empowerment leads to a control-adverse style and increased fraud" [84, p. 40]. Structural upheavals present a window of opportunity for criminals. Burgess [85], Clifford Shaw and Henry McKay [86] utilized the theory of social disorganization to describe increased incidents of crime in transition zones. Recent research posits that the likelihood of crime increases in environments undergoing rapid transformation [87]. As the education industry on all levels experiences major upheavals across functions (human resources, technology, data, instructional learning, data management), sectors (public and private reform) and mediums (brick and mortar versus online), it is not an exception to this observation.

Collusion at Senior Levels

In addition to structural change, the attitudes and behaviors of high-level authorities can prevent or exacerbate fraudulent activities. The Treadway Commission [88] states that "historically most major frauds are perpetrated by senior management in collusion with other employees" [89, p. 5]. In fact in its report, the AICPA has found that "many financial statement frauds have been perpetrated by intentional override by senior management of what might otherwise appear to be effective internal controls" [90, p.1]. Internal controls may be breached with ease when the fraud has been carried out by executives with access to privileged data and technology.

Examples of collusion and corruption at senior levels involve principals and education service providers conspiring to commit federal program bribery, aiding and abetting, and conspiracy to launder money intended to reform the lowest performing schools. As an example, a principal admitted to "funneling public school funds to nearly 1,000 consultants, local businesses, parents, family and friends" [176, para. 15]. The vendor implicated was charged with billing the Detroit Public Schools (DPS) $2.7 million "for school supplies that were never delivered with the help of principals who approved his phony invoices in exchange for kickbacks" [177, para. 10]. Ultimately 14 people were charged. In a separate case, an art gallery owner, a former executive director of the DPS Risk Management Department, and nine others were indicted for bilking $3.3 million from the Detroit Public Schools through a sham wellness program" [176, para 20]. On the east coast, a former District of Columbia Public Schools (DCPS) employee uncovered $19.4 million in contract overruns charged to DCPS by Chartwells for student food service from 2008 to 2012 leading to a qui tam suit.

Outsider Demographics

The National Working Group on Fraud, on behalf of the United Kingdom Association of Chief Police Officers (ACPO) defines external, or outsider fraud as "fraud which is perpetrated by individuals outside of the organization and covers activities such as theft, deception, and computer hacking" [91, p. 1]. The Association of Certified Fraud Examiners adds that external fraud is committed by third parties to include vendors, contractors or individuals [92]. Thirty-nine percent of the fraud cases in education that were ultimately brought to trial by the U.S. Department of Education, Office of the Inspector General resulted from outsider fraud. Within this outsider pool, 46 percent were lone actors, 39 percent operated in a ring or group, while 15 percent involved family members (husband/wife or mom/dad and son/daughter combinations) [93].

All Outsider Charges	Count
Financial Aid Fraud	37
Mail Fraud	14
Wire Fraud	11
Aggravated Identity Theft	7
Making False Statements	7
Identity theft, use of False Identification, Use Identity of another person	6
Conspiracy to commit Wire Fraud	4
Conspiracy to commit Student Loan Fraud	4
Conspiracy to commit Mail Fraud	4
Conspiracy to commit Financial Aid Fraud	3
Filed false federal tax returns	3
Bank Fraud	3
Mail Fraud	2
Theft of public funds from financial student aid and public property	2
Forged documents	2
Recruitment of straw students	2
Perjury	2
Conspiracy to defraud the US	2
Benefits Fraud	1
Fraud	1
Felon in Possession of a Firearm	1
Mishandling and Stealing	1
Mortgage Fraud	1
False Misrepresentation	1
Larceny	1
Conspiracy to access Florida A&M computer	1
Concealment	1
Conspiracy to Murder overseas	1
Conspiracy to provide material support to designated terrorist organization	1
Filed fraudulent financial info, False claims	1
Conspiracy	1

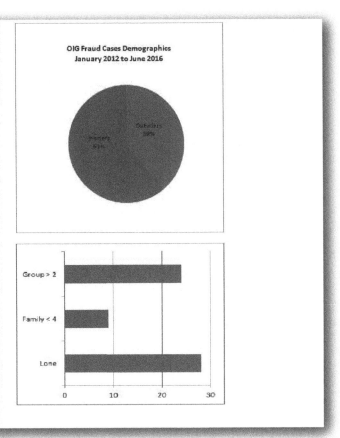

Table 6. Types of Outsider Cases: By Charges 2012- 2016 [93]
Source: Office of Inspector General, U.S. Department of Education, 2012-2016

Admissions Fraud

In 2014, 12.0 million students under 25 years of age and 8.2 million over the age of 25 enrolled in U.S. colleges and universities [180]. At the same time, the number of international students enrolled in U.S. colleges rose 8% from the previous year to nearly 900,000 students, according to the Institute of International Education [94, p. A5]. By 2015, the institute reported a 10% increase to 975,000 [179]. Competition for admission is increasingly fierce as elite colleges and universities reportedly reject up to 95% of their applicants [181]. In recent years, admissions fraud on college entrance exams has been uncovered in China and South Korea [182]. American post-secondary institutions are unprepared. "With only one in four schools having a clearly defined policy on what "fraud" looks like in the admissions process, it's clear that most colleges and universities don't recognize the problem," [183, para 3].

Residency, Visa and Immigration Fraud

Residency fraud occurs when parents of another state or locality illegally enroll their children in another district or state where the quality of public education and safety conditions are considered higher in comparison to those existing in one's own area of legal residency. "Many of the 88,000 kids in the District of Columbia's public and charter schools actually live in Maryland" [184, para 1]. Residency, Visa and immigration fraud may be perpetrated by both insiders and outsiders. In 2014, a fraud ring processing fraudulent student visas enabled "tens of thousands of foreign students" to become permanent residents of Australia [95, p. 1].

Australia is not alone. Ten years ago, David North [96], a Center for Immigration Studies Fellow, alerted federal authorities to Visa and immigration fraud vulnerabilities in the U.S. He divides visa fraud into three categories:

1. individual students who drop out of legitimate universities to become illegal aliens on their own;
2. visa mills, which are distinctly illegitimate establishments; and
3. employees of legitimate universities who misuse their positions to convert legitimate foreign students into illegal aliens [96, p. 1].

North maintains that insider employees participating in Visa fraud, "are more rarely caught" [96, p.1]. Further, after instituting internal disciplinary hearings leading to student withdrawals, educators prematurely close cases. It is rare when former students fraudulently entering the U.S. are turned over to the federal government for prosecution. The consequence should lead to **permanent** inadmissibility to the United States due to prior fraud or misrepresentation, according to the Immigration Nationality Act of 1965 [97].

The harm caused by falsified academic transcripts, forged credentials, and diploma mills extends far beyond the victim organizations to border management. ICE HSI Erik Johansson, an evaluator of foreign credentials in Sweden and interviewed by Tobenkin [98, p. 39], explained,

"We have seen roughly 195 cases of degrees from problematic universities from 1999 to the present and more than half of the cases we have seen are diploma mills from U.S. institutions or that claim to be from a U.S. university. The message I would give is that we would welcome some U.S. federal interest in these matters. This does concern the U.S. as well" [98, p. 39].

Student Visa Fraud Links to National Security Threats

Porous internal control systems and records management in the education sector may increase the threat to human life and national security. Of the 9,000 schools certified to accept foreign students, 150 have participated in closed investigations as potential visa mills, according to Counter-terrorism and Criminal Exploitation Unit Chief Brian Smeltzer [162]. Visa fraud in the education sector threatens national security. Special Agent Smelzter testified before the Senate Committee on Homeland Security and Governmental Affairs, saying "approximately 36 convicted terrorists came to the country using various forms of student visas" [163, p.11].

Institution	State		Institution	State
			Avtech Institute of Technology	NJ
World Christian Theological University	CA		Uceda School West New York	NJ
			Uceda	NJ
Dessin Design College	CA		Herkimer Fulton Hamilton Otsego BOCES	NY
Hongik International University	CA			
Horizon Institute	CA		Blanton-Peale Graduate Institute	NY
Embassy CES Language Training Center	CA		Metropolitan Business Institute	NY
California University of Business and Technology	CA		New York General Consulting, Inc.	NY
			The University of Findlay	OH
Long Beach Flight Academy	CA		The Rock School	PA
Stanton University	CA		Washington Baptist University	VA
Sangha & Laity Training Program	CA		Stratford University	VA
Diablo Valley College	CA		Tysons College	VA
Language Consultants International, LLC	CO		American College of Commerce & Technology	VA
Uceda	FL		IGlobal University	VA
Orlando Language School	FL		Wisconsin Lutheran Seminary	WI
UNILATINA	FL		CCB School of Atlanta	N/I
Faith Baptist Christian School	FL		Central Baptist Christian Academy	N/I
Orlando Academy School of Health Professions	FL		Austrian Flight Academy	N/I
			English Time Language School	N/I
Illinois Eastern Community Colleges	IL		California Ezra Bible Academy	N/I
Hult International Business School	MA		Doroops College Services	N/I

Image 8. Schools with Closed ICE Investigations involving Potential Visa Mills (an investigation does not imply criminality as the school may have been an unwilling victim)
Source: U.S. Immigration and Customs Enforcement (September 30, 2015).
Response to ICE FOIA Request dated July 5, 2015 [164].

For background, the "Student Exchange and Visitor Program (SEVP) managed by U.S. Immigrations and Custom Enforcement allows 1.3 million students and visitors to stay in the United States in order to study or work" [165, p.59]. An outgrowth of the Hearing led by Senator Coburn was the conclusion that "poor management of the student and visitor visa programs invites a potential risk to national security even murder. In the past, people plotting terrorist attacks, including several of the 9 /11 hijackers, were in the United States on student visas" [165, p.60]. This is not new. The U.S. Government Accountability Office referenced the Student and Exchange Visitor Program indicating that "DHS needs to take actions to strengthen monitoring of schools" [166, p. 1]. This conclusion was a follow up to the April 2011 report

> "on the need for close monitoring and oversight of foreign students, and that some schools have attempted to exploit the immigration system by knowingly reporting that foreign students were fulfilling their visa requirements when they were not attending school or attending intermittently" [167].

Cases of Fraud, Mismanagement and Abuse by Level

A review of U.S. Department of Education, Office of Inspector General [99] [100], Department of Justice [101] [102], the Securities and Exchange Commission [103] [104], and state criminal and civil cases reveal processes at risk for fraud, mismanagement, and abuse [105] [106] [107]. This level of threat varies by education levels as noted below.

Risk	Red Flag	Level	Actor
Program Fraud	Inability to verify student/family eligibility, attendance, and/or participation, inflated invoices, invoices not traceable to a good or service, fake and/or falsified documents, employing under-qualified instructors inconsistent with requirements	S, PS	IR
Contract Fraud	No bid contracts, collusion, invoices not traceable to a good or service, Vendor invoices lack detail	S, PS	IR, OR
Enroll Fraud	Student do not meet entrance criteria, excessive number of students that fail to meet the 'continuing enrollment' status (poor grades, attendance, accounts in arrears), failure to conduct random audits and on-site visits to verify significant changes, inability to verify student/family eligibility, and attendance	S, PS	IR
Embezzle	Ghost vendors, fake accounts payables, fraudulent reimbursements, inflated time sheets, re-routed refund checks, vendors with same address	S, PS	IR
Payroll fraud	Inflated time sheets, ghost employees, employees with same address, no deductions for payroll taxes, outliers for overtime, work longer than 24 hours in one day, inconsistencies in start/termination dates, employee matches with vendor, drawing unauthorized compensation from multiple campuses	S, PS	IR
False Claims	Falsified documents, forged records, false certification of 90/10 rule	S, PS	IR
Cash theft	Failure to timely report and review grant receipts and disbursements	PS	IR
Material Misstate	Misrepresentation of job placement rates, overstatement of job potential	PS	IR
Visa fraud	Selling of educational documents allowing foreigners to obtain US student visas and work in the US while providing almost no instruction, lack of master schedule, failure to maintain attendance records	PS	IR
Diploma mill fraud	Offers credential without class, test, study or independent research requirement	PS	IR, OR
Financial aid fraud	Visible signs of altered financial documents, interest and income dividends are zero on tax returns, unresolved discrepancies among various sources, forged signatures, inaccurate and/or mismatched, social security numbers, falsified loan promissory notes, lack of citizenship documentation	S	IR, OR
Identity theft	Lack of identity theft program, failure to develop process/procedure for verifying student identities upon registration, fake, forged or altered identification documents on file, address discrepancies, invalid phone numbers, returned mail, same address used by multiple non-affiliated students (family, sorority, etc)	S, PS	IR, OR
Credit card fraud	Altered cards, larger than usual transaction, card not physically available, use of card to non-authorized vendors/retailers, for non-authorized purchases, lack of systems to review statements and reconcile against receipts, purchases or advances made in states, countries outside of the usual transaction zone	PS	IR, OR
Plagiarism	Varying tenses are present, certain phrases inconsistent with document style, complex concepts inserted in the document in an illogical manner, incorrect and/or incomplete listing of sources, a fact checker identifies plagiarism	PS	IR
Falsified research	Reproduced data does not generate the same results	PS	IR
Records tampering	Altered, missing documents, untimely submission of documents, contents do not match digital version or vice versa, changes in data without supporting documentation, excessive data access overrides, data access outside normal operating hours, reports of stolen passwords	S, PS	IR
Residency fraud	Lack of residency documents, altered documents	S, PS	OR
Academic fraud	Summative and/or standardized exam results inconsistent with formative assessments, class grades, language proficiency, attendance, student does not met objective criteria for entrance	S, PS	IR, OR
No show classes	Students obtain course grades, credit or credentials without attending class, completing an independent project, taking an exam, or completing course work	S, PS	IR
Student Debt Relief Scams	Telemarketers, email spam, direct mail, radio, television and online promotions	PS	OR

Image 9. Functions at Risk for Fraud by Level and Perpetrator Threat [108]
Source: T. Mead (2015). Risk Assessment Data Quality and Security for School and Campus Records. Unpublished Manuscript. Legend: S-Secondary Level, PS- Post Secondary School Level; IR- Insider/Internal Risk, OR- Outsider/External Risk

Perspectives of Fraud in Education

Criminologists understand that fraud conjures up a number of meanings in criminal law. For instance, fraud, as broadly defined includes

"(1) acts aimed at objects other than the misappropriation of property (such as the deprivation of honest services, obstruction of governmental functions, and obtaining of unjust advantage), and (2) acts committed by means other than deception (such as breach of trust, conflicts of interest, and exploitation) [109, p. 52].

Unfortunately, expanded definitions of fraud can not be fully enforced within the education sector until it has obtained credibility and legitimacy in the general public. Green and Kugler [109] argue

White collar criminal offenses, such as bribery, gratuities, perjury, false statements, and fraud, reflect a kind of moral ambiguity that is lacking in the case of many more familiar street crimes. Whether a given actor will be punished as a criminal, or admired as a successful businessperson, politician, lobbyist, or witness will often depend on nuanced moral judgments and subtle distinctions in facts [109, p. 58].

Against this backdrop, the attitudes about fraud in education will be fully explored in the following section.

Attitudes about Cheating, Plagiarism and Falsified Research

Cheating on standardized exams, plagiarism and falsifying research are behaviors specific to the education sector and are often deemed harmless and victimless. Traditionally, students and research subjects are rarely informed, if at all on assessment results, its myriad end uses, and the decisions impacted. This occurs even though their experiences serve to drive the assessment and events researched. Without an inherent feedback loop built into the system, the harm to the victim is not reported, verified or investigated. Increased educator fraud is associated with "high stakes testing" [110, p. 1]. This occurs when student scores on standardized tests are considered as factors for teacher evaluations and school performance matrices. Penalties and rewards are exacted based upon performance indices. To examine deception, the Scientific American Mind posed the question, "Why we Cheat?" and provided the rationale that "Everybody does it" [111]. Explanations from the microbiologists Fang and Casadevall [111, p. 30-31] ranged from the physical size of the brain (a larger neocortex) to increased competition.

Varied Responses to the Discovery of Fraud

Consider below, the varying resolutions for these cases with similar allegations around student grades and data tampering.

Case 1

A Chicago teacher pled guilty to misdemeanor computer tampering after it was determined that she had accessed a school's computer system illegally to change grades of students who were on the school's athletic ineligibility list [112].

Case 2

A computer teacher in New York was charged with twelve counts of falsifying business records in the first degree, a class E felony and seventeen counts of forgery in the second degree, class D felony. In addition to changing student's grades and standardized test scores, there were allegations that the defendant adjusted attendance records. These acts were part of a scheme to isolate and molest students under his care. In this regard, the perpetrator was also charged with three counts of endangering the welfare of a child, and one count of forcible touching; both class A misdemeanors and three counts of sex abuse in the third degree, class B misdemeanors [113].

Case 3

Five teachers in Philadelphia were charged with racketeering, perjury, tampering with public records, and forgery for allegedly changing or providing answers to students on standardized state tests [114].

Misdemeanor Reform

Educators are not alone in their desire to show clemency. The National Association of Criminal Defense Lawyers [115] recommended that misdemeanor cases with little impact upon public safety be set aside, reduced, and resolved with lesser penalties [116]. Further, the results of misdemeanor cases are not transparent. For every 1 million convictions for felonies (rape, murder, drug crime and robbery) there are more than 10 million misdemeanor cases in the United States filed each year [117]. Due to this volume, some states fail to allocate resources to record, track, and analyze misdemeanor data. "Data about them are sparse" [118, p.1].

Pace of Increase in Education Costs Far Exceeds Increase in Cost of Living

The exorbitantly high cost of higher education can be a contributing factor to increased incidents of data, computer-assisted, and white collar crime in education. For instance, households in the U.S. held more than $914 billion in student loan debt in 2012 in comparison to $750 billion for auto loans and $672 billion in credit card debt [119]. Experts tout the value held in education and consider it an investment [120]. However, in "Ivory Tower", it was reported, "tuition has risen since 1978 by 1,120 percent, and during that same period state funding for colleges has declined by 40 percent" [121].

Non-proportional Federal Contribution to University Revenue

From the perspective of the potential buyer of educational services, the cost is high. In comparison, school officials can become enticed by the excessive federal contribution to overall revenue. The federal government guarantees about 90% of the $1.3 trillion of student loan debt as estimated in August 2016, by *Investopia* [180]. Ohio University economist, Richard Vedder speculated that for every dollar of grant funding received, university systems increase tuition by 35 cents [122, p. A14]. Similarly, a New York Fed study found that for every dollar obtained in direct and subsidized loans, tuition prices are raised by 65 cents. For every one dollar granted from Pell federal funds, tuition increased by 55 cents [122].

Poor Economy

Enforcement experts find that increased financial pressures such as personal debts, declining home values, stagnant salaries, and dropping stock prices increase the risk for fraud [123] [124].

Secondary Level Education Reform

School reform has hastened the introduction of data-driven, results-oriented approaches to performance without corresponding control measures. Kaufmann [125]) says such practices may have "spurred change, although not in unambiguously positive ways" [125, p.1]. This is particularly acute with regards to the growth of the charter school movement and the lack of federal oversight. In 2004, the U.S. Department of Education, Office of Inspector General conducted a review of charter schools. It found that a federal program office with oversight for state compliance with charter schools' access to federal funds had not yet been established [126].

Variability of Teacher Preparation Program Curricula

There is considerable range of curricula lacking consistency. Seventy-one percent of newly hired employees entering the teaching profession are prepared at traditional institutions of higher learning. Twenty-one percent are trained in traditional institutions in a non-traditional setting. Eight percent are prepared in alternative programs located at non-traditional institutions [127]. Darling-Hammond, et al writes

> "Unlike the curriculum of other professions which has some coherence of substance and pedagogy, the teacher education curriculum is widely distributed but rarely coordinated. Many of those who teach teachers do not think of themselves as teacher educators.... And most have little preparation for the task of educating teachers" [128, p. 12].

Randi Weingarten, president of American Federation of Teachers (AFT), a union representing 1 million members, indicated a preference for a teacher residency program, similar to the practice found in the medical and counseling profession [129]. A residency program would provide ample time to instill highly demanded skills.

In 2013, the Association of American Colleges and Universities surveyed 318 employers to identify the skills in demand. Employers placed the greatest priority on ethics, intercultural skills, and capacity for professional development. Ninety-six percent of the employers identified ethical judgment and integrity as important, while seventy-six percent said it was very important.

University systems, state education commissioners, state and district superintendents, local education agency administrators and principals too may deem ethics, integrity, and strong moral character as important attributes for educators. There appears, however, to be a lack of synchronization between the demands of the market and output. Burant, Chubbuck and Whipp (2007) theorized that teacher education programs must emphasize moral sensitivity alongside content knowledge [132]. Campbell (2008) provided even harsher criticism: "Teacher education neglects the teaching of ethics" [133, p. 372].

Employers are not the only group to gain from ethical judgment and moral integrity. Students, particularly minorities and the poor, benefit also. Gore et al (2007) conducted a longitudinal study of 3,000 students during a three-year period and found that minority students from lower socio-economic backgrounds benefited the most from instructors who held high expectations based upon ethical and moral principles [134].

Variability of Alternative Pathways to Educator Licensure

To address a projected shortfall in the nationwide educator talent in the 1990s, alternatives to educator licensure were introduced. Many provided sparse training and meager support. To meet federal reporting guidelines during rapid build-up, some states included alternative candidates in their definitions of "highly qualified teachers" (HQT) even before candidates completed minimal training [135, p.93].

The suspected practice of falsified reporting to imply educator preparation and experience did not alarm regulatory authorities. To the contrary, the federal government may have been complicit in misreporting by lowering the baseline previously established for HQT. The U.S. Department of Education prepared a report to the U.S. Congress highly critical of the research-based, best practices for certification. Factors known to increase teacher preparation: attendance at schools of education, coursework in education, and student teaching were presented as possible options; not mandatory requirements [136].

Variability of Ethical Framework in the Teaching Profession

Keith-Spiegel et al [137] argued that ethical teaching involves the avoidance of actions and inactions that may cause students educational or emotional harm. Opportunities to self deal, tamper with grades and exams, and falsify applications for federal funding have not been dampened by the industry. Professions with fiduciary responsibilities such as securities dealers, stockbrokers, psychiatrists, physicians, social workers, certified public accountants, and attorneys have formed national ethics standards to guide professional behavior and prevent self dealing according to Hutchings [138]. He writes,

> "American Bar Association , original Cannons of Professional Ethics adopted in 1932, the model code of professional responsibility was adopted in 1969, or the American Psychological Association , developed in 1952, the American Counseling Association, first published in 1961, the American Medical Association, adopted in 1847, American School counselors Association, first adopted in 1984" [138, p. 13-15].

Conversely, individual educators must school themselves on state and municipal codes to maintain career mobility. Without a national standard for ethics, Hutchings reasoned that decision-making threatens to become spontaneous and capricious. He warned that the absence of national standards poses grave risk to educators and is not in the best interest of students. Hutchings developed the "Ethical Equilibrium" model illustrating the balance between dispositional, regulatory, and ethical frameworks [138, p. 9].

A 2004 Rand Report recommends improving accountability by adopting self-regulating systems used in the legal profession. "The legal accountability model is largely based on notions of processional accountability which entail controlling entry into the procession, mandatory capacity-building, self-policing, and protecting client concerns" [139, p.xv].

Growing Trend Toward Lex Loci Arguments

Educators greatly impact student outcomes. Evaluators found that there was a 52 percentile point difference in student scores when instructed by either a high performing or low performing teacher for three consecutive years [140]. Impact extends beyond matriculation. It has been determined that students with one year of ineffective teaching at the secondary level can lose $1.4 million in lifetime earnings [141].

As such, educators are vulnerable to litigation. It has been postulated that educators and schools have a fiduciary responsibility to students in their care [142]. If so, the industry is wholly unprepared for such responsibility.

Oversight Reductions Due to Secondary Employer Profile Shifts

Shifts in employer profiles have resulted in government oversight reductions. Brewer and Hentschke [143] say the speed with which charters have entered the market confines the reach of government. The government has traditionally protected the public from abuse and self-dealing, demanding regulatory compliance.

> "Because of the coupling of public operation with powerful ministries, employee unions and so on, the creation of privately-operated public schools enables governments to bypass these intransigent forces that make change from within so difficult. U.S. charter schools have been used as a vehicle to reduce stifling effects of over-regulation and union contracts, without directly challenging the constituencies that benefit from these" [143, p. 232].

Severns and Glueck [144] point to Washington, DC, Chicago, and New York City districts where billions were spent to embrace charters. These districts oversee schools that have been called 'holding pens' with large percentages of failing students, drop outs, and truant heading straight to jail, not to institutions of higher learning. The autonomy and increased decentralization demanded by the traditional schools to more directly compete with public charters results in the de-prioritization of policies and procedures to deter occupational fraud. This directional void leaves an educator class susceptible to ethical lapses in judgment and an industry ripe for fraud. For an idea of the magnitude of charter school operations in comparison to traditional public schools, please see the tables below.

The Highest Percentage of Charter Students by School District, 2012-2013

K-12 School District	Traditional Public School Enrollment	Charter Public School Enrollment	Percentage of Charter
New Orleans	9,414	36,126	79%
Detroit	49,172	51,083	51%
District of Columbia	45,557	34,674	43%
Flint City	8,472	4,781	36%

Source: 2013 Market Share Report, National Alliance for Public Charters [145]

The Highest Number of Charter Students by School District, 2012-2013

K-12 School District	Traditional Public School Enrollment	Charter Public School Enrollment	Percentage of Charter
Los Angeles Unified	534,611	120,958	18%
New York City	964,846	58,353	6%
Philadelphia	143,898	55,031	28%

Source: U.S. Department of Education, NCES, Common Core of Data (CCD) [146]

Shifts in Teacher Demographics

Twenty-five years ago, the number of years experience in education most often cited by educators was fifteen years, according to the National Commission on Teaching for America's Future [147, p. 10]. Today, one to two years is most frequently cited [148]. This has grossly impacted minority and poor public school students. Researchers show that inexperience undermines stability, hinders reform, and threatens student progress [148].

Job-embedded training in content, pedagogy, and ethics are critical. The study "Beginners in the Classroom: What the Changing Demographics of Teaching Mean for Schools, Students, and Society" [149] explored the reasons why new teachers leave education. The answer? Lack of support. Hanushek [150] found that an ineffective teacher can cost a student six months of learning annually. "In a single academic year, a good teacher will get a gain of one and a half grade- level equivalents, while a bad teacher will get a gain equivalent to just half a year" [150, p. 84]. Without support, ineffective educators may have a motive for participating in fraudulent activities.

Tenured to Adjunct Faculty Shifts for Post Secondary

The Association of Governing Boards [151] reported that 70 percent of higher education faculty nation-wide are adjunct or "contingent faculty." This is in stark contrast to almost a half century ago, when approximately 78.3 percent of higher education faculty were tenure-track and 21.7 percent were non-tenure track. Poor orientation, lagging recruitment schedules, job insecurity, low benefits, and inequitable salaries are employment conditions faced by adjunct faculty. Adjuncts' lack of orientation and limited access to professional development and formal assessments lower the quality of education. Without the identification of instructional deficiencies and the development of plans, student learning is negatively impacted. "From the moment they are first hired and continuing through their employment, they do not have access to resources such as funding to attend training and conferences to support their professional development" [151, p. 4].

Super-sized Political Influence and Donor Power in Education

Another factor responsible for the increase in fraud, white collar, and computer assisted crime in education is the super-sized political influence and donor power in education. As decision-making in education becomes more focused on data-driven solutions, distortion of data for one's political or financial purposes may become common place [152]. Pfeffer argues,

"For instance, if data are tabulated according to criteria that promote someone's factored decision, and that decision does not work out, he or she might be expected to suffer the consequences. In fact, however, such consequences are rarely visited on those who used information strategically" [152, p. 261].

Pfeffer asserts that there are three conditions contributing to power and influence:

1. the time lag between an organizational decision and the visible consequences of the decision,
2. the difficulty in assigning individual blame for an organizational decision gone awry, and
3. the collective unwillingness to analyze reasons for past failures.

As can be seen below, the lack of collective responsibility leads to denial of existing problems and faulty solutions.

Industry Denial of Potential for Fraud and Corruption

The education industry is not immune to fraud. In fact, it is ranks in the Top Five, according to the 2014 Global Fraud Study [153]. The education industry ranked fifth for reported cases of fraud, followed by retail and insurance. Fusco [154] and Segal [155] concluded that while fraud seemed pervasive, the sector appeared to deny its existence.

"One impediment to reform that no one is seriously studying in the debate over how to improve public schools are systematic fraud, waste and abuse. [That] this [is] missing is surprising because a number of school districts particularly large urban ones, have compiled impressive records of fraud and waste" [155, p. xxi].

The American Educational Research Association (AER) highlighted scholarly inquiries into education at its annual convention. More than 13,000 k-12 and post- secondary educators participated in 1,600 to 1,700 sessions based upon a telephone interview with Kimberly Ricks, Meetings Associate [156]. A search of the terms: "fraud," "crime," "misconduct," "cheating," "illegal," and "corrupt" yielded just 16 scholarly papers. Of those, 38 percent emphasized student misconduct; not adults. This finding is similar in an analysis of the proceedings 20 years ago. At the time, the education industry appeared to conspicuously deny the existence of fraud and corruption. "Of the 5,000 scholarly papers delivered at the 1995 annual meeting of the American Education Research Association, only a handful dealt with wrong doing by school employees," as reported in Fusco [157].

Beyond academia, on-the-ground educators can be found to express, "There are no ethical dilemmas in public education… because there are no ethics. There is no right or wrong. See nothing, hear nothing, report nothing, punish no one. Ethics does not exist," exclaimed a research participant [158, p. 34]. This finding is consistent with earlier research undertaken by Fusco [159] citing Fossey [160] from an article in *EdWeek* titled "Corrupt, mismanaged and unsafe schools: Where is the Research?"

On the horizon, however, there is promise of the convergence of the perceptions of organizational culture drawn upon real world experiences of educators with the abstract theories of academia. Barley, Meyer and Gash [161] observed that "academics and practitioners eventually came to view the importance of organizational culture similarly" [161, p. 53].

PART TWO

COMPUTER ASSISTED CRIME IN EDUCATION

Introduction

U.S. education institutions spent about $4.7 billion at elementary and secondary level and $6.6 billion on the post-secondary level for information technology in 2015 [1]. Even venture capitalists have forecast the prospects for higher than average earnings by infusing $1.87 billion of capital into the education sector 2014 [151]. Globally, technology represents $15 billion according to BMO Capital Markets [2]. The magnitude and speculative expectations may lend the market to increased risk for fraud, mismanagement, abuse and corruption.

There are many uses of technology in the education sector. According to the U.S. Department of Education,

> "Technology ushers in fundamental structural changes that can be integral to achieving significant improvements in productivity. Used to support both teaching and learning, technology infuses classrooms with digital learning tools, such as computers and hand held devices; expands course offerings, experiences, and learning materials; supports learning 24 hours a day, 7 days a week; builds 21st century skills; increases student engagement and motivation; and accelerates learning" [141, para 1].

Increased Internal and External Risks

The promise of improved performance, targeted interventions, reduced costs, and greater efficiencies from advanced technologies and increased capture, analysis, and use of data brings with it increased vulnerabilities [3] [4]. As student data accumulates, the risk of data breaches [5] [6] [7] and unintentional disclosure of personally iden-tifying private information (PIPI) increases exponentially. The private sector has rec-ognized the threat as they hold a vested interest in securing proprietary intellectual property and confidential customer information [8] [9]. Pouncing on opportunities, criminals in previous years have identified the education sector as the number one target for malware. From January to June 2010, "44% of all malware infections hit schools and universities" [10]. While the education sector has not remained at the top of the criminal's target list in 2015, there are trends showing that the threat is still very real [11]. Michael Oppenheim of FireEye, an internet security firm, estimates that 550 universities had experienced some type of data breach from 2006 to 2013, exposing confidential student and staff information [12].

Lack of Information Technology Expertise and Training
Due to the pervasiveness of the threat to PIPI, Congress proposed a Student Privacy Bill making data security mandatory [13]. It also strengthens the enforcement pro-visions of the Family Education Records Protection Act [14]. Why was the legisla-tion necessary? SANS Institute [15] reported upon a Computer Weekly survey of 638 public and private sector respondents. They discovered "in more than 63% of security breaches identified by respondents, human error was the major cause. Only 8% were purely technical failures." These numbers reveal that the human element is the weakest part of any security system [16]. This is particularly true for the edu-cation industry [17].

Failure of Preparation Programs to Teach Computer Skills
Almost 15 years ago, the Federal Trade Commission as cited by Willis and Raines cri-tiqued the antiquated systems and poor conditions of technology in education [18]. "There are thousands of buildings in this country with millions of people in them who have no telephones, no cable television, and no reasonable prospect of broadband ser-vices. They're called schools." While computer accessibility has greatly improved, the need to update educator knowledge with technology advances is critical. Further, the lack of educator training on access management and maintenance is an impediment to data quality and information security.

The paucity of technological acumen among educators is unjustifiable considering these contravening trends:

1. The use of data and technology holds the promise of helping students gain mastery of subject matter content. A six-year study completed by the State

Educational Technology Directors Association (SETDA) found that classroom incorporation of technological tools led to "positive academic results" [143, p.2]

2. The increased demands of data-driven decision making in policy, resource allocations, and evaluations of teacher effectiveness and program quality [144, p.5].

"Research suggests that pre-service teachers should be prepared to teach with technology, rather than just learning about technology" [19, p. 30]. These findings are supported by an International Society for Technology in Education (ISTE) study showing that "learning with technology is more important than learning about technology" [142, p. 16].

In a survey of 90 teacher preparation programs for The American Association of Colleges for Teacher Education, faculty respondents reported that 58 percent of teacher candidates were prepared to use computers as instructional aids in the classroom. During the same study, however, just 29 percent of the teacher candidates, when posed the same question felt ready to teach with computers [20]. To elucidate the reason for failure to prepare future educators, the Congressional Office of Technology Assessment hypothesized that there exists a "lack of expertise of many education school faculty" with computers [21].

Lack of Professional Development for Technology

In addition to inadequate preparation prior to hire, educators lack professional on-the-job training while employed. Borthwick and Pierson site a study by Bond (1998) finding that educators in Asian countries devote up to 60 days per year in professional development training [22, p. 11]. On the other side of the globe, Brown (2003) asserts (as cited by Borthwick, et al) that "new teachers in American public schools, on the other hand, are often turned loose in their classrooms, only to be heard from again on the day they quit" [22, p. 9].

Goldman, Cole, and Syer [23], found that computer labs are prominent in most schools and computers are situated in almost every classroom. Nonetheless, teachers have not made much use of technology. Trotter estimated that almost 40 percent of teachers have not integrated computer use into lesson plans at all [24]. By 2003, a study financed by the Gates Foundation recorded little change [25].

A decade later, an Information Technology Panel identified "updating IT professionals' skills and roles to accommodate emerging technologies and changing IT management and service delivery models" as the top priority for the education sector [26].

Absence of Basic Cyber Security and Ethics Training

The exertion of pressure to utilize computers in the classroom and to make data analysis available for the realization of gains in student learning weighs heavy upon educators. At the same time, the increased demand for student, parent, and public access to private information through vulnerable networks makes for an environment ripe for exploitation.

"Typically, the greatest security weakness of school districts is a lack of IT resources coupled with the need to provide greater access to the network.... In general K-12 IT systems tend to spend less on sophisticated protections than those of large corporations, making them easier to penetrate." [144, p.22].

"Banks and governments could be 'brought to their knees' by computer hackers because of the "weak link" represented by large numbers of staff who aren't properly trained in cyber security" remarks Professor Benham, visiting professor in cyber security management at Coventry University [145, para 1]. This statement is applicable to educational institutions in the United States.

As the following section will demonstrate, the lack of a formalized ethics training in education greatly heightens threats to cyber security. "To fully understand why the field of cyber ethics is important, one must first understand how to approach the study of general ethics" (Thorson, 2011) [28]. Inadequate ethics courses in professional educator certification programs, lenient enforcement of FERPA privacy protections, and inconsistencies in collection and reporting standards for PIPI data present conditions for increased risk for crime and self dealing. The National Cyber Security Alliance, for example, studied educator perceptions. Less than 25 percent of the respondents felt comfortable advising students on self protection against cyber predators, bullies, and identity theft [29].

Undisciplined Internet Use Linked to Malware and Theft

The National Bureau of Economic Research [30] analyzed 2003 to 2011 data from the American Time Use Survey showing that the typical American spent 13 minutes on the internet each day for leisure. Conversely, 1,300 college students reported spending 100 minutes daily [31]. In like manner, about 60 percent of the faculty reported weekly internet usage of four to 19 hours [32]. Beyond this mid-range category of faculty respondents, "another 40 percent reported being online for 20 or more hours, approximately three hours or more per week, or three or more hours per day" which is in excess of the norm for faculty users [32, p. 4].

In comparison to the typical American, educators and college students spend more time on the internet, making them (and the networks used) targets for malware. Malware is utilized for the purposes of grand theft and identify theft. In 2010, hackers stole $996,000 by inserting a virus into the authorization codes used by the controller at the University of Virginia. The scammers fraudulently wired money from the university's BB&T bank account to the Agriculture Bank of China [33].

Lack of pre-service and embedded on-the-job training pose significant threats. Training in the instructional uses, limitations, as well as the risks associated with computer technology is paramount. Reports of internet users receiving fraudulent emails show that "70% of internet users have unintentionally visited a spoofed website and that more than 15% of spoofed users admit to being phished" [27]. Professional development aimed at preventative measures can do much to thwart the unintentional release of confidential student information as well as unauthorized access to accounting and finance systems. Fraudulent emails are hard to detect with basic spam-filtering because they are designed to look like legitimate emails.

Adopted Technology Standards not Put into Practice

The National Council for the Accreditation of Teacher Education Programs adopted technology standards for teachers in 1998 [148]. The Association of School Administrators, in 2001 [149]. Yet, a coalition of organizations such as the Data Quality Campaign, American Association of Teacher Education Programs, the Council of Chief State School Officers, the National Association of (NASDTEC), the National Council on Teacher Quality, the National Education Association and WestEd determined these measures have not been applied consistently. The coalition has advocated for "teacher data literacy through state policy" while promoting and incentivizing ongoing technical training [34, p.1].

Inconsistencies in Communication from the Top

The lack of clear messaging increases environmental vulnerabilities to computer assisted crime. Jeffrey concluded that misconduct has a higher probability of occurring when victim organizations lack positive social reinforcers for employee emulation [35]. This involves positive social pressure from peers and role modeling to alleviate inconsistencies in spoken, written, and nonverbal communication concerning the protection of PIPI.

The highest caliber leaders create and support ethical decision-making by communicating and modeling high ethical standards [36]. "These top managers create and maintain an ethical culture by consistently behaving in an ethical fashion and encouraging others to behave in such a manner as well" [37]. The Association of Certified Fraud Examiners takes the concept a step further and says, "employees will do what they witness their bosses doing" [38]. Inherent within the expectation of role modeling and communication is the development of conduct codes that are clear, provide unambiguous language regarding acceptable behaviors and expected procedures, and are enforced [39].

Lack of Emphasis on Data Quality

On the secondary level, the U.S. Department of Education [40] reported upon several data quality problems. Lack of system interoperability, absence of uniform data definitions, data unavailability, inconsistent responses to data requirements across providers, longitudinal inconsistencies, data entry errors, and lack of timeliness were a few.

A 2005 analysis of the data reported to the Integrated Post Secondary Education Data System found significant data variances in the initial report submissions in comparison to revisions. "Staff totals for part-time employees with no faculty status" was overestimated by 30 percent; "Finance" was underestimated by 19 percent; and "Enrollment" data for part time students was overestimated by 11 percent [41].

By 2013, State Educational Technology Directors identified the following challenges: increased demand for communication relays between hardware and software applications; disparate data file formats; legal ambiguities surrounding the requirements for safeguarding PIPI; and lack of data standards [42].

As the education industry rushes to embrace data-driven decision making at all levels, there is an under-current of unease regarding the historical lack of data integrity and accountability. Susan Grajek, VP for Data Research and Analytics, EDUCAUSE has said, *"there is some doubt as to whether we really have what it takes to meet the expectations of analytics. It's not enough to have the infrastructure. **Is your data good enough? Do you have the data that you need, and is it any good?"** [43].*

Ineffective Internal Controls of Data Leading to Manipulation Allegations

The failure of management to address the complexities inherent in the validation of disparate data from multiple sources, differing file formats and structures is immense. The enormous task of data maintenance stored in hardware systems customized by multiple vendors for differing uses and the integration of information entered into software applications exacerbate data manipulation allegations. These problems span data used for finance/accounting, enrollment/registration, institutional development/research, exam administration/testing, and academic scheduling/grading.

For instance, students have filed lawsuits ranging from $5 million to $40 million alleging the payment of tuition for classes that were never held and the falsification of records to "enroll them and keep them enrolled so that government grant and loan dollars would keep flowing "[44][45][46]. Harvard University conducted an inquiry in 2010 of scientific misconduct concerning problems of "data acquisition, data analysis, data retention and the reporting of research methodologies and results" [47]. An El Paso Superintendent was sentenced to four years imprisonment, $56,600 in fines, and $180,000 in restitution for contract fraud and data tampering [48]. The Ohio Auditor charged Columbus City Schools District Superintendent for presiding over a culture of data manipulation alleging changed grades, deleted absences, and falsified dropout data [49]. Auditors in Washington, DC found that schools failed to maintain internal controls for graduation [50] and special education [51] data. Data tampering extends to scientific research with estimates up to 65% of retractions "due to misconduct" [52]. The failure of universities to control data led to overpayments of $222 million to 42,000 distance learners, who did not earn any academic credits during the payment period" [53].

"Big data represents all kinds of opportunities for all kinds of businesses, but collecting it, cleaning it up, and storing it can be a logistical nightmare" [146, para 1]. The challenge according to the Developer Network is to:

"extract the data, often from a variety of disparate systems, to transform that data, so that it is uniform in terms of format and content, and finally to load the data into a warehouse where it can serve as a basis for future business intelligence needs. It's very important that the integrity of the data is maintained" [146, para 4-5].

"Twenty-six states have designed and built or upgraded their data warehouses, or are in the process of doing so" [147, p. 1]. In reading through allegations of data tampering in the education sector, however, it becomes clear that much needs to be done to enhance the internal quality control measures (extraction, transformation, and loading) necessary to ensure data integrity.

Misreporting of Enrollment Data

When educational entities fail to report or misreport data, "the totals could be lowered by the missing amount or filled in with an assumed amount" [54, p.5]. Therefore, preliminary data when finalized may change as a consequence. Researchers at the U.S. Census Bureau noted that

> "reporting may be affected by incentives built into administrative requirements and funding formulas. For example, Michelle Fine (1991) noted that per pupil funding formulasinfluenced some New York City schools to encourage students to postpone official dropout from school until after the date at which student counts were submitted [54, p.8].

The rationale for misreporting enrollment data lies in federal funding methodologies. Depending upon the year, the U.S. Department of Education may invest between $70 to $80 billion annually on pre-k-12 education; the U.S. Department of Agriculture, $20.8 billion, for child nutrition funding; the Department of Health and Human Services, $9.3 billion for Head Start program support; and the Department of Labor, $5.7 billion, to provide aid for Youth Employment and Training Activities [55]. Enrollment data at the school, district or state level determines federal support for resources and staffing. Most funding is based upon a per pupil enrolled formula. Weighted formulas are then applied to enrollment, disability, income, and migration status. While there may be intentional over-reporting or misreporting of student enrollment driven by financial incentives, the next section demonstrates the perverse motivations for under reporting crime data.

Under-reporting of Crime Data

It is widely accepted that schools under and over-report required data elements as recipients of federal funding. This is executed to suit their own organizational needs. Concealed Campus [56] uncovered inconsistencies in Department of Education information when scrutinizing against FBI campus crime data [57] [58]. "The data are not directly comparable to data from the FBI's Uniform Crime Reporting System" . Please note that valid comparisons of campus crime are possible *only with study and analysis of the conditions affecting each institution*" [59]. The Department of Education now requires campuses to include crimes investigated and those un-substantiated. It mandates that schools disclose crime "from the past three calendar years as well as those going forward" [60].

Why is accurate crime data important? Timely attention to accurate crime data is used for planning and evaluating anti-crime alternatives. This process has been cited as reasons for New York City's reduction in reported crime [61]. Unfortunately, errors in crime data make crime resolution, investigation, prediction, prevention and the promotion of safety hard to achieve [62]. Campus crime is no exception [63] [64] [65][66]. Like many university systems, we are focusing on Clery compliance right now," said Stacey Sneed, Internal Audit Manager, Winston-Salem State University [67]. Accurate data and timely incident reporting will do much to prevent violence and promote safety in educational settings [68].

Month	City, State	School Name	Level
Jan	W. Lafayette, IN	Purdue University	College
Jan	Orangeburg, SC	SC State University	College
Feb	Raytown, MO	Raytown Success Academy	K-12
March	Savannah, GA	Savannah State University	College
April	Detroit, MI	E. English Village Prep	K-12
April	Griffith, IN	St. Mary Catholic School	K-12
May	Milwaukee, WI	Clark St School	K-12
June	Seattle, WA	Seattle Pacific University	College
June	Troutdale, OR	Reynolds H.S.	K-12
June	Benton, MO	Kelly H.S.	K-12
August	Newport News, VA	Saunders Elementary	K-12
October	Fairburn, GA	Langston Hughes H.S.	K-12
October	Marysville, WA	Marysville- Pilchuck H.S.	K-12

Image 11. 2014 Shootings in Schools Resulting in Fatalities [69]

Negligent Disclosure of Student Data Records- Internal Threat

Fraud, data manipulation, tampering, and misreporting are not the only risks associated with increased uses and expanded users data. Along with the promised advantages of improved performance, targeted interventions, and greater efficiencies; increased vulnerabilities exist. The unintentional disclosure or data breach of PIPI is a critical vulnerability [70 [71].

The causes of data breaches are varied. Sources range from database hacking, the accidental emailing of confidential information from a secure file to the wrong email address, and obtaining unencrypted files from a stolen laptop [72]. The FBI estimates that 85 to 97 percent of intrusions remain undetected [73]. In a study of 390 attacks, less than 10% of the managers reported the attacks [74]. In the education sector,

> "breaches can run the gamut from students hacking into school databases and changing their grades to instigating a denial of service attack to stop electronic testing to a major infiltration by cybercriminals who steal personally identifiable information such as Social Security and credit card numbers...Their multiple buildings are at times open to the public, allowing anyone to connect a device to their network, which makes the network incredibly difficult to secure" [148, p. 21-22].

The private sector has recognized the threat of true name identity theft. They have a vested interest in securing proprietary intellectual property and confidential customer information [75]. The negative attitudes held by customers of companies who have disclosed PIPI has been recorded by researchers [76]. To that end, it has proven costly. A Choicepoint data breach of 163,000 records led to $15 million in penalties in 2005 [77]. The unintended disclosure of names, social security numbers, addresses, dates of birth, and university identification numbers can be costly, both to the victim entity and the individual. Post-breach, educational institutions have signed contracts of up to $2.6 million to monitor the credit activity of victims impacted [78]. The average cost of up to $300 per compromised data record in the education sector makes this industry the "second most sector—behind only healthcare—for businesses with lost or stolen records globally" [79]. Additionally, for all companies impacted regardless of sector, there was a 23% increase in per record costs for breaches in comparison to costs incurred for similar breaches in the previous year [79].

In addition to the perceptions that there are no financial losses resulting from the disclosure of PIPI data; the lack of educator affinity with the student population and their families represents another explanation for the inadvertent release. Please see below, Image 12, a depiction of the myriad points where PIPI is vulnerable to exploitation.

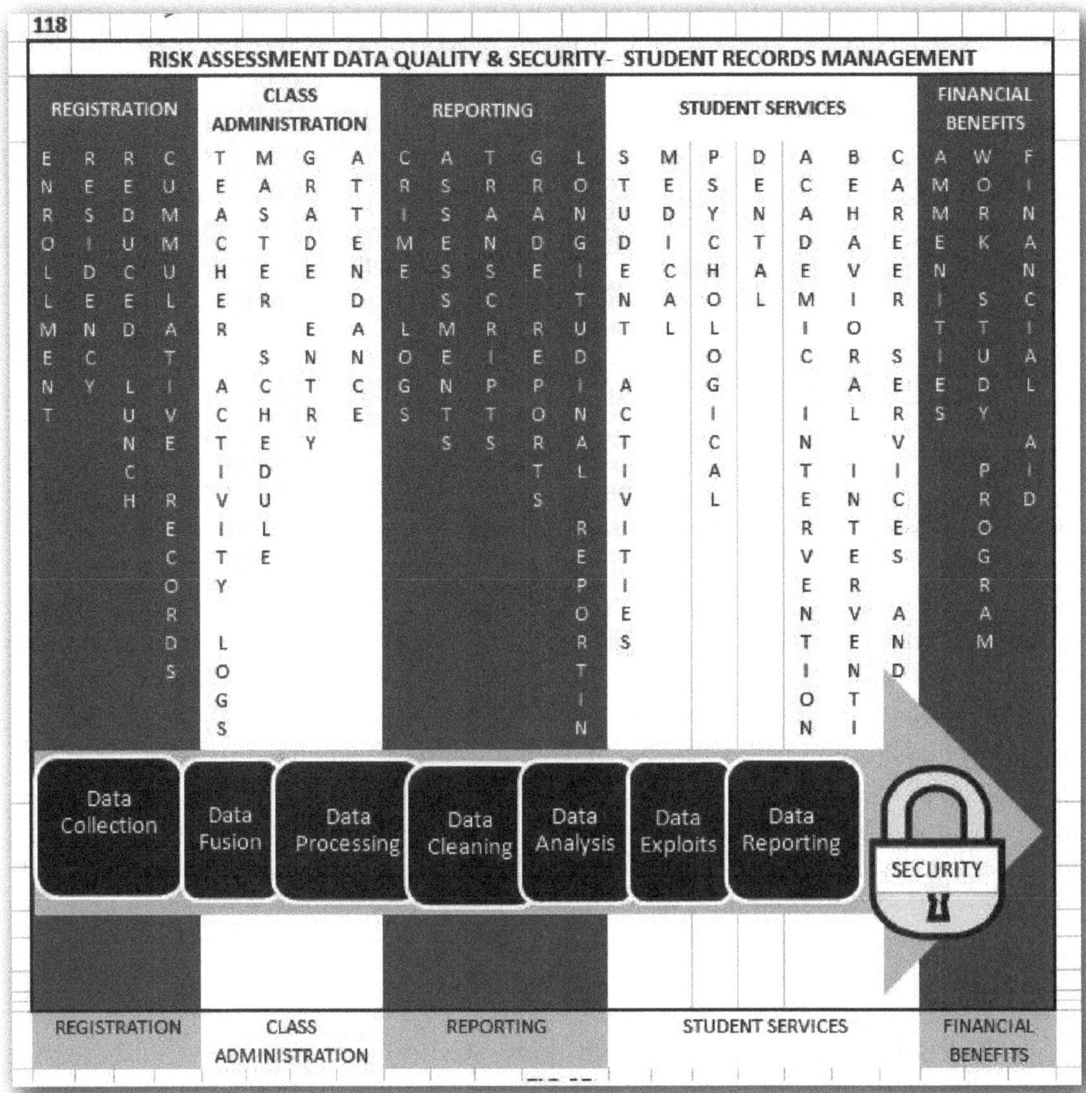

118

RISK ASSESSMENT DATA QUALITY & SECURITY- STUDENT RECORDS MANAGEMENT

REGISTRATION	CLASS ADMINISTRATION	REPORTING	STUDENT SERVICES	FINANCIAL BENEFITS

The table presents categories of data points arranged as vertical words beneath each heading:

REGISTRATION: ENROLLMENT · RESIDENCY · REDUCED LUNCH · CUMMULATIVE RECORDS LOGS

CLASS ADMINISTRATION: TEACHER ACTIVITY LOGS · MASTER SCHEDULE · GRADE ENTRY · ATTENDANCE

REPORTING: CRIMES LOGS · ASSESSMENTS · TRANSCRIPTS · GRADE REPORTS · LONGITUDINAL REPORTING

STUDENT SERVICES: STUDENT ACTIVITIES · MEDICAL · PSYCHOLOGICAL · DENTAL · ACADEMIC · BEHAVIOR INTERVENTION · CAREER SERVICES

FINANCIAL BENEFITS: AMENITIES · WORK STUDY · FINANCIAL AID PROGRAM

Process flow (left to right): Data Collection → Data Fusion → Data Processing → Data Cleaning → Data Analysis → Data Exploits → Data Reporting → SECURITY (lock)

REGISTRATION	CLASS ADMINISTRATION	REPORTING	STUDENT SERVICES	FINANCIAL BENEFITS

Image 12. Myriad Data Points Vulnerable to Exploitation [80]
Source: T. Mead, (2015). Risk Assessment Data Quality and Security for
School and Campus Records. Unpublished Manuscript [80].

Mismatch of Educator Talent versus Student Demographics

Studies show that the demographic mismatch between educators and public school students they serve has a negative effect on learning [81]. All educators serve as role models. Educators of all ethnicities and races can take advantage of "*insider*" cultural "*knowledge*" to motivate students toward academic progress. Minority teachers of the same ethnicity and socio-economic backgrounds as their students hold a "*humanistic commitment*" to positively impact the lives of minority students [81, p.2]. Some posit that this *'diversity gap'* explains the widening chasm of assessment scores and graduation rates existing between minority students in comparison to their nonminority peers [82, p.1].

The lack of relational interconnectedness can increase the threat of a data breaches. Researchers describe educational environments of incivility and insufficient mutual respect [84]. Lott [85] cited Opotow (1990, p.1) stressing that people perceived as *others* are believed to be, by extension, " nonentities, expendable, or undeserving; consequently harming them appears acceptable, appropriate or just" [85, p. 102]. In the absence of financial motives in contrast to the private sector, detached disdain reins.

Inequitable Technology Resources and Support for Rural and Urban Poor

In addition to the negative impact of educator mismatches for race and gender, researchers are on the cusp of understanding the negative effects of concentrated poverty and the inequitable allocation of school resources. "The percentage of U.S. students in high-poverty schools (poverty rates greater than 30%) doubled from 7% in 2007 to 16% in 2011. Decades of research demonstrate that concentrated poverty is a significant barrier to educational progress" [152, p.2].

This is particularly noteworthy in the budgetary areas of technology, data security and support. The National Center for Education Statistics reports that teacher computer and internet usage while at the school is largely determined by the school's poverty level [153].

"Teachers in schools with a school poverty level of less than 11 percent were more likely to use computers or the Internet "a lot" for creating instructional materials (52 percent) than teachers in schools with a school poverty level of 71 percent or more (32 percent). This pattern also held for teachers who used computers for administrative record keeping (43 versus 24 percent for the same groups) [153, para 4].

National pressure exerted upon rural towns and urban districts to increase technology use in the classroom in spite of limited access to technology support and resources pose grave dangers. These districts often assign one technology professional to several schools or expand the duties of related professionals (audio visual technician, librarian) to include technology. One frustrated parent reflected,

"Philadelphia schools don't just have a textbook problem. They have a data problem—which is actually a people problem. We tend to think of data as immutable truth. But we forget that data and data-collection systems are created by people. Flesh-and-blood humans need to count the books in a school and enter the numbers into a database. Usually, these humans are administrative assistants or teacher's aides. But severe state funding cuts over the past several years have meant cutbacks in the school district's administrative staff. Even the best data-collection system is useless if there are no people available to manage it" [154, para 40].

What types of confidential student data are vulnerable to subject to hacking and accidental disclosure?

Confidential Student Information Increases Identity Theft Risk

This section describes the types of data routinely collected, stored and reported upon by schools and universities that pose as security risks. Once confidential student information is divulged, the threat of child identity theft is so severe that the Federal Trade Commission (FTC) has provided consumer information briefs to the general public stating that, "a child's social security number can be used by identity thieves to apply for government benefits, open bank and credit card accounts, apply for a loan or utility service, or rent a place to live..." [86]. The FTC urges consumers to take **immediate action** if their child's information is being misused.

Due to the elevated threat, the Data Quality Campaign identified 83 legislative bills in 32 states introduced "to address emerging concerns" of threats to student data privacy [87]. This risk is not new. It was identified in a 2009 Children's Education Records and Privacy Report which determined that states collect much more data than required and store in vulnerable systems. The study concluded that "many states provide obscure, incomplete, or difficult to decipher information about their data practices and programs" [88]. The Pew Trust reported similar findings in 2013 [89]. These academic findings are representative of the real situations. In 2010, an unintentional disclosure of student names and disability status occurred at District of Columbia Public School Systems, leading the local union president to respond, "Parents and the Washington Teachers Union (WTU) would certainly want to know what steps will be taken by the city and the school district to correct the problem and ensure that such a breach can never occur again" [90]. Data was breached again less than 30 days later [91]. And, then again in February 2016. The District of Columbia is not alone. Breaches and unintentional disclosures are experienced at all levels.

Privacy Rights Clearinghouse, as cited by Journalist Dance of the Baltimore Sun [92] identified security breaches exposing millions of social security numbers, bank account numbers and personally identifying information for families applying for admission. See Table 13 below for a Threat valuation and risk assessment model.

Level of Risk	Threat and Vulnerability	Affected Personally Identifiable Private Information
High Risk	High Threat, High Vulnerability	Student Names, Social Security Numbers, Address, Date of Birth, Parent's Names, Disability Status
High Risk	High Threat, High Vulnerability	Students' individual data linked through the years with longitudinal data systems
Medium Risk	High Threat, Low Vulnerability	Redacted partially de-identified student data and aggregate data tables
Low Risk	Low Threat, Low Vulnerability	Anonymized data that cannot be linked across years and public aggregate data tables

Table 13. Level of Data Security Risk of Student Private Information [93] [94] [95]
Source: T. Mead, (2015). Data Security Risk in Education. Unpublished Manuscript [94].
Adapted from SANS Institute [93] and the Information Classification Hierarchy [95].

The table above identifies security risks by specific type and corresponding methods for treating the data to lower threat vulnerabilities [94]. For example, the highest risk, greatest threat, highest vulnerability category is described with the following characteristics: it exists when the collection, storage, and reporting of PIPI such as first, last name, middle initial, birth date, social security number, mother's maiden name, and so on. At this point, the data holds the highest value. Students are most vulnerable to identity theft where the data obtained by criminals can be directly used without modification.

Re-sale of Student Data without Consent
Standardized exam companies, College Board and ACT Inc., were sued for selling student PIPI data at prices of 30 to 38 cents per student record during 2011 to 2013. The complainant alleged consumer fraud, deceptive business practices, breach of written contract, invasion of privacy and misappropriation of confidential information, and unjust enrichment [96]. In an unrelated case, the Electronic Privacy Information Center sued the U.S. Department of Education for "promoting regulations that are alleged to undercut student privacy and parental consent" in 2013 [97].

Hacking of Student Data Records- External Threat
Sensing an opportunity, criminals target the education sector for malware. From January to June 2010, "forty-four percent of all malware infections hit schools and universities" [98]. By 2014, thirty colleges reported data breaches infecting the records of

almost 1 million students and staff [99]. The threat was so pervasive that in the sector that President Obama introduced legislation to deal with identity theft [100]. In 2015, Symantec Corporation [101] included education sector within the top five sectors susceptible to external data breaches and exclaimed that there were at least 1,359,190 identities exposed in the education sector alone. Please see the image below.

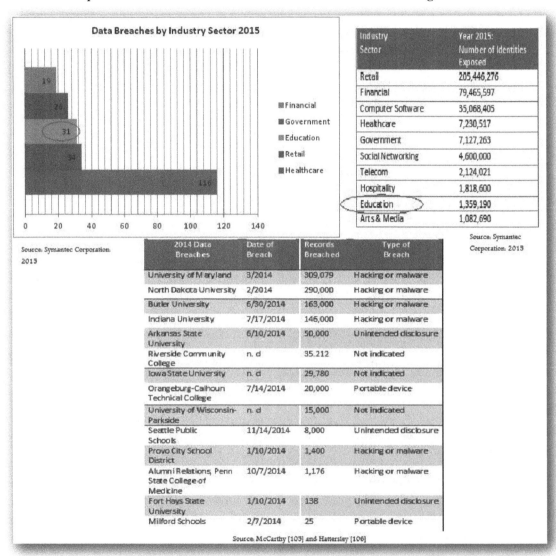

Image 14. 2015 Data Breaches by Industry Sector and Number of Exposed Identities [101] [105] [106]

Free Market Approach of Federal Government

In addition to new privacy legislation to protect student data, the Department of Education hired a Chief Privacy Officer and established a Privacy Technical Assistance

Center. The agency prepares Technical Briefs to inform educational institutions of best practices. Even so, it restricts the scope of the briefs. As a forewarning, it recognizes its limitations stating that the briefs "are presented as voluntary methods and not a one-size-fits-all solution; it is essential that each institution's data policies account for all applicable Federal, State, local and tribal laws, as well as its community's needs" [108] [109]. Without proscriptive and uniform data protection standards, the task becomes daunting for under-funded states and under-staffed districts and schools.

Lack of Enforcement Power

There are several federal Acts legislating the governance of confidential student information. The Family Educational Rights and Privacy Act of 1974 (FERPA) [110], the Fair Credit Reporting Act of 1970 (FCRP) [111], Gramm-Leach-Bliley Act of 1999 (GLBA) [112], Fair and Accurate Credit Transactions Act of 2003 (FACTA) [113], Health Insurance Portability and Accountability Act of 1996 (HIPAA) [114]; FERPA and FCRA will be emphasized here.

In 2014, the U.S. Department of Education issued guidance to protect student personal information and has proposed modifications to FERPA [115] [116]. FERPA is a federal privacy law that protects the privacy of educational records such as report cards, transcripts, disciplinary records, contact and family information, and class schedules. It gives parents and legal guardians the right to inspect, review, and request corrections. In many instances, educators must receive written consent from parents and legal guardians to release certain data. What happens when FERPA has been violated? Presently the Department "cannot take enforcement actions against improper disclosure" of private personal information by entities who collect, use, and record student personal information when the students are no longer enrolled. This includes state education agencies, post secondary agencies, research organizations, and student loan lenders receiving Department of Education funds.

Recent Changes to Family Education Records Privacy Act (FERPA)

Recent changes to FERPA have further increased the risk of unintentional disclosure of personally identifiable private information.

Gaps in Enforcement of FERPA

In addition to the significant changes in the FERPA, there are gaps in oversight and enforcement compliance. Please see below an analysis of FERPA. Please refer to the two tables below for a review of the significant changes to FERPA, privileges and corresponding obligations.

Significant Changes to FERPA
It is easier for state education agencies to share PIPI with other state agencies and external organizations without prior consent.
A state education agency no longer needs specific legal authorization to release local education agency PIPI data.
An education agency may disclose PIPI to a contractor, consultant, volunteer, or other party for outsources services after meeting certain requirements.
PIPI can be disclosed without prior consent for conducting studies to develop, validate, and administer assessments, student aid programs and to improve instruction.
An authorized representative may obtain access to PIPI to audit and evaluate program services. The authorized representative does not have to be under the direct control of the hiring body.

Source: FERPA, Recent Changes in Federal Regulations and State Compliance Moran [117] and Rinehart-Thompson [118]

Privileges	Without Obligations
Specific information must be recorded in the students records to describe the information that was disclosed and to who it was provided.	There does not exist a standardized system or report form for which to do so.
A parent or eligible student must be able to obtain information to whom their PIPI was disclosed upon review of the student's record.	There does not yet exist a uniform method, system or report for logging and identifying disclosures.
When schools publish student directory information, they are required to give public notice to parents and eligible students on the information types to be recorded and given the option to 'opt out.'	There does not exist a record-keeping method, system or report form to track 'opt outs' and submit to US Department of Education.
Any entity or individual authorized by a state or local education agency can obtain access without prior written consent to personally identification information from student's education records for audit or evaluation of federal legal requirements.	There does not exist a system to record the names of authorized entities or individuals obtaining PIPI, the date, duration period of the audit and/or evaluation.
Authorized representatives, when obtaining private student data are not held to strict standards of accountability for destroying records after use.	An accountability system for all holders, collectors, users and stores of PIPI has yet to be designed.
Under the 'studies exception' researchers are not required to sign agreements specifying the study's purpose, scope and duration. Nor are they required to destroy information upon study completion. They have the freedom to share personally identifiable student and parent information with other entities.	The parameters of sharing PIPI by researchers under the studies exception with external parties has yet to be defined.

Source: Mead, T. (2015). Privileges and Corresponding Obligations of FERPA. Unpublished Manuscript [119]. Based upon an analysis of Moran [117] and Rinehart-Thompson's [118] work.

Image 15. Significant Changes, Privileges of FERPA and Corresponding Obligations [119]

Noncompliance with the Red Flag Rule: Fair Credit Reporting Act

In addition to FERPA, an amendment to the Fair Credit Reporting Act (FCRA) requires that entities extending credit or reporting upon credit transactions confirm the identity of their customers and to establish programs to prevent identity theft. This is known as the Red Flags Rule. The Red Flags Rule is applicable to colleges, universities and training providers. Institutions of higher learning establish payment plans for tuition, room and board. These entities participate in federal loan programs such as the Perkins and Stafford. As such, the Red Flags Rule is applicable [120]. Many post secondary colleges and universities are unprepared and could face fines of up to $2,500 and civil penalties from the Federal Trade Commission (FTC). Grant Thornton reported in 2010,

"The Red Flags Rule (FTC 16 CFR 681) compliance deadline is approaching, and many higher education institutions are not prepared. This is largely because they 1) have never heard of the rule, 2) don't think they are covered by the rule or 3) have been distracted by other priorities" [121, p.1].

Predatory Practices Using Data to Target Minorities and Low Income Families

The U.S. Department of Education, under Title IV of the Higher Education Act provides financial support to low income students attending public, private nonprofit, and private for-profit colleges, universities, and career oriented schools [122]. Smith and Parrish [123] found that 80% of undergraduate students attending for-profit colleges and universities qualified for federal financial aid in comparison to 57% of undergraduate students attending traditional private and publically funded colleges. These statistics demonstrate that for-profit institutions serve comparatively more low-income students and members of under-represented minority groups than nonprofit institutions" [124, p. 12].

The use of Title IV has grown considerably through the years. Halperin [125] reported that for-profit and career schools receive about $33 billion of Title IV financial assistance annually. The College Board [126] determined that these students receive 25% of all Pell Grants and 25% of all direct loans to students. This is a dramatic increase from 1997. Just $18 billion were distributed to support approximately seven million students [127].

In spite of taxpayer investments in students attending for-profit institutions, the U.S. Senate Committee on Health, Education, Labor and Pensions [128] uncovered poor student outcomes. A two-year investigation found that "more than half of the students who enrolled in those colleges in 2008-9 left without a degree or diploma" [128, p.1]. The Committee asserted, "by 2009, at least 76 percent of students attending for-profit colleges were enrolled in a college owned by either a company traded on a major stock exchange or a college owned by a private equity firm. These demands for financial returns are contraindicated by the investment necessary to provide a high quality education [128, p.1]. As examples, HELP analyzed the staffing structure of for-profit colleges and found that the ratio of recruitment staff to student services staff was 2.5 to 1. Smith and Parrish [129] determined that "for-profit institutions spend nearly one-quarter (23%) of their revenue on marketing and recruiting, while spending just 17% on actual instruction" [129, p. 7]. The funds allocated to marketing and recruitment expenses in comparison to those for student services can lead to "poor student outcomes. Many for-profit institutions frequently find themselves in the news, characterized as unscrupulous or predatory, leading to questions about the propriety of government support for some for-profit institutions" [130, p. 121].

Student Debt Relief Scams

In 2005, about nine million Americans turned to credit counselors for help lowering their debt. Many are debt relief scammers. Unscrupulous "counselors compound problems, offering improper advice, engaging in deceptive practices, or charging exorbitant fees [131, p.13]. To date, federal and state regulators have filed more than 500 enforcement actions against mortgage debt relief companies. So far, authorities have filed suit against ten bucket shops. The way in which the scams operate is not unique to the financial aid industry. Companies advertising student financial aid and other debt relief services send promotions by email and direct mail to targeted individuals. They also announce deals on the radio, cable television, and websites frequented by indebted college students. "Some [student] clients ended up in a worse position while paying the firm to solve their problems" [132, p.85].

As a background, 40 million Americans are indebted to institutions for approximately $1.3 trillion for student loans. The Consumer Financial Protection Bureau estimates that 8 million borrowers are already in default. Wasik implies that the US Department of Education is partly responsible, citing the Department's 2014 Office of Inspector General report which criticizes the agency for lacking a "comprehensive plan or strategy to prevent student loan defaults" [132, p.84].

Distance Learning

Online and distant learning are receiving increased acceptance in both elementary and secondary school systems and post secondary [133] [134]. The Office of the Inspector General for the U.S. Department of Education emphasizes the risk of fraud, computer-assisted crimes and identity theft in distance learning programs. At each stage of the learning process: from admission and financial aid applications, course registration, grade calculations, coursework completion, academic records maintenance to tuition payments occur over the internet without any face-to-face meetings. Further, distance programs are not required to verify student identities. Complications arise when identities are stolen and accomplices are recruited to increase the magnitude of the scheme. In fact, individuals operating rings

"target mainly lower-cost institutions because federal student aid awards easily cover tuition resulting in a higher award balance (known as a refund) paid to the student and intended for educational expenses such as books and room and board. It is these financial aid refund awards which the fraud ring participants seek. The student applicants have no intention of pursuing a degree, and often are not even eligible for federal student aid because they do not have a legitimate high school diploma or GED. The participants take a cut of the financial aid refund proceeds and the turn the remainder over to the ringleaders" [135, p. 1].

Elementary and Secondary
In 2009-2010 school year, approximately 1.3 million high school students enrolled in distance learning courses [136]. This represented a fourfold increase from 2004-2005. At the time, there were about 300,000 enrollments.

Post Secondary
According to the U.S. News & World Report [137], "more than 6.1 million students took at least one online class during fall 2010; a 10.1 percent increase over the year before." While the growth as abated, it is significantly higher than the growth rate in higher education overall [138].

Changes in Federal Audit and Monitoring Requirements
The Office of Management and Budget (OMB) made three changes in federal audit and monitoring requirements for federal grantees.

The first change was "to increase the funding threshold for non-federal audits to $750,000" from $500,000 [139, p. 16]. As a result, about "5,000 non-federal entities will be relieved of the single-audit requirement" [140].

The second change was to require an analysis of potential grantee risk prior to award. The five criteria used to determine risk are: financial stability, previous federal grant experience, existence of an internal control system, prior performance, and adverse

information (Discretionary Grants Handbook, as cited by Kwak and Keleher [139]..
The 2013 OMB guidance discussed above is in alignment with the U.S. Department of
Education 2014 policy for conducting pre-award risk reviews [139, p. 18]).

The third was a consolidation of eight separate sets of guidance into one to "elimi-
nate duplicative and conflicting guidance, encourage efficient use of information
technology and shared services, strengthen oversight, and provide for consistency and
transparency" [140].

The reduction of 5,000 single audits annually as indicated by the first change has the
potential to increase risk for fraud and computer-assisted crime due to non-detection.
The second and third change fail to consider data protection, network, and systems
security risk as critical factors when assessing the overall organizational pre-award risk.

PART THREE

THE FRAUD PRISM

Purpose of this Chapter

The purpose of this chapter is twofold. First, in presenting a new Fraud theory, it emphasizes the internal occurrence of mail and wire fraud, white collar crime, bribery, kickbacks, larceny, theft, embezzlement, money laundering, deprivation of honest services, and corruption committed by educators and service providers who possess educational credentials. These insiders use their employment and/or inside access to commit fraud. Second, this chapter examines the conditions in the education sector that entice insiders and outsiders to conspire together or act individually to target educational institutions for criminal activities.

The Fraud Prism™

The Fraud Prism™ [1] represents a new meso theory bridging micro and macro explanations for fraud and criminality. This theory has been used throughout this book to describe and better understand detection, enforcement, prosecution, and prevention of white collar [2] crime and criminals in the education sector. While the Fraud Diamond [3] and its predecessor, the Fraud Triangle [4], are universally accepted concepts for describing fraud, they are insufficient for analyzing fraud perpetrated by educators and others employed in an educational setting. They are inadequate for evaluating why schools and universities are often targets by outsiders.

The statement of causation is best illustrated by a visual image of a prism. The Fraud Prism ™ is three dimensional and is viewed through the risk lenses of certainty of discovery, enforcement, and prosecution. These factors have the power to bend one's perception of the traditional elements used by criminologists to explain fraud and related crimes. They are rationalization, incentive, opportunity, and capability.

The internal calculations of the certainty of discovery, enforcement, and prosecution ultimately determines whether fraud will be committed. "When people have the opportunity to commit a crime, they weigh the downside such as the risk of getting caught and punished and being stigmatized by society against the upside" [5, p. 41]. This new theory relies upon an incentive based economic model of crime to analyze, explain and describe the way in which individual perceptions and "attitudes toward risk affect the extent of illegal behavior [6, p. 3].

This theory applies to internal criminals (educators, staff, and management), external criminals and organizations (vendors, crime syndicates); for schools and universities can be victims of fraud or perpetrators of fraud by way of administrative practices and through their governing board, administrators, faculty, and staff.

In the education sector, the perception of detection is low. This attitude may be associated with an increased threat for fraud, white collar, data, and computer-assisted crime [7] as depicted in the image below.

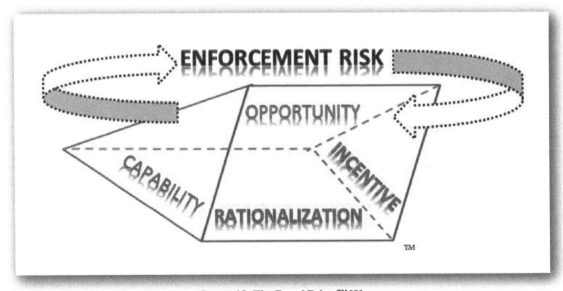

Image 16. The Fraud Prism™ [8]

The Fraud Prism Theory [8] may be tested, measured, disproved and extends beyond a mere statement of belief.

As with all theories, the Fraud Prism, is underpinned by the propositions used to interpret the relationship between two or more concepts. Each will be discussed in greater detail in subsequent sections of this chapter.

Propositions

1. When potential perpetrators perceive the risk of discovery is low, the threat of white collar crime increases.
2. When potential perpetrators perceive the risk of enforcement is low, the threat of white collar crime increases.
3. When potential perpetrators perceive the risk of prosecution is low, the threat of white collar crime increases.
4. When potential perpetrators perceive that there exists an environment of undisciplined computer, data, and technology use, the threat of white collar crime increases.

Hypothesis Statements and Variables

Ho1: The independent variables: perception of discovery risk, enforcement risk, and   prosecution risk influence the dependent acts of fraud and related white collar crime.

Ho2: The independent variables: perception of discovery risk, enforcement risk, and prosecution risk influence perpetrator behavior.

Further research needs to be undertaken to determine if the relationship between the independent and dependent variables are cause and effect, causal, or correlational.

Three Variables Associated with Enforcement Certainty

The probability of crime discovery, investigation, due process, and punishment and the time elapsing between phases greatly impacts a potential criminal's assessment of risk [9].

The lack of clarity regarding offenses and the diversity of resolutions like administrative, civil, and/or criminal proceedings have fostered occupational fraud, including an environment whereby computer-assisted crime and fraud by outsiders is feasible. The higher the certainty of crime discovery, the immediacy and severity of punishment and the likelihood of public condemnation before one's peers, the higher the enforcement risk [9]. This sentiment was foretold almost a decade ago. Nichols and Berliner [10] issued the following warning:

"But it we continue to monitor public education with high states tests when we know full well that we should expect distortions and corruptions of the measurement system; we will be requested to regularly investigate how such distortion and corruption occurs and determine who is responsible and we will also be required to severely punish miscreants when we find them" [10, p. 165].

This is striking because, for "persons who have much to lose," a slight increase in the likelihood of crime discovery, prosecution, and punishment produces a risk they are unwilling to take [11, p.30].

Risk of Discovery

There are several reasons why the discovery risk of fraud and computer-assisted crime in education is perceived as low. First, crime in general often goes undiscovered. Baumer and Lauritsen [12] found that less than half of all crimes are detected by the justice system. Second, while most crimes go unreported to police due to non-detection, others are detected and resolved outside of the criminal system. Therefore, they are not included in the official crime statistics [13]. Third, while most fraud is committed with computers, most computer-related crimes probably go undetected [14]. The Australian Federal Police (AFP) estimated that about 80% of computer-assisted crime victims "were completely unaware that an offense involving their system had been committed" [14, p. 2]. Fourth, computer-assisted crime affords extra layers of protection for the criminal. Anonymity buffers the criminal from the victim, giving the criminal more time to perpetuate the crime. Further, the crime and harm to the victim may remain hidden indefinitely, making prosecution remote [15].

Breadth and Depth of Fraud

Fraud can be perpetrated across departments spanning several functions. Front office activities of pre-admissions, registration, master scheduling, grant reporting, and matriculation are vulnerable. For back office operations, the risk of fraud does not diminish. Administrators, vendors, and outsiders exploit vulnerabilities in payroll, data management, information technology, finance, procurement, and operations. Please see Images 17 and 18 for sample organizational charts with circles denoting particularly problematic areas. For detailed discussions on fraudulent actions, please refer to subsequent sections.

Image 17. Sample Elementary & Secondary Organizational Chart

Principal					
AP Academics			AP Operations	AP Student Services	
Chair CTE Business	Chair Humanities	Chair STEM	Business & HR Manager	Chair, Spec Education	Chair Guidance
	English	Science	Finance	IEP	Records Mgmt
Business	Social Studies	Engineer	Grants Mgmt	Para professionals	Attendance
CTE	Foreign Language	Math	Security		Discipline
	Music	Health & PE			

Image 18. Sample Post Secondary Organizational Chart

President							
			Assistant to President	VP Strategic Planning	Chief Invest Officer	Public Affairs Officer	
Faculty Dean	College Dean		VP of Operations		Provost & Treasurer		VP Alumni Relations
Chairs	Associate Deans		Facilities	Dining Services	Admissions	Research Support	Reunion
Center Directors	Honor Code	Academic Resource	Risk Management	General Counsel	Financial Planning	Budget Office	Major Gifts
Graduate Program	Registrar	Counselor	Safety	Human Resources	Information Technology	Financial Aid	Annual Giving
Athletics	Campus Life	Campus Safety	Auxiliary Services	Real Estate	Controller	Library	Gift Planning
					Planned Giving	Treasury	Corporate Gifts
					Institute Research		Info Systems

Source: T. Mead (2015). Risk Assessment Data Quality and Security for
School and Campus Records. Unpublished Manuscript [16].

49

Lack of Historical Studies

Criminologists utilize case-based reasoning to detect and solve crime. This process involves the analysis of each new incident. A comparison of the incident to previous incidents with similar attributes is undertaken. In time, for every successive incident presented, associated attributes are added to the knowledge base, incorporated into the rule set, and new patterns are identified or old ones are expanded [17]. In the absence of historical studies and compilations of fraud cases in education, the discovery of crime becomes particularly difficult. Crime fighters do not have an archive of cases readily available for comparison. Nor do they have criminal profiles, red flags or crime symptoms to use for preventive alerts. Case theory has not been fully developed. These limitations make organizations more vulnerable. The criminals who commit crime in an education setting are therefore less prone to detection, capture, and prosecution.

Lack of Longitudinal Data

To emphasize the importance of historical studies, longitudinal, and quantitative data, the Institute for Fraud Prevention, when questioned about fraud in education has said, "The Membership does not discount the need for research into fraud in education; at the same time, other concerns are a priority, especially given the areas of concern regarding about being able to identify and locate enough data on education fraud to derive meaningful statistical inferences" [18].

Need for the Reprioritization of High Level Enforcement

A count of the U.S. Department of Education crime data reports from 1999 to 2013 as discussed in Chapter 1 show that fraud in education is on the increase [19]. However, the FBI "doesn't generally become involved [in] these cases." Rather the FBI when "resources allow—assist our partners at the Department of Education and other agencies in rooting out some of the more egregious offenders" [20, p. 1].

The FBI [21], the Association of Certified Fraud Examiners, [22] [23] and others [24] have identified common fraud scams prevalent in particular industries. Health care fraud is identified using patient demographics, treatment details and services, policy and claim information, benefits and amount [25]. Retail fraud; by reviewing date/time stamps, transactional data, payment history and account age [26] [27]. securities fraud; involves exams of accounts receivable, allowance of doubtful debts, and net sales figures ratios [28]. In a review of the literature and investigation reports, the manner in which fraud in education can be discovered; with the exception of financial aid fraud, has not yet been uncovered.

Risk of Enforcement

Enforcement involves the detection, deterrence, investigation, punishment, and resolution of violators of policies and law. Whey used effectively, it compels day-to-day obedience and adherence to established norms. Monitoring, evaluation, inspection, and control represent components of an enforcement system.

School Policing

White-collar criminals often begin to exhibit violent tendencies when left un-checked and inadequately monitored [134]. They may become dangerous red collar criminals. This leaves our vulnerable school-age children and young adults at grave threat for harm and no source of reliable protection. Criminologists have not yet collected metadata to develop criminal profiles to determine the point within the spectrum white collar criminals morph to red. Nor have they identified with specificity, the illegal acts most prevalent in the education sector that may uncover latent tendencies toward violence. Without the standardized research and routine collection of data, one may never know.

There are 19,000 sworn law enforcement officers supported by $750 million in federal funding posted in American schools in 2009 [135]. Their priority has been to support the disciplining of students for strict obedience to school policy while simultaneously thwarting violent crime. These school-based resource officers have the skill set to monitor and investigate all crimes; whether committed by adults or youth. The Harvard Review reports that the focus, however, has been on the criminalization of students [136]. There exists a reform movement to reduce the presence of law enforcement in schools [137]. As such, this author proposes a gradual shift in officer scope to student protection, albeit from other students or from any and all adults including educators, staff and parents. Some of the other enforcement methods used to lower the threat of crime follows.

Monitoring Systems

"Monitoring follows a management model with a focus on improving day-to-day project operation" [29, p.45]. Educational institutions spend roughly $2 billion annually to assess student mastery of content knowledge, inform instruction and improve curriculum. Often standardized summative exams are used as a foundation [30]. The results of student data are then used as one factor for evaluating teacher effectiveness [31]. The next phase in the continuous improvement cycle are observations and on-site monitoring. This is done to verify adherence to program plans and to evaluate organizational effectiveness. Regulatory bodies use these systems too for ensuring compliance with educational industry standards, state and federal laws and regulations Fitz-Gibbon [32] added "improvement begins with locating problems" [32, p.50]. An analysis of organizational effectiveness represents the final process and identifies areas that show a misalignment to industry standards, deviations from stated plans, misallocations of funds and resources, and noncompliance with regulations and laws.

Two continuous improvement cycle concepts are presented here. The first, as represented by Image 19 was developed by this author in the context of educational systems. The second image is based upon the McKinsey 7 (Seven) Factors and is illustrated in Image 20.

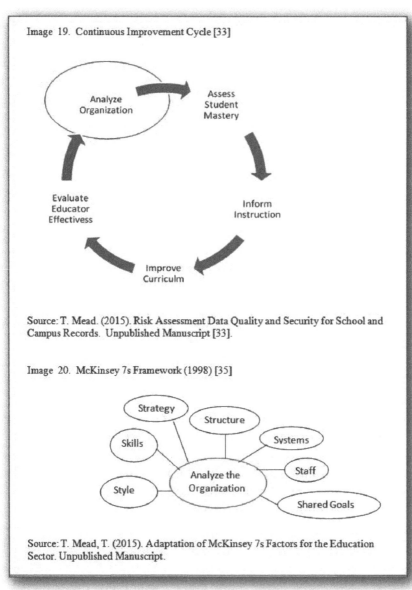

Image 19. Continuous Improvement Cycle [33]

Source: T. Mead. (2015). Risk Assessment Data Quality and Security for School and Campus Records. Unpublished Manuscript [33].

Image 20. McKinsey 7s Framework (1998) [35]

Source: T. Mead, T. (2015). Adaptation of McKinsey 7s Factors for the Education Sector. Unpublished Manuscript.

The continuous cycle of evaluation and improvement was best articulated by Lockheed and Verspoor as cited in Kamens and McNeely [34],

"Achievement testing at the primary level can provide indicators of student attainment of principal educational objectives: functional literacy and numeracy. When combined with monitoring systems on costs, student flows, material inputs and staff, achievement data enable managers to identify schools and districts that are performing well and those that are not . . . and to identify areas of the curriculum where improvements are needed" [34, p. 410].

The improvement cycle is not a new concept. McKinsey & Company developed the 7s Framework as a model for analyzing organizational effectiveness in the business domain [35]. Of the seven factors, this author labels 4s as macro organisms largely impacting the organizational ecosystem (strategy, systems and structure) and 3s as micro organisms influencing individual attitudes, values and behaviors (staff, skills, style and shared values).

Federal Grants Monitoring
In the 1990s, the U.S. Department of Education utilized a "gotcha" mentality for monitoring grants "to increase the number of audit findings and produce large monetary recoveries from recipients of federal funds" [36, p. xii]. A decade later, its enforcement policy transitioned to the use of "audits, monitoring and technical assistance to identify difficult problems and strengthen the underlying program and development of effective corrective action for the future" [36, p.xii]. By 2015, the IBM Center for the Business of Government advised the U.S. Department of Education to integrate risk mitigation with monitoring of program plans, implementation, policy, and standards [37].

State Grants Monitoring
The federal government affords states considerable autonomy for monitoring subrecipients of federal grants. While a reasonable assurance standard must be used, the frequency, content, duration, or format (onsite audit, limited scope desk audit, or other means) are not mandated. The lack of specificity is a crucial weakness. "Good monitoring also allows the project to be effectively evaluated; therefore it is a continuous process and periodic surveillance (for both observation and vigilance) of the project implementation" [38, p. 33].

Third Party Year-end Evaluations

"Evaluation uses a research model to assess the extent to which project objectives have been met or surpassed" [38, p.45]. In 2014, the state education agency in the District of Columbia requested an investment of $2.19 billion or 20.4% of the District's budget for public education. This amount was almost two times higher than the investment into public safety ($1.19 billion) and was second to human support services ($4.3 billion) according to the FY2015 Budget Hearing [39]. And yet,

> "these funds may be going towards unsuccessful and wasteful programs that provide no benefit to DCs traditional and charter public schools and their students. Currently, no formal evaluation system of external support organizations exists within DC. By creating a rigorous evaluation system, DC s OSSE [state education agency] will be able to more efficiently target its limited funding to beneficial organizations" [40. P. i].

The importance of a robust control system cannot be understated. More than a decade ago, the U.S. General Accounting Office testified that the Department of Education's "weak internal controls led to instances of fraud and other improper payments" [41, p. 1]. By 2014, the U.S. Department of Education assured that there were no significant weaknesses found in its internal controls of operations, financial reporting and systems. Even so, former Secretary Duncan acknowledged that the Department still had "internal control- and compliance related issues, such as those identified by our auditors and the management challenges raised by the Office of the Inspector General" [42, p. 44].

Controls System

Field monitoring, on-site investigation, and year-end evaluations are uniquely separate though fully integrated aspects of a controls system. These processes are used to compel adherence to laws, regulations, and policies. Of the three, a key similarity is shared among monitoring and investigations. The timeliness of the findings allows for incorporation into current year operations. Such feedback can positively affect programming in near real time. On the other hand, program evaluations are conducted by third parties at the end of the funding year. As such, identified shortcomings are not corrected prior to end-of-year program closeout. While there are many similarities between the audit and monitoring functions in comparison to investigations; the primary differences as illustrated in Image 21.

Investigations are conducted using deductive reasoning (if, how, why, and with whom) illegal and fraudulent acts have been committed while completing routine tasks as outlined in Image 22. Finally, upon the conclusion of an investigation, reports may be turned over to prosecutors to prove the intent to deceive. Image 23 depicts a sample listing of behaviors traditionally used to prove the intent to deceive. Deceptive intentions form the foundation for criminal fraud charges.

Image 21. Audit and Investigation Comparisons [44] [45]

Conceptual Element	Monitoring and Audits	Investigations
Preconception of Wrong-doing	No	Yes
Goal	Verification of compliance	Un/substantiation of Allegation
Why conduct a _____?	Mandatory legal requirement	Reaction to an event
Nature	General	Critical and in-depth
Common Methods	Self reports, independent review of financial statements, and site visits to observe operations	Independent search/collection of evidence, document review, on-site observation, interrogation, inquiry and inspection
Document Review Scope	Test mathematical accuracy Non-statistical sampling	Thorough examination of documents
Sequence	Occurs before investigation	Occurs after an Audit/Monitoring Visit
Basis	Standards, Principles, Policies and Procedures	Rules of Evidence, Civil and/or Criminal Procedure
Report	Reports of Opinion and/or Findings	Investigative Report to Un/substantiate Allegations
Confidentiality of Report	Not generally	Yes

Source: Auditing: Principles and Practice (2015) R. Kumar. & V. Sharma, p. 490 [44] and L.W. Voma (2008). *Fraud Risk Assessment*. John Wiley & Sons, Inc. Hoboken, NJ [45].

Image 22. Sample Fraudulent Acts by Profession [70]

Profession	Daily tasks	Illegal Behavior
Cashier	Operating a cash register	Theft
Accountant	Completing a federal/state tax return	Filing false tax return
Physician	Prescribing medication	Prescription fraud
Attorney	Using power of attorney	Elder financial abuse
Financial Advisor	Investing client funds	Embezzlement

Source: T. Mead, (2015). Fraudulent Acts by Profession: A Comparative Study. Unpublished Manuscript [70].

Image 23. Behaviors to Prove Intent to Deceive [129]

Behaviors	
Document Tampering	Document Forgery
Destruction of Evidence	Confession
Concealment of Evidence	Lies and False Statements
Falsifying Documents	Behavior Patterns
Financial Gain	Testimony of Co-conspirator
Testimony of Direct Witness	Obstruction of Justice

Source: Adapted from University of Louisiana Office of Internal Audits and Ethics Liaison https://internalaudit.nsula.edu/fraud-awarenes [129

To prevent fraud, computer-assisted and data related crimes, monitoring, investigations, and evaluations are integral elements of a control system. Without consistent and uniform programs of evaluation, investigation, and monitoring for detecting fraud and noncompliance; social disapproval, one of the most potent methods for deterring criminal activities, is not fully exploited [43].

Social Disapproval Threatened

Laws are used to dictate the rights and obligations individuals have to one another as they live, work, and play in a collective society. On the other hand, "social norms provide a mechanism by which people through consensus, recognize and adhere to" [46, p. 24]. Individual compliance with societal laws, regulations, and policies are based upon the perception that family and friends will disapprove of them when socially accepted behaviors are violated and laws are broken.

In addition to research by Wrong [47], Nelissen and Mulder [48] completed research involving 84 participants. They concluded that social disapproval was more effective for obtaining compliance than the threat of monetary penalties. Wrong, as cited by Grasmick and Green [49] found that individuals are "especially motivated by the desire to achieve a positive image of self by winning acceptance or status in the eyes of others [49, p.328].

Monitoring, evaluation, and investigation identify prohibited conduct, target bad actors, express disapproval, retrain the workforce, and review institutional effectiveness. Communication strategies are examined to determine weaknesses in the way in which employees are informed of policies, procedures, and processes.

Risk of Prosecution

"Many crimes that are committed never result in an arrest, so arrests are not good measures of how many crimes are committed by individuals" [50, p. 133]. This is particularly true in the education sector whereby occupational fraud is resolved through disciplinary proceedings. This is unfortunate. Grasmick and Green [51] found that formal legal penalties leading to the rejection of family and friends can be the single greatest deterrent. Formal penalties and the adoption of moral codes of conduct can inhibit potential criminality. They argued that "in order to deter, actual threats of legal punishment must be communicated to individuals" [51, p.325].

Fear of Legal Punishment

Punishment, as described by philosophers (1) is burdensome, (2) the burden is intentional, (3) it is imposed upon someone found to be guilty, (4) it expresses public condemnation, and (5) it is imposed upon the guilty by a legal authority [52]. Regrettably, legal policy academicians de-emphasize the harm caused by fraud and endorse lenient sentencing [53].

When white collar crime and fraud are reduced to misdemeanors for reasons of clemency; fear of punishment can be reduced and thus the threat of social ostracization is minimized. The outcomes of misdemeanor cases are not transparent. For every 1 million convictions for felony there are more than 10 million misdemeanor cases in the United States filed each year [54]. Due to the sheer volume and lack of focused public attention in comparison with felony cases, some states fail to allocate resources to record, track, and analyze misdemeanor data. "Data about them are sparse" [54, p.1].

Even when cases are escalated to the criminal court system, the National Association of Criminal Defense Lawyers recommends the resolution of "misdemeanors that do not impact public safety to penalties that are less costly to taxpayers" [55, p.7]. They rationalize that taxpayers spend an average of $80 per inmate each day to jail offenders for these lesser crimes [56].

"Fraudsters view their crimes as being victimless, not dangerous to society and causing no visual or physical damage to anyone or anything" [57, p. 44]. Some theorists go to the extreme to argue against the imposition of **any** punishment against wrongdoers. "In part, there is a trade-off between punishment and other methods of social control. To the extent that this is so, non-penalty methods are preferable as long as they do not have other significant drawbacks" [58, p.92]. This mis-conceptualized definition of victimless crime has been adopted by the education industry.

Righton Johnson, an attorney sitting in on the interrogations of the Atlanta educators convicted of racketeering was interviewed by the New Yorker magazine [59]. He explained that teachers participating in the fabrication, altering and tampering of student answer sheets "thought they were committing a victimless crime [59]." Victimless crime represents one of the five types of crime that include violent, property, white collar, organized and victimless. Fraud and computer-assisted crime negatively impacting students in an educational system has been considered 'victimless.' For example, assessment results equip educators with information to differentiate instruction based upon student needs. Test scores are used by administrators to direct resources where they are needed most. Finally, policy makers analyze student test results to craft legislation and develop policies to address structural deficiencies.

Criminologists consider consensual crime like prostitution, illicit sex in some states and gambling as victimless crime. For the term "refers to behaviors in which people engage voluntarily and willingly even though these behaviors violate the law" [60]. Clearly minor students and parents do not knowingly consent to low quality educational programming and mismanagement of educational service brought about by fraud and computer assisted crime. As with all victims of crime, students are appropriately protected by the Crime Victims' Rights Act, 2004 [61].

Elementary and Secondary. Allegations of insider fraud within elementary or secondary school setting are rarely escalated to the criminal courts. Traditionally, educator fraud cases often resulted in disciplinary actions such as reprimands, suspensions, demotions, void and suspension of contracts [62], loss of license and job [63]. Jacob and Levitt [64] predicted that substantiated allegations of educator cheating results in mere disciplinary action.

Post secondary. Fraud occurring on the postsecondary level was no different. Tobenkin [65] found that the prosecution of admissions, enrollment fraud, and document forgery were uncommon. "Hampered by legal concerns, administrative resource limitations, and fears of bad publicity, many universities decline to pursue legal action against even egregious fraudsters" [65, p. 42]. Postsecondary administrators hold internal administrative and disciplinary hearings. These hearings tend toward leniency as the officers rendering judgment are not impartial or independent and atypically have backgrounds in criminology.

At all levels of education, criminals have resorted to perjury and even obstruction of justice and witness tampering to avoid legal punishment. Beccaria [66], a classical theorist, asserts that "the certainty of punishment—not the severity—deters people from criminal acts as well as the length of time lapsing from conviction to punishment. According to Jeffrey [67] when applied inconsistently, the "improper and sloppy use of punishment does not deter or rehabilitate." In contrast with these canons, the retention of pension benefits sends a different message to would be criminals employed and operating within the education sector.

Retention of Pension Benefits

The Governing Staff researched pension forfeitures, observing that 50% of the states in the United States have adopted pension forfeiture clauses for crimes committed [68]. The other half, therefore, allow public employees to retain their pensions regardless of the reason for their employment separation. In states where pensions can be forfeited; a criminal conviction does not result in automatic forfeiture. Some states require a felony conviction, others only misdemeanors. Granular details exist to exclude educator pensioners by reserving the revocation of pension benefits to state officeholders, elected officials and legislators, or narrow the scope to crimes committed in relation to their specific duties.

Committed to Obey the Law

As discussed in the previous chapters, education professionals are no less committed than their colleagues in other industries to obey the law. The ambiguity and multiplicity of federal and state statutes and regulations makes it difficult to abide.

Image 24. Sample Listing of Federal Laws Impacting Education [69]

Federal Law	Year Enacted
Educational Research Act	1954
National Defense Education Act	1958
Vocational Education Act	1963
Economic Opportunity Act	1964
Higher Education Act	1965
Elementary and Secondary Education Act	1965
International Education Act	1966
Education Professions Development Act	1967
Elementary & Secondary Education Assistance Programs Extension	1970
Education Amendments of 1972, 1974, 1978, 1995	1974
Family Education Rights and Privacy Act	1974
Youth Employment & Demonstration Projects Act	1977
Career Education Incentive Act	1977
Department of Education Organization Act	1979
Student Loan Consolidation and Technical Amendments Act	1983
Education for Economic Security Act	1984
Carl D. Perkins Vocational Education Act	1984
Safe Schools Act	1984
Montgomery GI Bill- Active Duty	1985
Hawkins-Stafford School Improvement Amendments	1988
Stewart B. McKinney Homeless Assistance Amendments Act	1988
Student Right-to-Know and Campus Security Act	1990
School Dropout Prevention and Basic Skills Improvement Act	1990
National Literacy Act	1991
School-to-Work Opportunities Act	1994
Chart School Expansion Act	1994
Individuals with Disabilities Education Act	1997
Workforce Investment Act	1998
College Scholarship Fraud Prevention Act	2000
No Child Left Behind Act	2002
American Recovery and Reinvestment Act	2009*
Every Student Succeeds Act	2015*

Source: National Center for Education Statistics, 2003 [69]. *After publication

Rationalization

Unlike other professions, fraud in education is an abstract concept. Seldom has fraud been drilled down to concrete individual actions, sanctions, and legal penalties. The U.S. Department of Education, Office of Inspector General, offers the following

> "fraud occurs when education grants are not applied for, received, or spent for their intended purposes, generally through theft, misappropriation, or false statements. Fraud can occur in applying for a grant, such as if false information is provided on the grant application. Fraud can also occur during performance of a grant, such as through false assertions on a performance report, theft or misappropriation of grant funds, or certain types of lack of performance under the grant. Fraud also happens when grantees try to cover up underlying problems by creating false documents, by destroying documents, or by not being truthful with investigators or others. It's important to recognize that there can be fraud even if no money has been received, such as when false information is provided in a grant application, and that type of fraud should also be reported, investigated, and prosecuted" [71, p. 1].

Rationalization occurs when potential criminals convince themselves that there are no inconsistencies between their values and fraudulent activities. A white collar criminal may find it much easier to rationalize than a street criminal. How so? Typically, white collar crime, fraud, and corruption are committed in office settings, by people with higher social status in respected positions. White collar crimes involve spreadsheets of finance, performance, and documents. These have not historically caused bodily injury or damage to physical property. However, any action committed in violation of a federal, state, county, or municipal law is a considered a crime that may be prosecuted and punished accordingly. Society has viewed white collar crime as a victimless crime. There are legal policy academicians de-emphasizing the harm caused by fraud. They endorse lenient sentencing because of white collar crime's historical distinction as non-violent [72]. "Fraudsters view their crimes as being victimless, not dangerous to society and causing no visual or physical damage to anyone or anything" [73]. They say to themselves, "No harm has been done, so therefore, illegal activity is consistent with my values." Fraudsters in the education industry may rationalize their illegal activity in much the same manner.

Pace of Rise in Education Costs Far Exceeds General Rise in the Cost of Living
To establish, operate and maintain an entity of higher learning requires a plethora of resources. As such, competitive forces to drive down the cost of tuition, room, and board are virtually nonexistent as the "entry into the market is fairly tightly controlled" [74, p. 12]. High market entry costs coupled with high demand can prompt fraudulent activities by insiders. Further, "in a globalized, information-based economy, higher education—whether it takes the form of a certificate, a two-year degree, a four-year degree, or beyond—is increasingly necessary for the American workforce" [75, p. 24]. The lifetime earnings of college graduates greatly exceed non-college graduate earnings. This may provoke potential students to commit fraud.

The exorbitantly high cost of education without viable means with which to pay has been a contributing factor to increased incidents of white collar crime in education.

For instance, households in the U.S. held more than $914 billion in student loan debt in 2012 in comparison to just $750 billion for auto loans and $672 billion in credit card debt [76]. Experts tout the value held in education and consider it an investment [77]. However, "tuition has risen since 1978 by 1,120 percent, and during that same period state funding for colleges has declined by 40 percent" [78]. Likewise, outsiders and some insiders may collude to commit fraud with little chance of detection.

As it relates specifically to educators, poor working conditions and low salary levels in comparison to peers may represent just two reasons why an educator may rationalize that fraudulent behavior is worth the risk.

K-12 Salary
The National Education Association (NEA) reports that teachers have a lower starting salary than other professions requiring similar skills and responsibilities [79]. Generally, teachers are hired at a starting salary that is 33% less than their similarly suited colleagues.

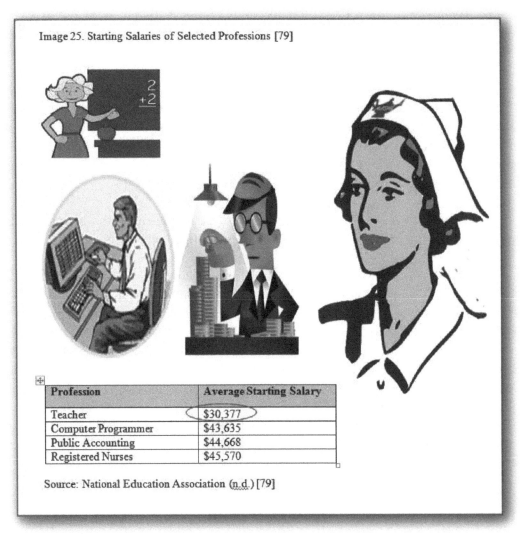

Image 25. Starting Salaries of Selected Professions [79]

Profession	Average Starting Salary
Teacher	$30,377
Computer Programmer	$43,635
Public Accounting	$44,668
Registered Nurses	$45,570

Source: National Education Association (n.d.) [79]

As teachers invest more years into teaching and gain experience, the pay gap widens. The annual pay for teachers "has fallen sharply over the past 60 years in relation to the annual pay of other workers with college degrees," adding "the average earnings of workers with at least a four-year college degree are over 50 percent higher than the average earnings of a teacher" [79, p. 1].

Teachers and support personnel "often work two to three jobs to make ends meet" [79, p. 5]. The Center for American Progress posted similar findings [79]. Many teacher who are heads of households with ten years experience of qualify for federal assistance. In addition to welfare, more than 20 percent of teachers in eleven states hold a second job to earn more money [80]. Further, "today's beginning teachers, who are discouraged by long vesting period, and the fact that they are asked to accept low pay today in return for a large pension at a distant end of a long career" [81, p.5].

This conclusion conflicts with the U .S. Bureau of Labor Statistics (USBLS) [82]. Lawrence Mishel, President of the Economic Policy Institute explained that the method by which USBLS calculates teacher salary is based upon the days worked (190 official school days divided by five, resulting in a 38 week work year) in comparison to the 48 to 52 weeks worked by non-educators. Thus, there is an under-estimation of teacher hours worked annually and a significant over-projection of teacher salaries based upon a hypothetical hourly wage rate.

Contingent Faculty in Higher Education
Contingent professors represent 74.7 percent of US faculty [83]. The American Federation of Teachers interviewed 500 adjunct faculty [84]. Fifty-seven percent indicated inadequate salaries. Forty-one percent said their expectations for the job were not realized. The Association of University Professors [85] compared salaries for contingent and tenure track-ers. Based upon $2,700 earned each three-credit course (4 per semester), the annualized salary is $21,600 in contrast to the average $66,000 starting salaries for tenure-track. Segran [86] cited a *New York Times* article whereby an adjunct "has been reduced to sleeping in her car, showering at college athletic centers and applying for food stamps" [86, p.1].

Incentive
A common incentive to commit a crime occurs when a person's earned income is not adequate to meet the desires, wants, or needs of an individual.

Bonus and Rewards
On an international scale, Eckstein [87] of the International Institute for Educational Planning, stressed that global educational reforms "are frequently submitted to abuse and even systematic corruption" [87, p. 34]. In the U.S., "the prevalence of cheating is shown to respond to relatively minor changes in teacher incentives" [88, p. 846]. School pressures include the threat of punishment for low test scores and the oppor-tunity for reward in case of high scores. These findings were mirrored by the Atlanta Public Schools Special Investigator's Report [89] and cited in Kaufmann [90]:

> "intense fear of failure to meet annual performance targets for student achieve-ment, culture of fear, retaliation and intimidation, failure of principal and ad-ministrative leadership and the use of an incentives policy" [90, p. 6].

Teacher competitive pressures and working conditions, considered secondary incentives, were cited by Kaufmann and included the desire

> "to be first and nobody wanted to be last' and to move up to older more prestigious grade levels, teaching lower grades were perceived as a demotion. Educators who participated in fraud and corruption were awarded after-school posts and preparatory periods if participated and conversely, were assigned to problem classes or not given the opportunity to move to teach students at higher grade levels, if refused to participate" [90, p.7].

Poor Qualifications and Experience to Meet Aggressive Goals

While reform introduces a myriad of incentives, it simultaneously liberalizes the certification and entry experience requirements for teachers. A U.S. Department of Education survey cited in the *New York Times* found that 25% of teachers in secondary public schools "lacked academic qualifications in the subject they teach, particularly in poorer school districts" [91]. The problem is compounded as younger, less-experienced teachers were more likely to cheat than those more experienced [92].

Lack of Classroom and Teaching Experience

"Classrooms in schools with teachers who graduated from more-prestigious undergraduate institutions were also less likely to cheat; classrooms in schools with younger teachers were more likely to cheat" [93].

Opportunity

Crimes such as negligent fraud, constructive fraud, and fraudulent misrepresentation do not require proof of intent to deceive; deceptive intent can be inferred from motive and the opportunity [94]. A key aspect of white collar crime is the pressure caused by perceptions that (1) "everybody does it, so I will too", (2) "there is no one to judge me critically," and (3) "no one to stop me." Why is criminal behavior likely in an educational setting, considering that the general public holds the highest regard for educators, particularly grade school teachers? [95].

Differential Association

Edwin Sutherland (1978) posited that social interactions in an intimate setting among law-abiding citizens and criminals lead to the adoption of criminality by the law-abider. Further as criminal activities increase, the skill level increases, as does the complexity of the crime. This theory, "Differential Association" was developed in collaboration with Donald Cressey. The five major elements of differential association conclude that criminal behavior is learned

1. not innate or inherited,
2. through interactions with other people,
3. within intimate, personal groups,
4. and the more the criminal behavior is practiced, the better one becomes at committing crime,
5. and will occur when perceived rewards are assumed to be greater than when not committing a crime [96].

With regards to insider/internal risk of fraud, the author points to Jeffrey [97] who added role modeling to Sutherland's association hypothesis as factors for criminality. Jeffrey theorized that there are incidents of crime, fraud, and misconduct in schools, in part, because crime-ridden schools lack positive social reinforcers and role modeling for students and educators to do what is right in comparison to similarly situated schools. Schools with comparable student populations, educator workforce, and urban challenges experience reduced risk for crime because they actively use positive social pressures and role modeling for deterrence [97].

Management's Unclear Messaging

Executives situated at the pinnacle of an organization are expected to use communication and role modeling to support ethical decision-making [98]. "These top managers create and maintain an ethical culture by consistently behaving in an ethical fashion and encouraging others to behave in such a manner as well" [99, p. 2]. The Association of Certified Fraud Examiners adds, "employees will do what they witness their bosses doing" [100, p.1]. Creating and enforcing clear conduct codes, modeling acceptable behaviors, and communicating expected procedures are paramount responsibilities for management in the deterrence of crime [101].

Weak Internal Controls and Lenient Oversight

The failure of top managers to model and communicate acceptable behaviors, identify impermissible conduct, and to enforce them place schools at grave risk for fraud. According to the Association of Certified Fraud Examiners [102],

"there are many different forms of misconduct that go on in the workplace and are observe by employees every year. Yet, many employees do not report this unethical conduct. Only 55 percent of employees said that they reported misconduct they observed in the workplace; a 10 percent drop from the previous survey conducted in 2003" [102, p.4].

Reasons given for not reporting: employer failed to take corrective action, disclosure of complainant identity, whistleblower retaliation, and uncertainty of whom to contact. "Employees who witnessed their company actively following its code of ethics were the *most* likely to report misconduct in the workplace, according to the 2005 National Business Ethics Survey [102, p. 4].

Reductions in District OIG Independence

Three of the largest public school districts, the cities of New York City, Chicago and Los Angeles established independent enforcement agencies to change the perceptions of lenient oversight and to formally impose societal pressures. These agencies are known as inspectors general. They provide oversight for educational programming [103]. Their primary purposes are to detect, deter and investigate fraud, waste and abuse. They are staffed by professional auditors and investigators. They maintain independence and are not supervised or managed by the centralized school system. By the early to mid start of the millennium, however, the inspector general office of New York City lost some of its independence from school management since its mayoral takeover in the summer of 2002.

Inadequate Self Regulatory and Policing System

The mission of self regulatory accreditation has evolved to gatekeeper. The federal government refers to the accreditation seal as an entry point for access to $130 billion in student loans and grants [104]. Accreditors are relied upon for the independent evaluation of organizational quality. Even so, accrediting bodies are not mandated by law to (a) publically disclose accreditation reports, or (b) divulge peer reviewer identities for specific colleges. The appearance of a conflict of interest can arise as (c) member institutions can pay more than $1 million for accreditation [105].

On the macro level, private and publicly-held companies, non-profits, federal and state governments, as a matter of course, warn job applicants that

"Only education or degrees recognized by the U.S. Department of Education from accredited colleges, universities, schools, or institutions may be used to qualify for Federal employment" (Office of Personnel Management) [106].

As a matter of course, parents, families and students at the micro level rely upon accrediting information as a value-added criteria and cost benefit analysis to determine for which school to apply based upon future earnings potential.

The power held by accrediting bodies is vast. Even so, Belkin and Fuller [104] found that accreditors rarely revoked accreditation to low performing schools. In response, accreditors say that their "assessment[s] are aimed at helping schools improve, rather than weeding out schools with low graduation rates or high student-loan default rates" [104]. The operational decision to remain reticent and resist change may be in the best interests of member organizations at the macro level. However on a micro level, failure to evolve has dire repercussions. Complainants in a January 2015 lawsuit filed against UNC-Chapel Hill and NCAA "seek unspecified damages and ask for the formation of an **independent commission to review, audit, assess and report on academic integrity** in NCAA- member athletic programs and *certify* member-school curricula as providing comparable educations and educational opportunities to athletes and non-athletes alike" [107].

Limited Resources for Federal Oversight

In 2014, the U.S. Department of Education restricted federal funding access to seventy-six colleges because of the severe risk posed to students and taxpayers [108]. At the same time, an additional 455 institutions were placed on a less severe list. The U.S. Department of Education [109] [110] does not review all grant programs managed by grantees that are non-compliant. The Department limits the list of entities to review based upon these priorities:

1. High cohort default rate or dollar volume default,
2. Significant fluctuation in Pell Grant awards or FSA loan volume,
3. State reported deficiencies or financial aid problems,
4. High annual dropout rates, and
5. Risk for noncompliance with administrative or financial requirements.

The U.S. Department of Education's approach is to target 20 of the most severe cases (from 544 cases) for increased financial monitoring. This increased oversight represents less than 4% of the most severe cases and does not consider institutions in need of increased monitoring or support for program or data quality [109] [110].
Collectively, "the 50 states and the District of Columbia reported $603.7 billion in funding collected for public elementary and secondary education" [111, para 8]. State and local governments generally provide "91 percent of all funding" for education [111, para 8], leaving the remaining 9 percent of discretionary spending approximating $70 billion provided by the federal government [112] [113].

Stringent accountability systems may do much to reduce the likelihood of fraud. Barnes and Webb cite two sources to support the statement such as Leatherwood and Spencer (1991) found that heightened management controls reduce employee misconduct [114]. Further, Turner and Stephenson (1993) found that "lax" management attitudes and ineffective policies have the opposite effect [114].

Oversized Mega Donor Class Influence
According to Dissent [115], private foundations wield considerable influence over the public pre-k to secondary education sector. To show support, they donate up to $4 billion each year. Three major funders, the Bill and Melinda Gates Foundation, Eli and Edythe Broad Foundation, and the Walton Foundation are identified as the 'giants' in the field. While their initiatives may be noble, "the cozy environment undermines all players—grantees, media, the public and the foundations themselves. Without honest assessments, funders are less likely to reach their goals [115]. One researcher, cited by Barkan [115] exclaims that "academics, activists, and the policy community live in a world where philanthropists are royalty...." As these major donors are boosters of projects promoting public charter schools, high stakes testing, and teacher merit pay, studies to evaluate their effectiveness may not be as independent as has been the custom.

> "Researchers themselves compete fiercely for the right to evaluate high profile reform initiatives. Almost without exception, the evaluators are hired by funders or grantees... most evaluators are selected at least in part because they are perceived as being sympathetic to the reform in question" [115].

Capability
Possession of certain skills, tools, and traits are necessities for committing fraud. A 2009 study [116] presented student stories of teachers behaving unprofessionally. In the most egregious cases, illegal behaviors were unearthed among the most ineffective teachers (as perceived by their students).

> "Illegal conduct by adults serving as educators does not always get addressed by supervisors and other administrators in ways that would prevent such damaging acts from reoccurring." ... "A teacher's misconduct my go unreported, dismissed, or even unrecorded in records" [116, p.6].

The capability to commit crime is impacted by access. Access to cash receipts, data and technological infrastructures is often overlooked. A potential criminal may possess the skills to commit a crime, but without access, the idea is not acted upon. Further, when employees are adequately supervised, crime can be prevented.

Poor Classroom Supervision
As some educational leadership programs may provide training in labor law, negotiations, and personnel policy, finding the time to supervise employees has been a challenge. Chait (117) found that "many schools currently lack the staff capacity—both in

terms of expertise and staff hours—to observe all of their staff and write up their findings throughout the year" [117, p. 9].

Poor Management Training

In addition to inadequate supervision, school leader programs have not been designed to meet the needs of candidates. Reference materials are outdated and are not aligned to generally accepted practices of leadership AACTE [118], Copland [119], Elmore [120], Lumsden [121], McCarthy [122], Murphy & Vriesenga, [123]. Modern curricula to address current challenges presented by the workers in the workplace is required. For example,

"To prevent some teachers from demonstrating unprofessional behaviors in the classroom, we need to do a better job providing quality teacher preparatory programs, embedding character-building and work ethics training in these programs [124, p. 10].

Top Level Access and Authority

Capability within top management involves using one's inside knowledge, access and authority for controlling resources and directing subordinates to commit illegal acts.

Some of the ways in which this capability is manifest are: top level access to secure information, possession of the highest administrative privileges to override internal controls, the authority to circumvent subordinates, and dissuade resistance. In 2011, KPMG [125] described the typical insider fraudster with the following characteristics: male, aged 36 to 45 years, holding a senior management position in the function of finance or finance related. The typical insider perpetrator according to KPMG had been employed with the same entity for 10 years or more and colluded with another perpetrator to commit the crime.

This author analyzed the January 2012 to June 2016 OIG Investigative Reports of cases prosecuted in the education sector and noticed several similarities. The most cited positions were Chief Executive Office or C-Suite Executive, the majority of perpetrators prosecuted were male (in a female dominated industry) and the age range indicated most often was between 50 to 59 years. The age ranges of 40 to 49 and 60 to 69 years were tied as the second highest age group of captured criminals for fraud in education. Finally, most insiders (unlike in the private sector) elected to carry out their crime as an individual (51%) rather than collude with others (30%, non-related group of two or more individuals, or 15% related group of at least two family members). Please refer to Image 26 for additional details.

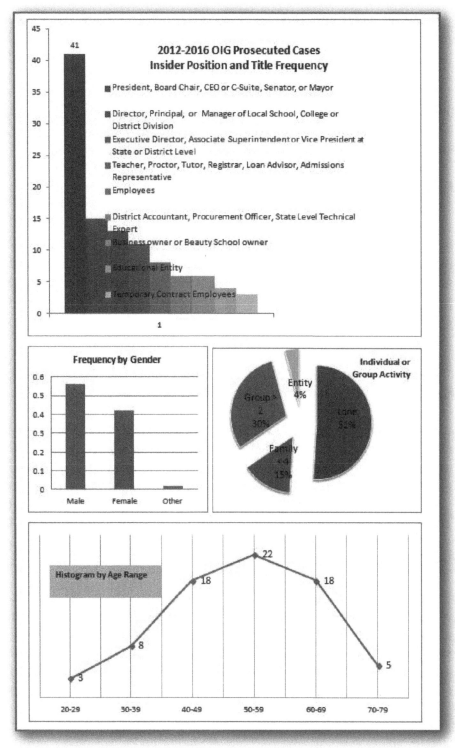

Image 26.   Insider Fraudster Profiles in the Education Sector [126]

As discussed in Chapter 1, based upon this authors analysis, the characteristics publicized for insider fraudsters identified in the 2012 to 2016 OIG Investigation Reports closely mirror those of the typical white collar criminal described by KPMG. Beyond those cases compiled and prosecuted by the U.S. Department of Education, OIG, in separate cases, school district superintendent leaders in El Paso, Texas; Atlanta, Georgia; and Camden, New Jersey were alleged to have either awarded themselves unauthorized performance bonuses, manipulated student enrollment, participated in a grade fixing scheme, falsified student transcripts, tampered with state standardized assessments and/or instructed subordinates to do so [127] [128].

Prelude to the Fraud Prism™ Paradigm

The previous sections of this book set illustrates how the Fraud Prism™ [129] builds upon the situational crime prevention theory of Cornish and Clarke [130] and Shaw, McKay [131] and Simpson's [132] earlier theories of social disorganization and upheaval. It seeks to portray an environment that "prompts, provokes, pressures, and permits" insider educators and outsiders to commit fraud and computer-assisted crime [133, p. 41].

> "The immediate environment suggests that in many cases situations are important not because they provide information about the likely outcome of a behavior which is the basis of opportunity reduction [crime prevention] but because they actively bring on behavior [133, p. 63].

Using the Fraud Prism as a foundation, the final segment of this book presents mega, macro and micro solutions for preventing fraud and computer-assisted crime.

PART FOUR

MEGA, MACRO, AND MICRO SOLUTIONS

Introduction

Proven fraud prevention theories assert that people obey the law because they (1) have a moral obligation. They want to (2) avoid social disapproval and (3) avoid legal punishment [1]. These decisions are more than binary absolutes. Researchers [2] have determined that individuals use a gradient scale to answer life's perplexing problems. Fraud is situated in the gray area. Taken singularly, altering documents, tampering with data, and falsifying certifications may not be criminal acts. Add the intention to knowingly deceive for personal or institutional gain and they become fraud. The same can be said for conspiracy. The education sector has been hesitant to pinpoint where unethical and immoral acts morph to criminality. Green and Kugler [3] argue,

> "The ability of criminal law to stigmatize, to achieve legitimacy, and to gain compliance ultimately depends on the extent to which it enjoys moral credibility and recognition in the broader lay community [3, p. 33]."

Three factors influencing fraud prevention relate to punishment: its certainty, severity and time. Classical theorists posit that the certainty of punishment—not the severity—deters criminality [4]. The length of time lapsing from discovery, arrest, prosecution, conviction and punishment reduces its effectiveness [5]. Industry upheaval, porous regulations, and mismanagement can effectuate fraud. Further, punishment when applied improperly and inconsistently will not deter or rehabilitate [6]. This chapter takes an expansive view to explore the solutions for fraud and computer assisted crime.

Public Mood and Public Policy

The degree to which individuals perceive the certainty and severity of punishment may be largely dictated by the public mood [7] [8]. "Punishment gives concrete expression to the public mood in a structured way" [7, p. 102]. Brooks says,

> "punishment is not merely something that happens to criminals, but it is something that the public communicate to them. Crimes are those activities that the public denounce, and the formal statement of their denunciation is punishment [7, p. 102].

Individual anxiety, frustration, fear, contempt, and anger influenced by economic downturns and systemic inequities impress upon the public mood. When experienced collectively, they "function as an interrupt system" [7, p.34]. To reset the political discourse, citizens demand action. The Pew Research Center (2015) interviewed 6,000 participants. They found that "22% say they are *angry* at the federal government; 57% are *frustrated* and 18% say they are *basically content*" [9, p. 9]. Twenty percent opined that government programs were "*well-run*" and "just 19% say they *can trust the government always or most of the time*, among the lowest levels in the past half-century" [9, p.4]. The collective negative affect has impacted governance as exhibited by the following legislative actions.

Dodd Frank and Consumer Financial Protection Act 2010

After the 2008 housing bust, "poll after poll showed that Americans wanted to hold Wall Street to account for the Great Crash" [10, p. 378]. A Bloomberg poll showed that 56% of the respondents agreed with the statement that

> "individuals in Wall Street banks whose actions helped cause the financial crisis should be punished by the federal government by limiting their compensation or banning them from working in the industry" [10, p. 378].

The Consumer Financial Protection Bureau (CFPB) was created to reinforce rules for banks, credit unions, payday lenders, debt collectors and foreclosure relief programs.

Bipartisan Campaign Reform Act 2002

This Act was established after multiple Congressional attempts to eradicate corruption and influence peddling failed. Senator John McCain has said,

"'Questions of honor are raised as much by appearances as by reality in politics, and because they incite public distrust, they need to be addressed no less directly than we would address evidence of expressly illegal corruption" [11, p. 92].

Almost 15 years later the Act is believed to have "fundamentally reshaped our political system, far more so than the recent decision in McCutcheon v FEC, which struck down overall limits on federal political contributions, or the decision in Citizens United" [12].

Computer Fraud and Abuse Act 1984, 1996 and 2001
This Act strengthens cyber security. It makes it unlawful to "knowingly access a computer without authorization, exceeding authorized access, transmit a harmful component of a program, information, code, or command" [13].

Banking Act 1933
The Banking Act of 1933 was intended to "restore confidence in the banking system" [14, p.1]. It addressed the market speculation that precipitated the depression, high employment and suicide [15].

Federal Education Fraud Prevention: Mega Level
Mortgage fraud can be used to conceptualize fraud in education. Total mortgage debt in the United States stands at $8.09 trillion [16]. From 1997 to 2005, financial institutions reported to enforcement authorities a 1,411% increase in suspicious activities relating to possible mortgage fraud; debtors entering into agreements with no intention of payment [17]. Criminals commit financial aid fraud under similar pretexts. U.S. consumers held more than $1.12 trillion in student loan debt in 2014 [18] up from $914 billion in 2012. Of this amount, the U.S. Department of Education, Office of the Inspector General estimated that from 2009 to 2012, about $187 million of financial aid funds may have been lost due to fraud [19]. Like the capital markets sector, citizens demands for increased accountability in government-funded programs resulted in these legislative actions.

College Scholarship Fraud Prevention Act of 2000

This Act deters fraud by increasing federal penalties (imprisonment and fines up to $500,000) and removing the homestead exemption. It requires the Attorney General, the Secretary of Education and the Federal Trade Commission (FTC) to publish fraud prevention information on a website to raise awareness [20, p. 418].

Campus Security Act of 1990 Amended 2008

The Campus Security Act requires colleges to report campus crime statistics, security measures, alerts, and to certify its campus security policy [20, p. 415].

Violations Against Women Act of 2014

This Act requires colleges to record crimes for dating, domestic violence, sexual assault, and stalking. The criteria for disciplinary proceedings, timelines, and possible sanctions must be indicated. They are also required to train students and employees on sexual assault prevention [21].

Single Audit Act of 1984 Amended 1996 (A-133)

Grantees spending $750,000 or more in a calendar year must present audited financial statements to the federal government. This is mandated to prevent federal fund mismanagement.

> "Traditionally the A-133 Audit has been the federal government's way of obtaining reasonable assurance via an independent third party auditor that institutions are being good stewards of federal award funds and are in compliance with applicable federal, state, sponsor, and other award-specific regulations [22, p.6].

Noncompliant entities undergo heightened financial monitoring. The areas examined: accreditation, administrative capabilities, fiscal responsibility and severe audit findings. In 2015, there were 560 schools at the post secondary level on the watch list [23].

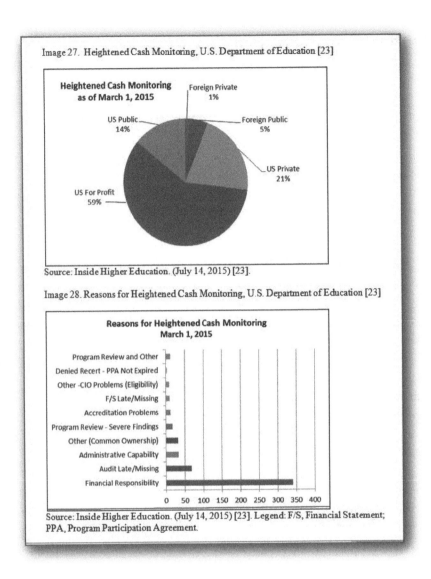

Image 27. Heightened Cash Monitoring, U.S. Department of Education [23]

Heightened Cash Monitoring as of March 1, 2015

- Foreign Private 1%
- US Public 14%
- Foreign Public 5%
- US Private 21%
- US For Profit 59%

Source: Inside Higher Education. (July 14, 2015) [23].

Image 28. Reasons for Heightened Cash Monitoring, U.S. Department of Education [23]

Reasons for Heightened Cash Monitoring March 1, 2015

- Program Review and Other
- Denied Recert - PPA Not Expired
- Other -CIO Problems (Eligibility)
- F/S Late/Missing
- Accreditation Problems
- Program Review - Severe Findings
- Other (Common Ownership)
- Administrative Capability
- Audit Late/Missing
- Financial Responsibility

0   50   100 150 200 250 300 350 400

Source: Inside Higher Education. (July 14, 2015) [23]. Legend: F/S, Financial Statement; PPA, Program Participation Agreement.

Public Disdain for Education Fraud

Using federal enforcement codes as a backdrop, state prosecutors investigated the following.

Elementary and Secondary Education

- 35 Atlanta Public School System educators were charged with 65 criminal counts of false statements, theft by taking, and racketeering [24]. An El Paso district superintendent was sentenced to four years imprisonment, fined $56,600 and ordered to repay $180,000 for contract fraud and data manipulations [25].

- Five Philadelphia School district educators were arrested for "perpetuating a culture of cheating" on state exams [26] [27]. They were charged with tampering with public records, perjury, forgery, and criminal conspiracy. Similar allegations were raised in the Camden, New Jersey school system [28].
- The Columbus City Schools (Ohio) was found by the state auditor [29] to orchestrate fraud involving changed grades, deleted, and falsified dropout rates [30]. The Federal Bureau of Investigation joined the investigation [31].
- A Chicago Public Schools superintendent pled guilty on charges of 20 counts of mail and wire fraud for receiving financial kickbacks to help her former employer secure "no bid" contracts [32].

Post Secondary

- St. John's University president resigned after a federal probe accused him and the dean of fraudulently obtaining $1 million from the school [33].
- A Columbia University accounts payable clerk and an accomplice stole $5.7 million by redirecting payments intended for New York Presbyterian Hospital. They received prison sentences for up to 21 years [34].
- A Columbia University professor manipulated and falsified research data. She created fictitious people and organizations for confirmation. The professor was found guilty of 21 counts of research misconduct. Nine of her studies were falsified, fabricated, plagiarized, or unreplicable [35].
- A Pennsylvania State University professor applied for federal funds using plagiarized and falsified research. He was charged with federal fraud, making false statements, and money laundering and ordered to repay $660,000 in grant proceeds. He received a 3.5-year prison sentence [36].

Universities respond to the risk of fraud by establishing Internal Audit and Compliance (IAC) Departments. Many IACs are narrowly scoped; to facilitate external audits and promote internal control. Some IACs exercise a broader reach. IACs in the North Carolina and Tennessee university systems process reports of misappropriation, mismanagement, fraud, waste and abuse [37] [38]. A sample policy from Winston Salem State University, Internal Audit Department describing illegal acts follow [39].

1. **Misappropriation-** the intentional, illegal use of property or funds of another entity for one's own use or other unauthorized purpose, by any person with a responsibility to care for and protect another's assets (a fiduciary duty).
2. **Mismanagement-** an instance or act of wrongly or incompetently carrying on a business or organizational affair.

3. **Waste-** an act or instance of spending or using carelessly or inefficiently.
4. **Fraud-** an act or instance of deceit, trickery, or intentional perversion of the truth in order to induce another to part with something of value or to surrender a legal right; an act of deceiving or misrepresenting.
5. **Abuse-** an act or instance of wrongful or improper use of authority.

From 2011 to 2015, state and district education agencies have handled academic test fraud in the manner described below.

Georgia State Board of Education (Atlanta Public Schools)	
Under the Authority	The Governor controls the Office of Student Achievement (holds auditing powers) separate from the Department of Education Special Investigators with the State Bureau of Investigation (a former Attorney General and Former DeKalb County District Attorney with subpoena powers and two independent law firms)
Cost Estimates	• $3 million for investigations • $698,000 for attorneys • $738,000 to tutor kids victimized by cheating • $2.4 million to 'idled' teachers impacted by the allegations • 60 State agents, attorneys, paralegals • 2,200 interviews and 800,000 document reviews
Penalties	**Criminal:** • Racketeer Influenced and Corrupt Organizations Act (RICO) • Making false statements and writings • False swearing (perjury) • Theft by Taking • Influencing Witnesses
New York State Department of Education	
Under the Authority	New York State Education Commissioner, The Office of School Personnel Review and Accountability- receives open cases from Assessments Department
Cost	• $1 million • Seven members of Test Security and Integrity Unit
Penalties	**Administrative Penalties** • Suspension, Denied Tenure • Not allowed to participate in testing • Storage of test items rescinded • Warning letter, Letter of Reprimand • Disciplinary 3020a charges • Annual training mandated • Report submitted to Superintendent, Attorney, or Administrative Trials Unit **Civil Penalties** • Fined 1 week pay • Fined $5,000 • Civil prosecution
District of Columbia , (Office of the State Superintendent of Education)	
Under the Authority	Mayor of District of Columbia Assessment Department, Division of Data, Assessment and Research under the Chief of Staff at the Office of the State Superintendent of Education
Cost	$200,000 to $400,000 annually
Penalties	**Personnel Penalties** • Re-testing within the test cycle period (potential costs to LEAs) • Deny, suspend, revoke, cancel, restrict the issuance or renewal of teaching/ administrative credential either indefinitely or for a set term not less than one year • Administrative fine, not to exceed $1,000 for each violation **LEA & School Penalties** • Score Invalidation • Payment of any expenses incurred by the LEA/SEA due to the violation • Administrative fine of not more than $10,000 for each violation • Test booklets held in abeyance • Monitoring

Source: T. Mead, (2014) International Academic Integrity Conference [40].

Image 29. State Response to K-12 Educator Cheating Scandals [40]

In the same vein, federal prosecutors joined with the U.S. Department of Justice and the Securities and Exchange Commission to utilize the Federal False Claims Act to enforce the proper use of federal funds and to take enforcement actions against fraudsters. A sample listing of enforcement actions follows.

Civil False Claims Act 31 U.S.C. Section 3729

The Civil False Claims Act was established in 1863. It is the primary vehicle for obtaining punitive damages and penalties from those defrauding the federal government. It was amended to increase damages from double to treble and to raise civil penalties to $11,000 for each claim [41].

Year Settled	Institution	Settlement Amount
2016	Bard College	$4,000,000.00
2015	Education Affiliates	$13,000,000.00
2014	Education Management	$100,000,000.00
2013	ATI Enterprises	$3,700,000.00
2013	Test Quest	$1,700,000.00
2013	American Commercial Colleges	$2,500,000.00
2013	US University	$700,000.00
2012	Education Holdings/Princeton Review	10,000,000.00
2012	Norwich University	$1,200,000.00
2012	NY Institute of Technology	$4,000,000.00
2009	University of Phoenix	$78,500,000.00

Image 30. Educational Entity Federal False Claims Settlements [42]
Source: T. Mead. (2015) . Risk Assessment Data Quality and Security for
School and Campus Records. Unpublished Manuscript [42].

Federal Fraudulent Claims for Student Financial Aid 20 U.S.C. Section 1097 (a)

The US Justice Department and the Securities and Exchange Commission use the Federal False Claims Act [43] to prosecute organizations and individuals conspiring to defraud the government. It is used to punish federal financial aid loan recipients who make false statements and commit fraud. In most instances, to prove fraud requires proof of the intent to deceive. The government, however, only needs to prove that material statements were made knowingly and willfully [44]. The person submitting a falsified application does not need to be the beneficiary. "Criminal liability under federal law extends to knowingly and willfully causing the funds to be disbursed to a third party by fraud, false statement, or forgery" [45].

Using the McKinsey 7S model as a foundation for problem solving, the following fraud prevention initiatives have been identified on the macro level and involve strategy, structure, and systems [46].

Fraud Prevention Initiatives: Macro Level

Effective fraud prevention programming requires the study of the organization. The governing body, strategy, structure and systems represent the basic organizational framework [47].

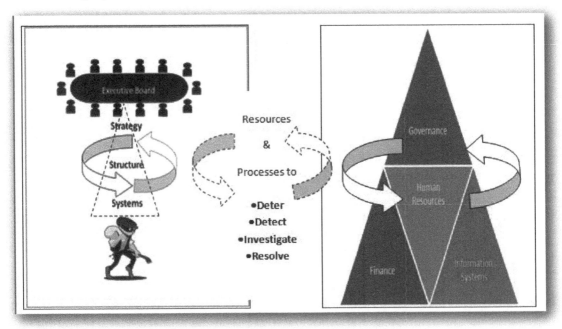

Image 31. Internal Governance and Detection [49]
Source: T. Mead. (2015). Risk Assessment Data Quality and Security for School and Campus Records. Unpublished Manuscript [49].

On a macro-level: fraud, computer- assisted and white collar crime prevention is directly proportional to federal, state, self regulatory and executive bodies' conceptualization of fraud. Perceptions of problem scope will determine the amount of fraud prevention resources allocated for eradication. "Lack of effective corporate governance seriously undermines any fraud risk management program" [48, p.3].

Strategy

Tone at the Top: External Accreditation Agencies

There are more than twelve self-regulatory agencies assessing the quality of education. U.S. Senator Lamar Alexander, Chair of the Senate Education Committee has asked, "Are accreditors doing enough to ensure that students are learning and receiving a quality education [50]?" Perhaps not. Of the 3,000 schools accredited over a 40 year period, only nine percent were reported to have lost accreditation by 2014.

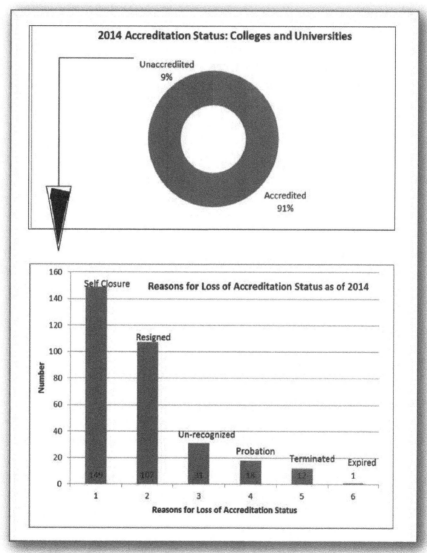

Image 32. 2014 Accreditation Status: Colleges and Universities [50]
Source: Belkin, D. Fuller, A. (June 27-28, 2015). *Accreditors of Colleges Weighing Crackdown.* The Wall Street Journal [50].

There are reform efforts by the American Council of Trustees and Alumni and the U.S. Department of Education to motivate accreditors to develop more rigorous standards and assessments. As investigations by the *Wall Street Journal* indicated, a mere 30 institutions were placed on probation or lost accreditation status spanning almost a half century period. The desired outcome is to help regulators weed out underperforming schools [50].

Tone at the Top: Internal Executive Board

The absence of positive social reinforcers and role modeling of ethical decision-making put organizations at risk for staff misconduct and insider fraud [51]. Trevino (1999) found that effective organizations use social reinforcers for exerting positive social pressures and crime deterrents [52]. Top leaders are expected to create and support ethical decision-making across all organizational levels. Communication and the active role modeling are critical [53]. "These top managers create and maintain an ethical culture by consistently behaving in an ethical fashion and encouraging others to behave in such a manner as well" [54] The Association of Certified Fraud Examiners builds upon the concept saying, "employees will do what they witness their bosses doing" [55].

Policy Development

Most people do not need reminders of the consequences of illegality to obey the law [56] [57] [58]. McCabe [59] advocates for the acknowledgment of laws and regulations, descriptions of appropriate behaviors and consequences of misconduct to address fraud. As do federal agencies; U.S. Government Accountability Office [60] [61], and the U.S. Department of Education, Office of Inspector General [61] [62] [63] [64] [65] [66] [67].

Compliance

Compliance programs represent a formalized method for reinforcing adherence to federal, state law, regulations, and corporate policies. To establish an effective compliance program, one must understand the underlying employee attitudes in conflict with conformity. Image 33 illustrates an adaptation of the Wortley [68, p. 66] classification system for preventing fraud. In addition to the factors devised by Wortley, this author has added Rewarding Compliance. Research in the compliance field assert that "incentives help drive behavior" [69, p.1].

Controlling Prompts	Controlling Pressures	Reducing Permissibility	Reducing Provocations	Rewarding Compliance
Controlling Triggers	**Reducing inappropriate conformity**	**Setting ground rules**	**Reducing frustration**	**Aligning compliance with strategy**
regulations accountability measures enforcement	cross-function, generation teams, mentors	ethics, integrity, data security, info technology, prevention training, signage	open door policy, EAP, assess jobs identify gaps of responsibility	discuss at executive board meetings, weave compliance into strategic plan
Providing Reminders	**Reducing inappropriate obedience**	**Clarifying responsibility**	**Reducing unhealthy competition**	**Increasing compliance visibility**
employee orientation handbooks training staff affirm conduct codes	set up tip line systems whistleblower support instill culture of integrity	embed fraud prevention tasks into all job descriptions embed prevention into SOP	train C-suite, managers and supervisors provide resources to support goals	hire integrity champion in C-suite, regular compliance updates, create task force
Reducing inappropriate imitation	**Encouraging compliance**	**Clarifying consequences**	**Respecting territory**	**Increasing opportunities for compliance reward**
rapid response to tip line and incident reports inform stakeholders of resolutions	routine reviews of employee handbook frequent employee evaluations set up alerts	inform of sanctions for fraud, data breaches and computer crimes across multiple mediums and vehicles	new hire fit applicant screening IR follow through	design and implement reward program to provide individual, unit and departmental recognition, reward, and benefits for compliance
Setting positive expectations	**Reducing anonymity**	**Personalizing victims**	**Controlling environmental irritants**	**Penalizing miscreants**
role modeling signage for prevention job satisfaction surveys	Identity authentication log data entries delineate responsibilities	inform of associated costs of fraud depersonalize the entity	employee wellness programs match skills with responsibilities	set up detection system and rigorous enforcement program, showcase consequences of noncompliance

Image 33. Classification Table of White Collar Crime Prevention in Education [70]
Source: T. Mead, (2015). Classification Table of White Collar Crime Prevention
in Education. Unpublished Manuscript [70]. Legend: EAP, Employee Assistance
Program; SOP, Standard Operating Procedures; IR, Incident Report

It is vital for educational institutions to establish compliance programs. Federal sentencing guidelines [71] [72] proffer leniency to victim organizations when compliance programs are in place. The required elements of acceptable programs are:

1. Policies, procedures and controls
2. Compliance and ethics oversight
3. Due diligence
4. Employee education
5. Enforcement
6. Monitoring
7. Incident reporting

While the Sentencing Commission [71] can be a catalyst for establishing a compliance program, it has been criticized for enacting an amendment to reduce the minimum sentence for fraud. The U.S. Department of Justice argued that moves to reduce sentences "would be bad policy and ignores the *overwhelming societal consensus* in favor of harsh punishment for these crimes" [72, p.1].

Structure

Typical Educational Institution Organizational Structure

Typical organizational structures existing at the elementary and secondary levels and at the post secondary level were illustrated on Image 17 and discussed in prior chapters. The following sections offer descriptions for ways in which internal controls can be embedded throughout these structures to prevent and contain fraud.

Risk Assessment and Management of Risk

In 1995, President Clinton recognized the importance of risk assessment and created a cabinet level committee to study weaknesses in critical infrastructure [74]. By 2003, President Bush established the National Strategy to Secure Cyberspace [75]. Risk management is as vital today as before. Risk management involves an identification of vulnerable assets and threats, the probability of a threat occurring, its impact and an analysis of possible losses incurred [76] [77]. It may not be deemed important in the education sector. The Association of Governing Boards and United Educators found that 60% of education administrators "do not use comprehensive strategic risk assessments to identify major risks to mission success" [78]. Strategic planning, non-withstanding; a top recommendation for preventing campus violence is to "conduct risk and safety assessments" [79, p. iii]. Image 34 adapted by this author depicts fraud prevention responsibilities.

Action Required	President						
	Vice President or Vice Principal of Operations						
	Investigation Internal Audits	Finance	Exec. Mgmt	Risk Mgmt	Public Relations	Human Resources	Legal
Internal Controls	S	S	P	S	S	S	S
Incident Reporting	P	S	S	S	S	S	S
Fraud Investigation	P					S	S
Law Enforcement Referrals	P						S
Lost Assets Recovery	P						
Fraud Prevention	SR	S	S	S	S	S	S
Internal Control Reviews	P						
Sensitive Cases	P		S	S		S	S
Press	S				P		
Civil Litigation	S						P
Corrective Action	SR		S	S			S
Monitor Recoveries	S	P					
Proactive Fraud Auditing	P						
Fraud Education	P				S		
Risk Analysis	S			P			
Case Analysis	P						
Anonymous Tip Line	P						
Ethics Line	S						P

Image 34. Sample Fraud Responsibility Matrix (ISACA, n.d.) [80]
Source: Adapted from the Information Systems Audit and Control Association.
Sample Framework for a Fraud Control Policy (n.d.) [80]. Legend: SR= Shared
Responsibility. S= Secondary Responsibility, P= Primary Responsibility

Internal Control Systems

"Internal controls promote efficiency, reduce risk of asset loss, and help ensure the reliability of financial statements and compliance with laws and regulations" according to COSO [81, p.1]. Departments such as operations, finance, admissions, athletics, alumni relations, and institutional research are most at risk for fraudulent activities. Internal control systems should be embedded throughout the structure and across functions to deter, detect, investigate and resolve fraud as illustrated on Image 31, to be found in prior chapters. The manner in which these controls can be embedded into functional areas are discussed below.

Manifestation of Internal Controls

Internal controls are materialized as resources in manpower (enforcement staff), infrastructure (hierarchal roles and responsibilities) and systems (human engineered and computer processes). Examples of internal control measures used to prevent fraud, white collar crime, theft and data tampering are: indicator tracking, multi-step authentication, multi-person/level approvals, multi-function approvals, multiple step verifications, account and data reconciliation, desk-top reviews, on-site monitoring, asset security, and segregation of duties.

Nagin argues that there is substantial evidence that increasing enforcement visibility significantly heightens the perceived risk of discovery and capture [83]. To add rigor for oversight and impose societal pressures, three of the largest school districts, New York City, Chicago and Los Angeles, established independent enforcement agencies. These agencies are known as inspectors general. They provide oversight for educational programming [84]. This author proposes similar enforcement agencies across the nation to be staffed by auditors and investigators independent of state and local school management and influence. The primary purposes of these offices would be to detect, deter, and investigate fraud, waste, and abuse.

Processes Embedded into Systems and Structures

Processes at risk for fraud are listed in Image 35. It identifies fraudulent acts perpetrated upon targeted documents in various departments. Without trained staff experienced in fraud symptom recognition in the education sector, detection and deterrence could be quite low.

Fraud Action	Department	Vulnerable Documents			
Alter, Falsify document	Finance	cash receipts	invoices	checks	
Forge signatures	Academic	transcripts	enrollment roster	attendance records	grade reports
	Human Resources	time sheets	expense reports	pay check	
Keep gifts	Alumni Affairs	donation logs	deposit slips	withdrawal slips	
Over/under state gifts	Alumni Affairs	donation logs	deposit slips	withdrawal slips	
Change eligibility status	Athletics	enrollment roster	transcripts	attendance records	grades discipline reports
Take cash	Athletics	ticket sales	retail sales receipts	expense reports	mileage logs
Inflate cash disbursement	Finance	invoices	cash receipts	paid logs	
Pilfer inventory, equipment, or supplies	Athletics	annual asset logs	bill of lading	YTD inventory	shipping receipts
	Operations	annual asset logs	bill of lading	YTD inventory	shipping receipts
	Facilities	annual asset logs	bill of lading	YTD inventory	shipping receipts
	Technology	annual asset logs	bill of lading	YTD inventory	shipping receipts
Create fictitious staff	Human Resources	employee lists	terminated lists	payroll history	benefits history
Create fake vendors	Finance	vendor lists	accounts payable	general ledger	invoices
Create fake students	Academic	admission registry	enrollment roster	attendance records	grade reports
Inflate hours worked	All Department	time sheets	vendor invoices	attendance records	
Keep withdrawn students	Academic	attendance records	grade reports	discipline reports	
	Financial aid	attendance records	grade reports	discipline reports	
Falsify grade, research, and transcript tampering	Institutional research	academic papers	peer reviews	Intervention records	data logs
	Admissions	Income statements	tax returns	transcripts	test scores

Image 35. Fraudulent Actions, Department and Targeted Documents [85]
Source: T. Mead, (2015). Risk Assessment Data Quality and Security for
School and Campus Records. Unpublished Manuscript [85].

Specifically concerning the deterrence, detection, investigation and resolution of test fraud, the following link analysis table has been presented.

Test Integrity Link Analysis			
Prime Subject	Second Subject	Activity Map	Indications of Issues
Coaching and Answer Sheet Tampering			
Teacher School and LEA Leaders	Test Proctor	Pre-test Instructional Activities, During test Administration	Wrong to right and overall erasures, consistency in response to items within classroom, high academic growth, smaller within classroom variation, drops in future results, mismatch in predicted result to actual, time stamp
Proxy Testing and Answer Copying			
Student	Parent	During- test Administration	Drops in future test performance, incident reports, high academic growth, smaller within classroom variation, mismatch in predicted result compared to actual
Unauthorized Access to Exam and Testing Materials			
Instructional Teacher Test Proctor	Parent Student School Leader	Pre-test Administration	Time stamp analysis, drops in future test performance, item difficulty performance mismatch within classroom, incident reports, high academic growth, smaller within classroom variation, mismatch in predicted result compared to actual
Abuse of Invalidations and Avoidance Participation			
School and LEA Leaders State Education Agency	Teacher Test Proctor	Pre-test Enrollment Data Verification, During test Administration Pre-test Student Anxiety/Avoidance	Large numbers of invalidations, increases in invalidations, invalidations with bias in prior or future scores, large number of un-attempted items/tests Grade level changes near window, mismatched grade and tests, suspension/expulsion at window
Misadministration of Accommodations			
Test Proctor Special Ed. Advisor State Ed. Agency	School Leader LEA Leader Teacher	Pre-test Instructional Supervision Activity During test Administration	Large volume of technical difficulty calls, and large volume of incident reports, Misalignment of enrollment/data and demographics with exam registration files, unexplained shifts in 'accessibility' and 'accommodations' terminology
Unauthorized Use of Electronic Devices and Confidentiality Breaches			
Student Test Proctor School Leader LEA Leader	Test Proctor Student	During- test Administration Post test Administration	Time stamp analysis, off-site monitoring flags, systems and network alerts, smaller within classroom and/or test unit variations Unexplained similarities and patterns in item responses, mismatch in predicted result compared to actual, unexplained internet traffic
Missing Materials			
School Leader LEA Leader	Test Proctor	Pre- test Administration Post test Administration	Inability to provide chain of custody and tracking documentation
Data Manipulations, False Certifications and False Statements			
School Leader LEA Leader State Ed. Agency	Test Proctor Teacher Parent	Pre-test Administration, During and Post- test Activity	Time stamp analysis, Mismatch in predicted performance compared to actual, Inability to provide chain of custody and tracking documentation, large volume of technical difficulty calls, large volume of incident reports, Misalignment of enrollment/data and demographics with exam registration files, unexplained shifts in 'accessibility' and 'accommodations' terminology, failure to respond to anonymous tips, Large numbers of invalidations, increases in invalidations, invalidations with bias in prior or future scores, large number of un-attempted items/tests Grade level changes near window, mismatched grade and tests, suspension/expulsion at window; weak role access controls

Image 36. Exam Security and Test Integrity Link Analysis [86]
Source: T. Mead, (2015). Link Analysis for Test Integrity and Exam Security. Unpublished Manuscript [86].

Desk top, On site Monitoring and Inspections

The United Nations Office on Drugs and Crime categorize monitoring, inspections, and evaluation systems as compliance mechanisms [87, p.45]. Monitoring and inspections take place during program implementation. In New York and Massachusetts, inspections are utilized for examining documents, interviewing teachers and administrators, and surveying parents according to the Brookings Institute [88]. Evaluations occur at year or program-end.

Post Secondary

The top ten findings for audits and program reviews of U.S. Department of Education federal grantees are listed below.

Image 37. 2014 Top Ten Audit Findings and Program Review Findings: Post Secondary Federal Student Aid [89] [90].

Rank	Audit Finding	Rank	Program Findings
1	Repeat Finding- Failure to Take Corrective Action	1	Verification Violations
2	Calculation Errors	2	Deficient Student Credit Balance
3	Inaccurate/Untimely Student Status Reporting	3	Deficiencies in Entrance/Exit Counseling* tied
4	Late Return of Title IV Funds	3	Title IV Refund Calculation Errors* tied
5	Verification Violations	4	Noncompliant with Crime Awareness Requirements* tied
6	Pell Over/Under Payment	4	Academic Progress Inadequately Developed/Monitored* tied
7	Qualified Auditor's Opinion	5	Inaccurate Recordkeeping
8	Deficient Student Balance	6	Late Return of Title IV Funds
9	Deficiencies in Entrance/Exit Counseling	7	Consumer Information Requirements Not Met
10	Untimely or Incorrectly Reported Grant Expenditures	8	Missing/inconsistent Student Files
		9	Pell Grant Over/Under Payment
		10	Inaccurate/Untimely Student Status Reporting* tied
		10	Lack of Administrative Capability* tied

Source: Barnett, E. and Weems, C. (December 2014). Session 33. Program Review Essentials and Top 10 Compliance Findings. U.S. Department of Education [89] [90].

Image 38. 2010, 2013 and 2014 A-133 Audit Findings at the Elementary and Secondary Level [94]

Audit Year	CFDA Program	Federal Program Name
2010	84.041	Impact Aid- Maintenance & Operations
2013	84.01	Title I Grants to Local Education Agencies
2013	10.555	National School Lunch Program- Cash Assistance
2014	84.173	Special Education Pre-school Grants

Source: Federal Audit Clearing House (2010, 2013, and 2014) [94]

Elementary and Secondary
The U.S. Department of Education funds educational initiatives under the Catalogue of Federal Domestic Assistance (CDFA) block programs in the 84.0 numbered series [91]. It involves Title I Grants, Migrant Education, Safe and Drug-Free Schools, Charter Schools, Twenty-first Century Community, State Grants, Educational Technology, English Language Acquisition, Mathematics and Science Partnerships, Improving Teacher Quality, Adult Education, Special Education, TRIO, Career and Technical Education, Rehabilitation Services, and Education Jobs Fund [92].

These funds support low income families, school libraries, and state education agencies for the purchase of textbooks, instructional materials, and supplemental education services. Research and professional development for teachers are also funded [93]. Auditors reported significant findings for the possible misuse of funds for years 2010, 2013 and 2014 for specific programs listed in Image 38 [94].

Findings and Corrective Action Plans for Systemic Improvements
Auditor [94] [95] and accreditor findings, data discrepancies [96] [97] and anonymous tips [98] [99] can identify systemic deficiencies and fraud. Subsequently, corrective action plans [100] are developed to address deficient areas [101]. The American Society for Quality [102] says such plans serve dual purposes. They are "powerful tools" for "fixing a problem that has occurred and preventive [for] fixing a problem that could occur [102, p.1].

Access Control Systems to Safeguard Confidential Information
To maintain security, industries must adopt measures to limit access to data files, informational reports, and systems infrastructure [103]. This requires the establishment of the highest data security standard espoused by the defense and intelligence sectors known as "defense in depth" [104] [105]. The Social Security Administration, Internal Revenue Service, U.S. Department of Education, and other agencies collect confidential taxpayer, beneficiary, dependent, and family information. In practice, Image 39, illustrates how defense-in-depth strategies such as non-disclosure and disclosure avoidance are used to protect confidential information.

Data Class	Personally Identifiable Private Information	Unintentional Disclosures from Human Error/ Malware	Present Federal and SEA Strategies	Comparable Federal Strategies
Top Secret	Student Names, Social Security Numbers, Address, Date of Birth, Parent's Names, Disability Status	University of Maryland	Primary Data Suppression	Non-Disclosure
Confidential	Students' individual data linked through the years with longitudinal data	DC Public Schools and the State Education Agency	Complementary Suppression	Disclosure Avoidance
Sensitive	Partially de-identified student data and aggregate data tables		Blurring and Perturbation	Disclosure Limitation
Un-classified	Anonymized data that cannot be linked across years and public aggregate data tables			

Image 39. Data Class, PIPI Treatment and Comparable Strategies Matrices [106]
Source: T. Mead, (2015). Risk Assessment Data Quality and Security for School and Campus Records. Unpublished Manuscript. Adapted from US Census Overview of Data Disclosure Policies; https://www.census.gov/srd/papers/pdf/rr92-09.pdf and http://fpg.unc.edu/sites/fpg.unc.edu/files/resources/reports-and-policy-briefs/DaSyDeidentificationGlossary.pdf [106]

Accountability measures are equally vital for the protection of personally identifiable private information. Keeping a record of every action performed by every system user is an absolute must. This "allows system administrators to hold users responsible for their conduct by keeping track of the actions they take" [109]. The Fordham Center on Law and Information Policy [110] advised organizations to:

1. conceal personal information through the use of dual database architectures,
2. require comprehensive agreements explicitly addressing privacy obligations for third parties,

3. limit information collection to data required by evaluative audits,
4. communicate access and permission policies,
5. maintain audit and user logs,
6. establish data retention policies,
7. make database structure and security programs be readily accessible and verifiable, and
8. appoint a Chief Privacy Officer at each state department of education.

Similarly, the Data Quality Campaign [111] prepared Fact Sheets encouraging states to:

1. take legal and moral privacy responsibilities seriously,
2. ensure limited access to student data,
3. consider FERPA as the "floor for protecting student privacy not the ceiling," and
4. take full responsibility for data protection system-wide.

Use System to Collect data and Conduct More Research

The saying, "What gets measured, get's managed" has been attributed to Drucker [112]. Internal control systems provide systematic measurement for deterring and detecting white collar and computer-assisted criminal acts. The data from these systems can be used to collect metadata for building perpetrator and victim agency profiles. Such information is vital for the development of a symptoms list and red flag alerts. Training and prevention programs are consequential products for informing others. The Institute for Fraud Prevention (IFP) was contacted in early 2015.

> "The Membership does not discount the need for research into fraud in education; at the same time, other concerns are a priority, especially given the areas of concern regarding about being able to identify and locate enough data on education fraud to derive meaningful statistical inferences" [113].

Fraud Prevention Initiatives: Micro Level

Fraud prevention initiatives on the micro level involve the deterrence of fraud at the individual decision-making phase. Research respondents to the Klepper and Nagin (1989) study indicated that they would take advantage of opportunities to disobey authorities, break rules, and commit illegal acts when they perceive low risk of criminal prosecution [114]. This is consistent with Williams and Hawkins'

(2010) argument that the threat of legal prosecution resulting from an arrest deters criminals [115].

The threat of legal prosecution extends beyond the intricacies of court hearings, sentencing, imprisonment, awarding and collection of fines. The negative consequences of a civil or criminal trial are experienced well into the future. Torny [116] cites work by Freeman (1991), Waldfogel (1994), and Bishway (1996) showing that job opportunities for individuals with prior offenses decreases by 15-30 percent. A fraud conviction can potentially reduce lifelong earnings by up to 40 percent [116].

To elucidate how fraud prevention initiatives can be designed to impact individual decision-making, the following McKinsey 7S factors: shared values, leadership style of mid level managers, staff, and skills are explored below [117].

Shared Values

Trice and Beyer (1993) identified these factors for influencing individuals operating within an organization: the shared vision of executive leadership, common values, beliefs and rituals, accepted performance norms, punishment, and reward systems [118]. The education industry ranked fifth for reported cases of fraud, followed by retail and insurance [119]. Historically, the education sector resolutely denied the existence of widespread fraud [120]. Psychologists, in the study of abnormalities, note that denial is an unhealthy coping mechanism [121]. Applied organizationally, Tedlow (2010) defines denial as "the unwillingness to see or admit a truth that ought to be apparent and is in fact apparent to many others" [122].

Organizational environments contribute to individual displays of dysfunctional behaviors by (1) "creating social conditions that promote violence by generating aggressive inclinations" and (2) lowering restraints against violent actions" [123, p. 281]. The threat of punishment is considered an inhibiting factor. Berkowitz, as cited by Van Fleet and Griffin (2006) found that dysfunctional behaviors such as theft and dishonesty can be minimized when systems are in place to control, restrain and halt employee actions and thoughts [124]. Kerr and Slocum (2005) adds the misalignment of stated shared values, performance measures, reward and punishment systems as factors [125].

"The reward system defines the relationship between the organization and the individual member by specifying the terms of exchange: It specifies the contributions expected from members and expresses values and norms to which those in the organization must conform, as well as the response individuals can expect to receive as a result of their performance. The reward system— who gets rewarded and why— is an unequivocal statement of the corporation's values and beliefs. As such, the reward system is the key to understanding culture [125, p.130].

As mentioned in Chapter Three, Jeffrey (1965) theorized that the absence of positive social reinforcers foster an environment ripe for crime [126]. Van Fleet and Griffin (2006) cite Glomb and Liao (2003) who theorized that individual behavior is guided by the attitudes and behaviors of individuals in one's immediate environment [127].

"The individual learns, then, by observing what others do and what they can or cannot "get away with". The structure, values, norms, and procedures of an organization, therefore, are vital for determining how individuals might respond to organization related situations" [127, p.702].

Staff, Organizational Climate and Culture

To ensure values alignment, a checklist showing relevant action steps across functional departments is offered below.

Action Step	C-Suite	Human Relations	Finance	Information Technology	Customer Service Public Relations
Develop authentic set of core values	■				
Appoint champion to personify core values	■	■	■	■	■
Establish policies that are value-driven	■				
Create quantifiable metrics based upon core value criteria	■		■		
Prepare strategic and operational plans based upon core values	■				
Translate core values into behaviors	■	■			
Integrate valued behaviors into standard operating procedures	■	■	■	■	■
Incorporate valued behaviors into required tasks and responsibilities	■	■	■	■	■
Communicate value-based behaviors to Recruitment managers		■			
Design communication strategy across all mediums to reflect core values	■				■
Identify referral and sourcing organizations based upon core values		■			
Use behavior-based interview questions		■			
Communicate core values to candidates		■			
Design training programs to educate staff on core values	■	■	■	■	■
Integrate core values into performance appraisal systems	■	■	■	■	■
Structure reward and punishment system around core values	■	■	■	■	■
Establish data analytics to identify deviations from core value metrics	■	■	■	■	■
Develop exit interview and dismissal criteria based upon core values	■	■	■	■	■

Image 40. Shared Values and Organizational Culture Alignment Checklist [128]
Source: T. Mead, (2015). Shared Values and Organizational Culture Alignment Checklist. Unpublished Manuscript [128] Legend: Shaded areas represents responsible action steps for the corresponding department C- Suite (CEO, COO, CIO), HR- Human Resources, Finance, IT- Information Systems, CS- Customer Service (Client Relations), PR- Public Relations and Communications

In addition to the identification of core values for encouraging and rewarding staff, an organization must also identify unacceptable behaviors and communicate the consequences. For specific examples of fraudulent actions by department and documents, please refer to Image 35. A list of actions used by prosecutors to prove the intent to deceive form the foundation for criminal fraud charges can be reviewed by referring to Image 23.

Public Awareness and Confidential Informant Recruitment

In pockets of education, there is a movement toward harsher penalties that are "so dreadful that the wrongdoer will not commit the offense" [130]. Educator awareness of the negative consequences of committing an offense is increased by publicly showcasing the actual infliction of the punishment upon the wrongdoer [131].

Campaigns to educate the public on fraudulent behaviors for which to look (as illustrated in preceding tables) can be effective. These campaigns publish guidance on what the public can do to prevent fraud, why they should act, and the resources available [132]. It informs the public of the individual burden inflicted upon the criminal and the imposed costs of the crime shouldered by society [133]. Anonymous tip lines can be set up for confidentially reporting a tip by email, phone and online web based portals. Incident reports, tips and complaints from law abiding educators [134] are effective methods for detecting potential fraud, mismanagement and abuse. "Researchers agree that about 70 to 80% of fraud losses are usually committed by the internal staff of an organization and that in most of the cases, they were eventually detected because somebody from the inside or outside blew the whistle" [135]. In light of this, a pipeline for the free flowing report of information must be established. Without such a pipeline, critical information remains undisclosed; and fraud, undetected. Even as entities install systems, employees may choose non-action. According to the Association of Certified Fraud Examiners [136],

"there are many different forms of misconduct that go on in the workplace and are observed by employees every year. Yet, many employees do not report this unethical conduct. Only 55 percent of employees said that they reported misconduct they observed in the workplace; a 10 percent drop from the previous survey conducted in 2003" [136].

According to the Ethics Resource Center (2011), 45 percent of employees observed misconduct in the workplace within the past year [137]. One-third of these witnesses did not report the misconduct. In a separate study, the top reasons for non-reporting include:

1. employee cynicism due to employer lack of responsiveness,
2. lack of clarity regarding the appropriate person for whom to inform,
3. divulgence of the identity of the complainant, and
4. retaliation by top management, supervisors and colleagues.

"Employees who witnessed their company actively following its code of ethics were the *most* likely to report misconduct in the workplace, according to the 2005 National Business Ethics Survey [138].

Increasing the probability that a crime will be discovered and reducing the length of time from discovery, to court proceedings, due process and ultimately punishment, greatly impacts a potential criminal's assessment of risk and therefore his or her behavior according to Albercht [139]. This author adds that organizations can deter internal criminality and avoid victimization by external parties with the adoption of a "zero tolerance" culture for fraud, white collar, and computer-assisted crime.

APPENDIX A

A ppendix A. Institutions on U.S. Department of Education Heightened Monitoring List as of 6-1-2016 [1].

Institution	Institution	Institution	Institution
Alabama State University	University of Canterbury	Star Career Academy	FINE Mortuary College
Central Alabama Community College	Ogle School Hair Skin Nails	Art Institute of Portland (The)	Little Priest Tribal College
Calhoun Community College	Phillips Graduate University	American University of Paris	Universidad Catolica Nordestana
University of North Alabama	Commonwealth of P.R Department of Education	Concorde Career College	Medical University of Silesia
University of West Alabama	Fortis College	Lincoln College of Technology	Queen Margaret University, Edinburgh
Marion Military Institute	Berks Technical Institute	Lincoln College of Technology	Fortis College
University of Mobile	N.E. Culinary Institute	Normandale Community College	Beacon College
Spring Hill College	National University College	Concorde Career College	Star Career Academy
Tuskegee University	Central Christian College of The Bible	Educators of Beauty College of Cosmetology	Bennett Career Institute
Lawson State Community College	Glenwood Beauty Academy	Art Institute of Philadelphia (The)	Acupuncture and Massage College
Creative Circus	AmeriTech College	Universiteit Van Amsterdam	Edinburgh Napier University
Emmanuel College	Concorde Career Institute	University of Melbourne	Fortis College
Spertus College of Judaica	Sisseton Wahpeton College	Concorde Career College	National Institute of Massotherapy
Kendall College	Southern Technical College	Alaska Bible College	ATS Institute of Technology
MacMurray College	Creative Circus	Concorde Career College	Fortis College
Shimer College	Art Institute of Seattle	Arkansas Baptist College	All-State Career
S. Illinois University at Carbondale	Florida Career College	Concorde Career College	Yeshiva Shaarei Torah of Rockland
Bethel College	Venango County Area Vocational Tech School	Lakehead University	Williamson Christian College
Iowa Wesleyan College	Fort Worth Beauty School	Empire College	Missouri College of Cosmetology North
Bethany College	KD Conservatory College of Film & Drama Arts	Utica School of Commerce	Lubbock Hair Academy
Bethel College	Magnolia College of Cosmetology	TONI&GUY Hairdressing Academy	Institute For Therapeutic Massage
Central Christian College of Kansas	Emmanuel Bible College	Art Institute of Atlanta (The)	Concorde Career College
Highland Community College	Fortis Institute	Lincoln College of New England	Southeastern College
Kentucky Wesleyan College	Florida Institute of Ultrasound	Fortis College	Southeastern Institute
St. Catharine College	JRMC School of Nursing	Pennco Tech	Southeastern Institute
Eastern Nazarene College	Center for Employment Training	Educators of Beauty College of Cosmetology	Carolina Christian College
Pine Manor College	Professional Skills Institute	St. Paul's School of Nursing	Total Look School of Cosmetology & Massage Therapy

Rochester College	Bay State School of Technology	University of King's College	David's Academy of Beauty
Kuyper College	Southern Institute of Cosmetology	Merrillville Beauty College	Carver Bible College
Finlandia University	Fortis College	University of P.R, Ponce	New Concepts School of Cosmetology
Anoka-Ramsey Community College	Academy of Radio & TV Broadcasting	Inver Hills Community College	Metropolitan Learning Institute
Riverland Community College	Fortis College	Colorado Technical University	Medical University of Gdansk
Bemidji State University	Institute of Beauty Careers	Art Institute of Fort Lauderdale (The)	Faith Evangelical College & Seminary
Central Lakes College	Indiana County Technology Center	Art Institutes International - MN	Ave Maria School of Law
Vermilion Community College	Le Cordon Bleu College of Culinary Arts in Chicago	Fortis Institute	Regency Beauty Institute - Cleveland
Hibbing Community College	Michigan Barber School	Metropolitan State University	Auguste Escoffier School of Culinary Arts

Itasca Community College	Concorde Career College	Rabbinical College of Long Island	Southeastern Institute
Minnesota State University, Mankato	University of Puerto Rico - Medical Science Campus	Dakota County Technical College	Shear Academy
Minneapolis Community and Technical College	Ponce Health Sciences University	Instituto Tecnologico y de Estudios Superiores de Monterrey	Auguste Escoffier School of Culinary Arts
Crossroads College	Spanish-American Institute	Sheridan College	Mid City College
Minnesota State University Moorhead	All-State Career School	Regency Beauty Institute	Northcentral University
North Hennepin Community College	Walden University	Hennepin Technical College	Maple Springs Baptist Bible College & Seminary
Rochester Community and Technical College	Institucion Chaviano de Mayaguez	Wichita Technical Institute	Charlotte Christian College and Theological Seminary
SW MN State University	Beauty Academy	Century College	American Academy of Traditional Chinese Medicine
St. Cloud State University	Joffrey Ballet School, American Ballet Center	London International Film School	Ecclesia College
Northland Community and Technical College	International School of Skin and Nailcare	PB Cosmetology Education Centre	Florida School of Traditional Midwifery
Minnesota State College - SE Technical	Art Institute of NY City	University of Queensland	Community Christian College
Winona State University	Ponce Paramedical College	American Academy McAllister Institute	University of Gloucestershire
Copiah-Lincoln Community College	Stratford University	Tom P. Haney Technical Center	Southern Technical College
Evangel University	Brownson Technical School	Thomas Jefferson School of Law	National Polytechnic College
Miles Community College	Inner State Beauty School	Cincinnati College of Mortuary Science	eClips School of Cosmetology and Barbering
Dawson Community College	Tri-State College of Acupuncture	University of Puerto Rico - Utuado	Buchanan Beauty College
Summit University of Pennsylvania	South Texas Vocational Technical Institute	University of Puerto Rico Bayamon Technical	Total Cosmetology Training Center

New York Theological Seminary	Academy of Hair Technology	Universidad Central del Este	Harrisburg University of Science and Technology
Dominican College of Blauvelt	Fort Berthold Community College	Pennsylvania Institute of Technology	New England College of Business and Finance
Webb Institute	Art Institute of York (The) - Pennsylvania	Technical Career Institutes	Ex'pression College
Johnson C Smith University	Le Cordon Bleu College of Culinary Arts	D'Jay's Institute of Cosmetology and Esthiology	Ecumenical Theological Seminary
William Peace University	Los Angeles ORT Technical Institute	SBI Campus - an affiliate of Sanford-Brown	Art Institute of Phoenix (The)
Cincinnati Christian University	Pennsylvania Institute of Taxidermy	Collins School of Cosmetology	Creative Hair School of Cosmetology
Hiram College	International Culinary Center	Pike Lincoln Technical Center	American Institute of Medical Technology
Wilberforce University	Beauty College of America	Taylor Business Institute	Raphael Recanati International School, Interdisciplinary Center
Eastern Oklahoma State College	Maryland University of Integrative Health	Roxbury Community College	Academy for Careers and Technology
Saint Gregory's University	Murdoch University	San Diego Christian College	Make-Up Designory
Multnomah University	CC's Cosmetology College	Rosedale Technical College	Academy of Natural Therapy
Keystone College	Infinity Career College	Hamilton Technical College	Charleston School of Law
Lutheran Theological Seminary – PA	Seminario Evangelico de Puerto Rico	Victoria University of Wellington	Academy Di Capelli
University of Valley Forge	Medtech College	University of Puerto Rico, Aguadilla Regional College	EDHEC Business School
Cheyney University of PA	College America Denver	Burlington College	Taylor College
Cairn University	Spartan College of Aeronautics & Technology	Birmingham City University	DiGrigoli School of Cosmetology
Allen University	Vatterott College	VEEB Nassau County School of Practical Nursing	Larry's Barber College
Bethel University	Crave Beauty Academy	University of Wales - Lampeter	Northcoast Medical Training Academy
Hiwassee College	Vatterott College	St. Paul's School of Nursing	Dominion School of Hair Design
Stevens Henager College	Miller - Motte Technical College	University of Auckland (The)	Coast Career Institute
Green Mountain College	Sanford-Brown College	Lincoln Technical Institute	Trident University International
Virginia Wesleyan College	Sanford-Brown College	TONI & GUY Hairdressing Academy	Total Image Beauty Academy
Saint Martin's University	Le Cordon Bleu College of Culinary Arts	Caribbean University	InfoTech Career College
Ohio Valley University	Academy of Cosmetology	Illinois Institute of Art (The)	International Professional School of Bodywork
University of P.R Central Admin	McNally Smith College of Music	National University of Ireland, Galway	Cozmo The School
University of Puerto Rico - Humacao University College	Hairmasters Institute of Cosmetology	Instituto Tecnologico de Santo Domingo	Borner's Barber College

University of P.R. Mayaguez	Virginia College	Hair California Beauty Academy	Cardiotech Ultrasound School
University of the Virgin Islands	Fortis Institute	Ogle School Hair Skin Nails	Frederick School of Cosmetology
Mesabi Range College	Fortis Institute	South University	San Diego Culinary Institute
Hebrew University of Jerusalem (The)	Fortis Institute	American Beauty College	Transformed Barber and Cosmetology Academy
North American Baptist Seminary	University of Puerto Rico Carolina Regional College	Capri Oak Forest Beauty College	International College of Cosmetology
Tucson College	EDIC College	Roxborough Memorial Hospital	New Life Business Institute
Daniel Webster College	Le Cordon Bleu College of Culinary Arts	Harrington College of Design	Northern California Institute of Cosmetology
McCann School Business & Techn	Head's West Kentucky Beauty College	Brown College of Court Reporting	Park West Barber School
Penn Commercial Business/Technical School	Remington College	Vatterott College	Toledo Restaurant Training Center
Miller-Motte Technical College	Fairview Academy	Briarcliffe College	Aerosim Flight Academy
Ridgewater College	Sanford-Brown College	Milwaukee Institute of Art & Design	Texas Beauty College
Minnesota West Community and Technical College	NewSchool of Architecture and Design	Art Institute of Colorado (The)	Flair Beauty College
Saint Paul College - A Community & Technical College	University of East London	Northern New Mexico College	Trinity School of Health and Allied Sciences
St. Cloud Technical and Community College	Studio Art Centers International - Florence	Concorde Career Institute	Atlanta Beauty & Barber Academy
Pine Technical and Community College	Regency Beauty Institute	Ben-Gurion University of the Negev	Pinchot University
South Central College	Aaron's Academy of Beauty	Med-Assist School of Hawaii	Preferred College of Nursing
MN State Community & Technical College	ABC Beauty College	Spa Tech Institute	Jose Maria Vargas University
Alexandria Technical & Community College	University of Sydney	Bramson ORT College	Laird Institute of Spa Therapy
George Corley Wallace State Community College - Selma	Southeast Missouri Hospital College of Nursing and Health Sciences	JFK Medical Center Muhlenberg Harold B. and Dorothy A. Snyder Schools	Eureka Institute of Health and Beauty
Lake Superior College	ITT Technical Institute	American InterContinental University	Barone Beauty Academy
Northwest Technical College - Bemidji	University of Debrecen	Sanford-Brown College	Cosmetic Arts Institute
Montclair Hospital LLC	Paul Mitchell the School Missouri Columbia	Art Institute of Houston	Salon & Spa Institute
California College San Diego	Rosel School of Cosmetology	Court Reporting Institute of St Louis	Southern California University SOMA
Phillips Beth Israel School of Nursing	Nouvelle Institute	Central School of Practical Nursing	Taylor Andrews Academy Of Hair Design

Saint Elizabeth Medical Center	Leech Lake Tribal College	Pennco Tech	Cosmetology College of Franklin County
Citizens School of Nursing	Springfield Beauty Academy	Fortis Institute	Aveda Institute of New Mexico (The)
W. PA Hospital School of Nursing	Carsten Institute of Cosmetology	National Conservatory of Dramatic Arts	Nashville Barber and Style Academy
University of Toronto	Taylor Technical Institute	Riverside College of Health Careers	American Technical Institute
University of Geneva	Atlanta Institute of Music and Media	Keiser University	Entourage Institute of Beauty and Esthetics
Brown Mackie College	Griffith University	Missouri School of Barbering & Hairstyling-St. Louis	Integrity College of Health
Rainy River Community College	Summit College	Concorde Career College	Hair Academy
Mid America Nazarene University	Francois D. College of Hair Skin & Nails	Harrison College	CyberTex Institute of Technology
University of P.R. Rio Piedras Campus	Everglades University	New Hope Christian College	Radians College
University of P.R. Cayey Univ. College	Ponca City Beauty College	Sanford-Brown College	RGV Careers An Institute for Higher Learning
University of Puerto Rico - Arecibo	Ohio College of Massotherapy	Instituto de Banca y Comercio	Helms College
Redstone College	CollegeAmerica - Flagstaff	Swedish Institute	FINE Mortuary College
Lincoln Technical Institute	New York Conservatory For Dramatic Arts (The)	Concorde Career Institute	SAE Institute of Technology-Miami
ITT Technical Institute	Southeastern College	Argosy University	NRI Institute of Health Sciences
Anoka Tech College	Miami Ad School	Middlesex University	S. Texas Careers Academy
Sanford-Brown College	Fond du Lac Tribal & Community College	Pentecostal Theological Seminary	Champ's Barber School
Medtech College	Modern Beauty School	Hobe Sound Bible College	Cole Holland College
Fountainhead College-Technology	Mesalands Community College	Fortis College	Universal Training Institute
Art Institute of Pittsburgh (The)	Le Cordon Bleu College of Culinary Arts	University of Westminster	East-West Healing Arts Institute
Chioffin Career & Technical Center	Unification Theological Seminary	Pittsburgh Career Institute	Bay Area Medical Academy
New England Institute of Art (The)	L T International Beauty School	Gene Juarez Beauty Schools	Setting the Standard Barber & Natural Hair Academy
Coyne College	American College of Hairstyling-Des Moines	Chattanooga College - Medical, Dental & Technical	Sherrill's University of Barber & Cosmetology
Concorde Career College	Blue Cliff College	Universiteit Utrecht	Cosmetology Training Center
Boston Baptist College	Lincoln Technical Institute - Hartford	Tyndale University College & Seminary	Unilatina International College
Spartan College Aeronautics & Technology	Advance Beauty Techs Academy	Portfolio Center-	MKG Beauty & Business
Star CCMareer Academy	Miami International University of Art & Design	Le Cordon Bleu College of Culinary Arts	Boston Baptist College

Source: U.S. Department of Education (June 1, 2016). List of Institutions on HCM as of June 1, 2016 [1].

APPENDIX B

Appendix B. US College Staffing Changes 1987-2011 (Only institutions with negative percent change in enrollment are listed).

APPENDIX C

Appendix C Schools and Districts with Significant Deficiencies and Material Weaknesses as of 12-31-2015.

College and State	Col B	Col C	Col D	College and State	Col B	Col C	Col D
Hobe Sound Bible College FL	75.00%	-60.00%	-61.50%	PA State University-Penn State Greater Allegheny PA	120.00%	85.70%	-41.10%
Morrison Institute of Technology IL	-50.00%	-25.00%	-63.40%	Concordia Theol Seminary IN	-88.90%	428.60%	-41.70%
Paul Quinn College TX	-29.40%	-30.40%	-71.00%	Lawrence Technological University MI	-56.90%	-75.00%	-41.80%
Lutheran School of Theoy at Chicago	-27.30%	200.00%	-71.70%	Little Big Horn College MT	100.00%	475.00%	-44.00%
Remington College-Tampa Campus FL	-63.20%	-23.50%	-78.30%	Jarvis Christian College TX	-40.60%	50.00%	-44.10%
Palmer College of Chiropractic-Davenport IA	100.00%	-32.10%	-93.80%	Saint Pauls College VA	50.00%	23.50%	-44.40%
Chester College of New England NH	NA	Will close	-100.00%	Lexington Theological Seminary KY	150.00%	0.00%	-45.20%
Metro Comm Col PN Valley MO	300.00%	788.90%	-100.00%	St. Andrews University NC	25.00%	95.70%	-46.80%
Sem- Immaculate Conception NY	200.00%	-33.30%	-100.00%	Heritage Christian University AL	NA	150.00%	-51.80%
Utah State University-College of Eastern Utah	125.00%	113.30%	-100.00%	Saint Vladimirs Orthodox Theo Seminary NY	300.00%	100.00%	-53.20%
Lon Morris College TX	16.70%	450.00%	-100.00%	Rockefeller University NY	54.40%	38.70%	-54.40%
Metro Community College-Maple Woods MO	16.70%	640.00%	-100.00%	Central Bible College MO	70.00%	433.30%	-55.30%
Ohio College of Podiatric Medicine	-27.80%	200.00%	-100.00%	Trinity Lutheran Seminary OH	-66.70%	200.00%	-55.30%
Texas 21	22	3436		WV University Institute of Techn	-44.80%	-40.20%	-58.20%
Hobe Sound Bible College FL	75.00%	-60.00%	-61.50%	University of Saint Mary of the Lake IL	NA	425.00%	-60.20%
Morrison Institute of Technology IL	-50.00%	-25.00%	-63.40%	Hiwassee College TN	10.00%	5.60%	-60.50%

SCHOOL/DISTRICT AUDITED	TROY SCHOOL DISTRICT-MI	MIO AUSABLE SCHOOLS-MI	C.O.O.R. INTERMEDIATE SCHOOL DISTRICT-MI
CLOVERDALE UNIFIED SCHOOL DISTRICT-CA	ALBION PUBLIC SCHOOLS-MI	CABOOL R-IV SCH DISTRICT-MO	SIERRA NEVADA COLLEGE-NV
UNITED CEREBRAL PALSY SEGUIN OF GREATER CHICAGO-IL	EAST JACKSON COMMUNITY SCHS-MI	ALLIANCE PUBLIC SCH-NE	RAPID CITY AREA SCH DISTRICT NO. 51-4-SD
MAHOMET-SEYMOUR COMMUNITY UNIT SCH DISTRICT NO. 3-IL	BIG RAPIDS PUBLIC SCH-MI	WINNEBAGO PUBLIC SCH DISTRICT #17-NE	JOHNSON UNIVERSITY-TN
WEST AURORA SCHOOL DISTRICT 129-IL	WHITE CLOUD PUBLIC SCH-MI	UMONHON NATION SCH DISTRICT #16-NE	CUERO INDEPENDENT SCH DISTRICT-TX
TAZEWELL-MASON COUNTIES SP EDUCATION ASSOCIATION-IL	SCHOOL DISTRICT OF THE CITY OF PONTIAC-MI	LINCOLN COUNTY PUBLIC SCH DISTRICT NO. 1-NE	NORTH KITSAP SCH DISTRICT NO. 400-WA
TUKWILA SCH DISTRICT NO. 406-WA	SCH DISTRICT WEYAUWEGA-FREMONT WI	SCHOOL DISTRICT OF ALTOONA-WI	

Sources: Appendix B The New England Center for Investigative Reporting, February 6, 2014 [174]. Legend: Column B Full time Administrators Percentage Change from 1987- 2011, Column C Full time Professional Staff Percentage Change from 1987- 2011, Column D- Student Enrollment Percentage Change from 1987- 2011. Only institutions with Column D negative percentage change greater than (-30%) were listed

Appendix C. A-133 Federal Audit Reports, Federal Audit Clearinghouse (8,802 Records Found, 230 were filtered for CDFA 84.0 only for the 8/2014 to 12/2015 reporting period, 26 were filtered for Conditions: Reportable Conditions/Significant Deficiency and Material Weakness

DEFINITIONS

(taken from Merriam-Webster.com, Dictionary.com, Thefreedictionary.com unless otherwise noted)

A-133/Single Audit/OMB A-133 Audit an organization-wide review, examination or audit of an entity that expends $750,000 or more of federal assistance received for its operations.

Access a process by which a system enables a user to view the information the asset contains (Pennington, 2010, Information Security Basics Cyber AWR-173W Course Notes).

Accountability the obligation of an individual or organization to account for its activities, accept responsibility for them, and to disclose the results in a transparent manner.

Accreditation the granting of power to perform various acts or duties; the act of granting credit or recognition, especially to an educational institution that maintains suitable standards. Accreditation is necessary to any person or institution in education that needs to prove that they meet a general standard of quality.

Act of fraud is a deceptive representation intended to induce another to give up property or legal rights.

Adjunct/ part time/ contingent faculty any instructor or professor teaching courses employed by a college or university for a specific purpose or length of time and often part-time; they are exempt from some of the responsibilities of fully employed university instructors (tenured).

Admissions fraud "when a person deceives, or conspires with others to deceive, another person or group of persons into believing that a claim [false information on an application regarding qualifications or experience, the provision of a fake certificate or reference to support an application, or the deliberate omission of relevant information, e.g. the non-inclusion of information regarding previous qualifications or relevant criminal convictions, or some other act of deception] made by that person or group is genuine when in fact it is false" (University of Edinburgh, para 2).

Aggravated identity theft occurs when someone "knowingly transfers, possesses, or uses, without lawful authority, a means of identification of another person" in the commission of particular felony violations."

Allegation a claim or assertion that someone has done something illegal or wrong, typically one made without proof.

Anonymize(d) technique in which sensitive data is hidden (Thorston, Cyber Ethics, Course Notes).

Audit can be federal or nonfederal and generally involves an official inspection of an individual's or organization's accounts, typically by an independent body.

Audit findings area(s) of potential control weakness, policy violation, or other issue identified during the audit.

Blurring a technique used to limit disclosure of personal information by converting continuous data elements into categorical data elements, aggregating data across small groups of respondents, and reporting rounded values and ranges instead of exact count to reduce the certainty of identification (U.S. Department of Education, Data De-identification Terms, (n.d., p.2).

Bribery "the offering, giving, receiving or soliciting of something of value for the purpose of influencing the action of an official in the discharge of his or her public or legal duties" (Free Legal Dictionary by FarLex).

CDFA refers to the Catalog of Federal Domestic Assistance, a government-wide compendium of federal programs, projects, services, and activities which provide federal assistance (GSA, n.d.).

C- suite refers to a corporation's most important senior executives; it gets its name because top senior executives' titles tend to start with the letter C (chief executive officer, chief operating officer, and chief information officer). In the education arena, these translate to State Superintendent, District Superintendent, President (of a college), Vice President, Principal, Assistant Principal.

Collusion occurs when two or more people agree in secret to defraud someone or to take something illegally.

Compliance the action or fact of complying with laws, regulations, policies, procedures and contracts.

Computer-assisted crime unauthorized use of a computer for personal gain, as in the illegal transfer of funds or to alter the data or property of others; the use of a computer to take or alter data, or to gain unlawful use of computers or services.

Conflict of interest "a term used in connection with public officials and fiduciaries and their relationship to matters of private interest or gain to them" (Black's Law Dictionary).

Consent occurs when people are made aware of all uses of their personal information before they agree for their information to be used by another person or organization (Thorston, Cyber Ethics, Course Notes).

Conspiracy "an agreement between two or more persons to engage jointly in an unlawful or criminal act, or an act that is innocent in itself but becomes unlawful when done by the combination of actors" (Free Legal Dictionary by FarLex).

Corrective action plan a plan that clearly describes measures to be taken to address any findings (nonconformities or deficiencies) identified during a program review, operational or financial audit that leads to recommended improvements.

Corruption dishonest or fraudulent conduct by those in power, typically involving bribery.

Crime any act committed in violation of a law that prohibits it and authorizes punishment for its commission (Wilson and Herrnstein, 1985, p. 22).
Gottfredson and Hirschi explain crime thusly, "acts of force or fraud undertaken in the pursuit of self interest" (1990, p. 15).

Criminal profile an investigative tool used by law enforcement agencies to identify likely suspects and analyze patterns that may predict future offenses and/or victims.

Cyber ethics is the study of moral, legal, and social issues involving cyber technologies (Thorston, Cyber Ethics, Course Notes).

Cyber security the state of being protected against the criminal or unauthorized use of electronic data, or the measures taken to achieve this.

Data breach as an incident in which personal private information has been viewed, stolen or used by anyone unauthorized or 'in excess of authorization' (Thorson, T. 2011).

Data tampering "the threats of data being altered in authorized ways, either accidentally or intentionally" (IGI Global, n.d.).

Debt relief service scam the act of targeting of consumers with significant debt by falsely promising to negotiate with their creditors to settle or otherwise reduce their repayment obligations (Kirchheimer, 2006, p. 13).

Defense in Depth the adoption of multi-layered mechanisms, embedded within differing systems of various types to provide backup and redundancies for each other for information security. Examples: network security (firewall), host security, and human security (user education, careful system administration, etc (Zwicky, Cooper and Chapman, 2000, p. 61).

Denial "the unwillingness to see or admit a truth that ought to be apparent and is in fact apparent to many others; the unconscious determination that a certain reality is too terrible to contemplate, so therefore it cannot be true" (Tedlow, R. S, 2010).

Deprivation of Honest Services any act or omission that "wrong[s] one in his property rights by dishonest methods or schemes and usually signify[ies] the deprivation of something of value by trick, deceit, chicane or overreaching" (McNally v. United States, 483 U.S. 350, 350 (1987) as cited by C.Doyle, 2010, Congressional Research Service).

Determination of findings a special form of written approval by an authorized official that is required by statute or regulation as a prerequisite to taking certain contract actions.

Diploma mill is a company or organization that claims to be a higher education institution but which offers illegitimate academic degrees and diplomas for a fee.

Disciplinary actions are reprimands, suspensions, demotions, void and suspension of contracts (U.S.A. Education Law, n.d.),   loss of license and job (Olson and Fremer, 2013).

Disclosure occurs when confidential information is revealed or divulged; it occurs whenever information that is intended to be confidential is accessed by unauthorized people or systems (Pennington, 2010, Information Security Basics Cyber AWR-173W Course Notes).

Disclosure avoidance refers to the efforts made to de-identify the data in order to reduce the risk of disclosure of private (U.S. Department of Education, Data De-identification Terms, n.d., p.4).

Discovery risk is impacted by accountability systems, monitoring programs, computer accessibility.

Disparate data any data that are essentially not alike, or are distinctly different in kind, quality, or character. They are unequal and cannot be readily integrated to meet the business information demand. They are low quality, defective, discordant, ambiguous, heterogeneous data.

Distance learning a method of studying in which lectures are broadcast or classes are conducted by correspondence or over the internet, without the student's need to attend a school or college.

Elementary school level a school for the first four to six grades, and usually including kindergarten.

Embezzlement the fraudulent taking of personal property by someone to who it was entrusted (Cornell University Law School, Legal Information Institute); the misappropriation of property after lawful possession (The Free Dictionary by FarLex).

Enforcement any system by which some members of society act in an organized manner to enforce the law by discovering, deterring, rehabilitating, or punishing people who violate the rules and norms governing that society" (New Law Journal, 1974, p. 358). Enforcement also includes "the act of compelling observance of or compliance with a law, rule or obligation" (Oxford Dictionaries.com).

Enforcement risk is impacted by the frequency (monthly, semi-annually, annually, every third yea) of monitoring programs, method by which sites are selected (random, sample or total pool), and the identity of the monitoring team (internal, third party, state, local or campus/school-based).

Enroll/enrollment to enter (someone) as a member of or participant in something; the act or process of enrollment, the number of persons enrolled, as for a course or in a school.

Ethics moral principles that govern a person's or group's behavior.

Ethical Equilibrium "a balance between dispositional framework, regulatory framework, ethical framework" (Hutchings, 2014, p. 9).

Evaluation is the systematic and objective assessment of an on-going or completed project, program or policy, and is design, implementation and results (Monitoring & Evaluation Brief, n.d.The World Bank. p. 1 Available:: http://siteresources.worldbank.org/INTBELARUS/Resources/M&E.pd)

External or outsider fraud " actions perpetrated by individuals outside of the organization and covers activities such as theft, deception and computer hacking(Association of Chief Police Officers, United Kingdom, Fraud-stoppers.Com, n.d.); "fraud which is perpetrated by individuals outside of the organization and covers activities such as theft, deception and computer hacking." (ACPO, n.d., p. 1).

False claim when a person knowingly makes an untrue statement (an assertion of a right to government money or property) or claim to gain a benefit or reward.

False statement a statement that is deceitful and untrue statement that is made for ulterior motives (Black's Law Dictionary).

Federal audit those conducted by the Government Accountability (GAO) Office of Inspector General (OIG) within The Department of Education (ED) (Discretionary Grants Handbook as cited by IBM Center for the Business of Government, 2015, p. 16).

Felony a crime, typically one involving violence such as rape, murder, drug crime and robbery; it is regarded as more serious than a misdemeanor, and usually punishable by imprisonment for more than one year or by death.

Forgery the crime of falsely making or altering a writing by which the legal rights or obligations of another person are apparently affected; simulated signing of another person's name to any such writing whether or not it is also the forger's name; action of forging or producing a copy of a document, signature, banknote, or work of art.

Fraud any intentional act or omission designed to deceive others, resulting in the victim suffering a loss and/or the perpetrator achieving a gain. It is a statutory or common-law tort action that allows for parties injured by fraud to take private actions in civil courts in order to recover damages" (U.S.A. Education Law, n.d.); a white collar crime that involves the following characteristics: a misrepresentation of a material fact, made knowingly with the intent to deceive, whereby an individual victim and/or victim organization relied upon the misrepresentation which ultimately resulted in injury or damage.

Fraudulent action activities whereby perpetrators and or organizations resort to deceptive acts, false suggestions, concealment of the truth, and other unfair means to violate trust.

Frustration the feeling of being upset or annoyed, especially because of inability to change or achieve something.

Grand theft is the intentional taking of others' property without their consent.

Grant means an award of financial assistance, including cooperative agreements, in the form of money, or property in lieu of money, by the Federal Government to an eligible grantee.

Grantee a person to whom a grant or conveyance is made.

Ground rules the basic rules or principles on which future actions or behaviors should be based.

Hacker, hacking an attacker or someone seeking to gain access to something illegally; the act of intentionally accessing a computer without authorization or exceeding authorized access (Pennington, 2010, Information Security Basics Cyber AWR-173W Course Notes).

Heightened Cash Monitoring "a step that the U.S. Department of Education, Federal Student Aid can take with institutions to provide additional oversight for a number of financial or federal compliance issues, some of which may be serious and others that may be less troublesome (Federal Student Aid, U.S. Department of Education, Available:: https://studentaid.ed.gov/sa/about/data-center/school/hcm)."

IDEA Individuals with Disabilities Education Act provides financial assistance for state and local school districts to support equal access to education for children with disabilities.

Identity theft the fraudulent acquisition and use of a person's private identifying information, usually for financial gain; a crime in which an imposter obtains key pieces of personal information such as social security or driver's license numbers in order to impersonate someone else.

Incident an event or occurrence.

Information security the practice of ensuring that information (i.e., facts, data, etc) are only available to specific individuals; to ensure that the entity has control over who, what, when, where, and how information is accessed and modified (W. Pennington, 2010).

Inspection on-site, physical examination of a property, commodity, project or program operations to confirm that it meets the standards of the contract, grant or cooperative agreement.

Intent "the exercise of intelligent will, the mind being fully aware of the nature and consequences of the act which is about (to be done, and with such knowledge and with full liberty of action, willing and electing to do it " (Blacks Law Dictionary).

Internal Control a process, effected by an entity's board of directors, management and other personnel, designed to provide reasonable assurance regarding the achievement of objectives in: effectiveness and efficiency of operations, reliability of financial reporting, compliance with applicable laws and regulations.

Internal, or insider fraud "the use of one's occupation for personal enrichment through the deliberate misuse or misapplication of the employing organization's resources or assets" (ACFE, Fraud 101, p. 1).

Investigate/investigation the process of trying to find out the facts about something such as a crime or accident in order to learn how it happened and who did it.

Job-embedded professional development/ teacher education "refers to teacher learning that is grounded in day-to-day teaching practice designed to enhance teachers' content-specific instructional practices with the intent of improving student learning" (as cited in Job-Embedded Professional Development: Issue Brief. April 2010, National Comprehensive Center for Teacher Quality, p.2).

k-12, K-12, pre-K-12 kindergarten (which may include pre-school) through twelfth grade

Kickback the seller's return of part of the purchase price of an item to a buyer or buyer's representative for the purpose of inducing a purchase or improperly influencing future purchases.

Larceny the crime of taking the goods of another person without permission (usually secretly), with the intent of keeping them (The Free Dictionary by FarLex).

Leakage a diversion of funds from some iterative process for "private gain"; refers to outflow from a circular flow of income model (Reinikka, R. and Svensson, J., 2001).

Link analysis a technique used to explain the relationships between entities in a criminal investigation.'

Longitudinal involving the repeated observation or examination of a set of subjects over time with respect to one or more study variables.

Mail fraud a crime in which the perpetrator develops a scheme using the mail to defraud another of money or property. This crime specifically requires the intent to defraud " (The Free Legal Dictionary by FarLex).

Malicious insider a current or former employee, contractor, or other business partner with authorized and/or unauthorized access to an organization's network, system, or data.

Malware refers to a category of malicious software, or any software that is intended to be harmful to a computer or its entire network (Thorston, 2011, Cyber AWR-175W-Information Security for Everyone Course Notes).

Material misstatement is the accidental or intentional untrue information that influences a major decision.

Material "means that the subject matter of the statement [or concealment] related to a fact or circumstance which would be important to the decision to be made as distinguished from an insignificant, trivial or unimportant detail" (Lect Law Library).

Metadata are a set of data that describes and gives information about other data.

Misappropriation the fraudulent appropriation of funds or property entrusted to your care but actually owned by someone else; the action of misappropriating something; embezzlement; to take (something, such as money) dishonestly for your own use.

Misdemeanor a minor wrongdoing; a non- indictable offense, regarded as less serious than a felony.

TONYA J. MEAD, MBA, MA

Misrepresentation the action or offense of giving a false or misleading account of the nature of something.

Money laundering the process of taking the proceeds of criminal activity and making them appear legal.

Monitoring a continuing function that aims primarily to provide the management and main stakeholders of ongoing intervention with early indications of progress or lack thereof in the achievement of results (Monitoring & Evaluation Brief, n.d. The World Bank. p. 1 Available: http://siteresources.worldbank.org/INTBELARUS/Resources/M&E.pd)

Mortgage fraud involves the overstating income, employment and salary, under-reporting expenses; and omitting liens, liabilities and alimony. These activities are material misrepresentation used to deceive lenders. Industry profiteers may collude with consumers by overstating the appraised assessment value, recruiting straw buyers, and participating in identity theft.

Murder the unlawful killing of another human being without justification or excuse (The Free Dictionary by FarLex).

National security "is a corporate term covering both national defense and foreign relations of the U.S. It refers to the protection of a nation from attack or other danger by holding adequate armed forces and guarding state secrets (USLegal.com)."

Non-federal audit those conducted by private firms. They generally involve a review of financial statements, expenditures, and internal control (Discretionary Grants Handbook as cited by IBM Center for the Business of Government, 2015, p. 16).

Norm "informal guideline about what is considered normal (what is correct or incorrect) social behavior in a particular group or social unit, formal rule or standard laid down by legal, religious or social authority against which appropriateness (what is right or wrong) of an individual's behavior is judged" (Business Dictionary).

Obstruction of justice any attempt to hinder the discovery, apprehension, conviction or punishment of anyone who has committed a crime (Ohio Bar Association).

Organization "is two or more people working together to achieve a common goal" (Griffin and Moorhead, p. 20).

Per pupil enrollment formula a formula used by states to distribute education money to school districts.

Perjury a crime that occurs when an individual willfully makes a false statement during a judicial proceeding, after he or she has taken an oath to speak the truth.

Permissibility permitted, allowable.

Personally identifying private information (PIPI); Personally identifiable information (PII); Sensitive personal information (SPI)   information that can be used on its own or with other information to identify, contact, or locate a single person, or to identify an individual in context. Any information about an individual maintained by an agency including (1) information that can be used to distinguish or trace an individual's identity, such as name, social security number, date and place of birth, mother's maiden name, or biometric (NIST, Special Publication 800-122, April 2010).

Perturbation a technique used to limit disclosure of personal information by making small changes to the data to prevent the identification of individuals from unique or rare population groups (U.S. Department of Education, Data De-identification Terms, n.d., p.5).

Phishing a technique used to gain personal information for purposes of identity theft, using fraudulent email messages that appear to come from legitimate businesses.

Plagiarism the practice of taking someone else's work or ideas and passing them off as one's own.

Post secondary education level the level of education that goes beyond secondary (high school) level.

Pre-k (pre-kindergarten school level) day care with some educational content for children younger than five, provided by elementary schools or preschools.

Pre-service training teacher education is the education and training provided to student teachers before they have undertaken any teaching.

Program review a method of oversight to evaluate the compliance with Title IV, HEA statute and resolutions to identify errors in compliance and liabilities owed. It served as a tool to improve future institutional capabilities (Prince, S.D., U.S. Department of Education, 2015 NASFAA Conference, July 19-22, 2015).

Program review findings instances in which an entity was found to have instances of non-compliance during a program review (Prince, S.D., U.S. Department of Education, 2015 NASFAA Conference, July 19-22, 2015).

Prompt cause (of an event or fact) or bring about (an action or feeling)

Prosecution risk is impacted by the mode selected for imparting justice (disciplinary, closed and/or open administrative hearing, civil court system, criminal court system, administrative dispute resolution, mediation).

Provocation an action or occurrence that causes someone to become angry or to begin to do something.

Public charter school a public school operating under a 'charter' or essentially a contract entered into between the school and its authorizing agency; the charter allows the school with significant operational autonomy to pursue specific educational objectives.

Public mood "distinct positive and negative components that citizens experience because of their membership in a particular political community" (Rahn, Kroeger and Kite, 1996, p. 31).

Punishment contains the following elements: (1) it is burdensome, (2) the burden is intentional, (3) it is imposed upon someone found to be guilty, (4) it expresses public condemnation, and (5) it is imposed upon the guilty by a legal authority (Hoskins, The Moral Permissibility of Punishment, IEP, n.d.).

Qui tam a type of civil lawsuit whistleblowers bring under the False Claims Act, a law that rewards whistleblowers if their qui tam cases recover funds for the government (Phillips & Cohen, LLP).

Racketeering "traditionally, obtaining or extorting money illegally or carrying on illegal business activities, usually by organized crime. A pattern of illegal activitiy carried out as part of an enterprise that is owned or controlled by those who are engaged in the illegal activity" (Free Legal Dictionary by FarLex).

Reasonable assurance the level of confidence that the financial statements are not materially misstated that an auditor, exercising professional skill and care, is expected to attain from an audit. It requires documentation and observations that are sufficient to conclude conformity to applicable laws, regulations and policies.

Red collar criminals "straddle both the white-collar crime arena and, eventually, the violent crime arena. In circumstances where there is threat of detection, red-collar criminals commit brutal acts of violence to silence the people who have detected their fraud and to prevent further disclosure (Brody and Kiehl, 2010, para. 18)."

Red flag/symptom a condition which is directly attributable to dishonest or fraudulent. It may result from the fraud itself or from the attempt to conceal the fraud (Wilson and Root, 1989, p. 22-9 and 22-10).

Redact to remove information from a document because you do not want the public to see it.

Residency fraud occurs when parents of another state or locality illegally enroll their children in other another district or state where the quality of public education and safety conditions are considered higher in comparison to those existing in one's own area of legal residency

Retaliation the punishment of an employee by an employer for engaging in legally protected activity, such as making a complaint of harassment or participating in workplace investigations. It can be manifest in the following ways: verbal abuse, employee termination or exclusion from important decisions and work activity (Employee Preferences for Reporting Manager Misconduct, Industry View, 2014, Software Advice Available: http://www.softwareadvice.com/hr/industryview/manager-misconduct-report-2014/)

Reward system "the allocation of compensation and benefits to employees that follow the standards, rules and procedures established" (Blacks Law Dictionary).

Risk a situation involving exposure to dander, harm or loss; an event that has a potentially negative impact and the possibility that such an event will occur and adversely affect an entity's assets, activities, and operations (IBM Center for the Business of Government, 2015, p. 12).

Risk assessment is a systematic process of evaluating the potential risks that may be involved in a projected activity or undertaking.

Risk management the continuous process of assessing risks, reducing the potential that an adverse event will occur, and putting steps in place to deal with any event that does occur; it involves a continuous process of managing- through a series of mitigating actions that permeate an entity's activities- the likelihood of an adverse event and its negative impact. Risk management address risk before mitigating an action, as well as the risk that remains after countermeasures have been taken (Government Accountability Officer, Report #GAO-06-91, December 2005, as cited by IBM Center for the Business of Government, 2015, p. 12).

Risk mitigation planning is the process of developing options and actions to enhance opportunities and reduce threats to program objectives (International Council on Systems Engineering, January 2010, INCOSE Systems Engineering Handbook, Version 3.2. NCOSE-TP-2003-002-03.2, p. 213-225).

Role model a person who serves as an example of the values, attitudes and behaviors associated with a role.

School district encompasses a specific geographical area with defined boundaries which serves to operate local public primary and secondary schools for formal academic or scholastic teaching in various nations.

School policing/ school resource officers are sworn law enforcement officers who are responsible for providing security and crime prevention services in the American school environment.

Secondary school level a school intermediate between elementary school and college and usually offering general, technical, vocational, or college-preparatory courses.

Sector an area of the economy in which entities (companies, nonprofit agencies, and other entities) share the same or a related product or service, operate in the same segment of the economy, or share a similar business type.

Self dealing is the conduct of a trustee, an attorney, a corporate officer, or other fiduciary that consists of taking advantage of his position in a transaction and acting for his own interests rather than for the interests of the beneficiaries of the trust, corporate shareholders, or his clients.

Self regulation rules and standards set by non-profit or appointed third party organization that represents the industry; compliance with these recommendations are voluntary (Thorston, Cyber Ethics, Course Notes).

Social disapproval the rejection and condemnation of a person for an action or behavior the group sees as wrong.

Spoofing an attack is when a malicious party impersonates another device or user on a network in order to launch attacks against network hosts, steal data, spread malware or bypass access controls.

Student learning outcomes the knowledge, skills and abilities that students have attained as a result of their involvement in a particular set of educational experiences.

Suppression a technique used to limit disclosure of personal information by removing data from a cell or a row in a table to prevent the identification of individuals in small groups or those with unique characteristics (U.S. Department of Education, Data De-identification Terms, n.d., p.5).

Teacher cheating accidently leaving multiplication tables on classroom walls, changing student responses on answer sheets, encouraging low performing students not to participate in order to obtain financial benefits.

Tenured is an arrangement whereby faculty members, after successful completion of a period of probationary service, can be dismissed only for adequate cause or other possible circumstances and only after a hearing before a faculty committee.

Terrorist a person who uses violent acts and threats to intimidate, coerce and frighten people in an area as a way of trying to achieve a political goal.

Theft the generic term for all crimes in which a person intentionally and fraudulently takes personal property of another without permission or consent and with the intent to convert it to the taker's use (including potential sale) (The Free Dictionary by FarLex).

True name identity theft obtaining access to someone's personal information to impersonate the person's identity.

Title I of the Elementary and Secondary Education Act (ESEA) provides financial assistance to local education agencies and schools with high numbers or high percentages of children from low-income families to help ensure that all children meet challenging state academic standards.

Title IV the college and university (post secondary) programs authorized under Title IV of the Higher Education Act of 1965 covers the administration of U.S. federal student financial aid programs.

Traditional public school is a school that is maintained at public expense for the education of the children of a community or district and that constitutes a part of a system of free public education commonly including primary and secondary schools.

True name identity theft obtaining access to someone's personal information to impersonate the person's identity.

Victimless crime include consensual crime like prostitution, illicit sex in some states and gambling, "refers to behaviors in which people engage voluntarily and willingly even though these behaviors violate the law" (Barkan, S.E., 2015).

Visa fraud/immigration fraud the fraudulent procuring, forging, or fraudulent of visas or other entry documents.

Whistleblower a person who informs on a person or organization engaged in an illicit activity.

White collar crime refers to financially motivated nonviolent crime committed by business and government professionals (Sutherland, E., 1939).

Wire fraud "fraud committed by means of electronic communication, as by telephone or modem" (The Free Legal Dictionary by FarLex).

Witness tampering the act of attempting to alter or prevent the testimony of witnesses within criminal or civil proceedings.

Zero tolerance the refusal to accept antisocial behavior, typically by strict and uncompromising application of the law.

WORKS CITED

Contact email: tonya@ishareknowledge.com

Executive Summary and Introduction

47. "Grand jury votes second superseding indictment charging five with conspiracy to murder overseas," US Department of Justice, US Attorney's Office, District of Minnesota. Minneapolis, MN, October 21, 2015.

48. R.G. Brody and K.A. Kiehl, "From white collar crime to red collar crime." *Journal of Financial Crime,* 2010, 17(3), p. 351-364. Available: https://www.ncbi.nlm.nih.gov/pmc/articles/PMC4235672/

1. "OIG Fraud Hotline: Fraud Prevention, "US Department of Education, Office of Inspector General, Washington, DC. Available: www2.ed.gov/about/offices/list/oig/hotline.html

2. Financing education: National, state and local funding and spending for public schools in 2013," US Department of Education, Institute of Education Sciences, National Center for Education Statistics, Washington, DC, January 25, 2016. Available: http://nces.ed.gov/blogs/nces/post/financing-education-national-state-and-local-funding-and-spending-for-public-schools-in-2013

3. National Priorities Project, Northampton, MA, "Federal Budget Tipsheet: Education Spending," Available: https://www.nationalpriorities.org/guides/tipsheet-education-spending/ and "Ten Facts about K-12 Education Funding," US Department of Education, US Department of Education Budget Service and the National Center for Education Statistics. Washington, DC, 2014. Available: http://www2.ed.gov/about/overview/fed/10facts/index.html?exp

4.   "Fast Facts," US Department of Education, Institute of Education Sciences, The National Center for Education Statistics, Washington, DC (n.d.). Available: http://nces.ed.gov/fastfacts/display.asp?id=84

5.   D. Halperin, "A Nation of Trump Universities: The Abuses of For-Profit Colleges," *The Republic Report*. August 28, 2013. Available: http://www.republicreport. org/2013/students-across-america-report-deceptions-for-profit-colleges/

6.   R.P. Pena,"Federal Lawsuit Accuses For Profit Schools of Fraud," *The New York Times*. February 19, 2014. Available: http://www.nytimes.com/2014/02/20/us/ lawsuit-accuses-for-profit-schools-of-fraud.html?_r=0

7.   C. Howard, "Donald Trump University Lawsuit is Lesson for All For Profit Colleges," *Forbes*. August 27, 2013. Available: http://www.forbes.com/sites/carolinehow- ard/2013/08/27/donald-trump-universitys-big-lesson-for-all-for-profit-schools/

8.   S. Wade, "Harvard Finds Scientist Guilty of Misconduct," *The New York Times*. August 20, 2010. Available: http://www.nytimes.com/2010/08/21/education/21harvard. html?_r=0

9.   S. Sanders, "Report Says UNC Grade Boosting Scandal Involved Fake Classes," *National Public Radio* (NPR). October 23, 2014. Available: http:// www.npr.org/blogs/thetwo-way/2014/10/23/358310267/report-says-unc- grade-boosting-scandal-involved-fake-classes

10.   Y. Kappes,"Former EPISD Superintendent Lorenzo Garcia gets 42 months, of- fers no apologies for scandal," *El Paso Times*. October 5, 2012.Available: http:// www.elpasotimes.com/episd/ci_21707413/former-episd-superintendent- lorenzo-garcia-sentenced-3-1

11.   D.Yost, "Interim Report of Student Attendance Data and Accountability System." The State of Ohio, Auditor of State. Columbus, OH, October 4, 2012.

12.   C.J. Willoughby, "Audit of the District of Columbia Public Schools' Graduation requirements." Government of the District of Columbia, Office of the Inspector General. Report OIG No. 06-2-25GA, Washington, DC. April 5, 2007.

13.   D.K Nichols, "Letter Report: Implementation Status of Auditor Recommendations Pertaining to Audits of Agencies Under the Purview of the Committee on Finance and Revenue (FR): Special Education," Government of the District of Columbia,

District of Columbia Auditor, Washington, DC, pg. 11, February 28, 2005. Available: http://dcauditor.org/sites/default/files/DCA1405.pdf

14. "Detroit Public Schools: June 30, 2014 Annual Report,"Office of the Inspector General, Detroit, MI, June 30, 2014. MI. Available: http://detroitk12.org/admin/inspector_general/docs/2014.06.30_Annual_Report.pdf

15. "Miami Dade County Public Schools: Annual Report 2013-2014,"Office of the Inspector General, Miami, FL, 2014. Available: http://www.miamidadeig.org/2015MDCPS/2014mdcpsAnnualReport.pdf

16. S. Richards, "Fraud Breeds Retractions," *The Scientist.* October 1, 2012. Available: http://www.the-scientist.com/?articles.view/articleNo/32687/title/Fraud-Breeds-Retractions/

17. "Final Audit Report," Report # ED-OIG/A07L0001, Office of Inspector General, Department of Education. Washington, DC, pg 3, February 2014.

165. "A Review of the Department of Homeland Security's Missions and Performance," Committee of Homeland Security and Government Affairs US Senate Committee Chair Tom Coburn 113th Congress. 15 January, 2015.

18. Association of Certified Fraud Examiners (ACFE), Austin, TX, " 2012 Global Fraud Study: Report to the Nations on Occupational Fraud and Abuse," 2013.

19. The Institute of Internal Auditors (IIA), The American Institute of Certified Public Accountants (AICPA), and the Association of Certified Fraud Examiners (ACFE), *Managing the Business Risk of Fraud: A Practical Guide*, 2013. Available: http://acfe.gr/wp-content/uploads/2013/10/managing-business-risk.pdf

20. M.G. Maxfield and E. R.Babbie, *Research Methods for Criminal Justice and Criminology*, 4th ed. Belmont, CA: Thomson Wadsworth, 2005.

21. L. Segal, *Battling Corruption in America's Public Schools.*, 1st ed. Cambridge MA: Harvard University Press, March 2005.

22. A.A. Fusco, *School Corruption: Betrayal of Children and the Public Trust*, New York: iUniverse, Inc. 2005.

23. E.H. Sutherland and D.R. Cressey, *Criminology*, Baltimore, MD: Lippincott, 1978.

24. "Class Notes," class notes for Cyber Law and White Collar Crime, Cyber-AWR-168W, Instructor T. Thorston, Texas A&M Engineering Extension Service, 2011.

25. D. T. Wolfe, D.T. and D.R. Hermanson, "The Fraud Diamond: Considering the Four Elements of Fraud," The CPA Journal. December 4, 2004. Available: http://www.nysscpa.org/cpajournal/2004/1204/essentials/p38.htm

26. F. C. Fang and A. Casadevall, "Why we cheat," *Scientific American Mind*. Vol. 24 No. 2. p. 31-37. April 2013.

27. D.R. Cressy, *Other People's Money*. Montclair, NJ: Paterson Smith,1973.

28. D.T. Wolfe and D.R. Hermanson, "The Fraud Diamond: Considering the Four Elements of Fraud," *The CPA Journal*. December 4, 2004. Available: http://www.nysscpa.org/cpajournal/2004/1204/essentials/p38.htm

29. D.R. Cressy, *Other People's Money*. Montclair, NJ: Paterson Smith,1973.

30. W.S. Albrecht, K. R. Howe, and M. B. Romney. *Deterring Fraud: The Internal Auditor's Perspective*. Altomonte Springs, FL: The Institute of Internal Auditors' Research Foundation, 1984.

31. J. Dorminey, S. Fleming, M.J. Krancher, and R. Riley. "The Evolution of Fraud Theory," *Issues in Accounting Education*. Vol. 27, No. 2, p. 555-579. American Accounting Association, 2012.

32. T. Mead, (2014, September 25). "The Educator Fraud Paradigm and Implications for Educators and Academia."Paper presented at the IAFOR North American Conference on Education 2014, Providence, RI (pg 61-82).Naka Ward, Nagoya, Aichi Japan 460-0008. Available: http://iafor.org/archives/proceedings/NACE/NACE2014_proceedings.pdf

33. Software Engineering Institute. *Insider Fraud in Financial Services*, 2012.Carnegie Mellon University, Pittsburg, PA. Available: https://resources.sei.cmu.edu/asset_files/Brochure/2012_015_001_28207.pdf

34. Association of Certified Fraud Examiners (ACFE), Austin, TX, " 2012 Global Fraud Study: Report to the Nations on Occupational Fraud and Abuse," 2013.

35. Association of Certified Fraud Examiners (ACFE), Austin, TX, " 2012 Global Fraud Study: Report to the Nations on Occupational Fraud and Abuse," 2013.

36. Association of Chief Police Officers, London, UK: "What is Fraud?" (n.d.). Available: http://www.fraud-stoppers.info/about/index.html

37. Association of Certified Fraud Examiners (ACFE), Austin, TX, " 2010 Global Fraud Study: Report to the Nations on Occupational Fraud and Abuse," 2011.

38. Association of Certified Fraud Examiners (ACFE), Austin, TX, " 2012 Global Fraud Study: Report to the Nations on Occupational Fraud and Abuse," 2013.

39. N. Amara and R. Landry, "Counting citations in the field of business and management: why use Google Scholar rather than the Web of Science," Budapest, Hungary: *Akademiai Kiado*, 2012. Available:http://www.akademiai.com/doi/abs/10.1007/s11192-012-0729-2

40. K. Kousha, and M. Thelwall, M. "Google Scholar citations and Google Web/URL citations: A multi-discipline exploratory analysis," *Journal of the American Society for Information Science and Technology*, Vo. 58, Issue 7, 1055-1065. May 2007. Available: http://onlinelibrary.wiley.com/doi/10.1002/asi.20584/abstract

165. "A Review of the Department of Homeland Security's Missions and Performance," Committee of Homeland Security and Government Affairs US Senate Committee Chair Tom Coburn 113th Congress. 15 January, 2015.

174. "Student and Exchange Visitor Program: DHS Needs to Take Actions to Strengthen Monitoring of Schools," Report # GAO-12-895T. Washington, DC. 24 July, 2012.

41. F.E. Crampton, F.E., R.C. Wood, R.C and D.C. Thompson, D.C. *Money and Schools.* New York, NY: Routledge, 2015.

42. L. Segal, *Battling Corruption in America's Public Schools.,* 1st ed. Cambridge MA: Harvard University Press, March 2005.

43. C. Ferraz, F. Finan, and D.B. Moreira, *Corrupting Learning: Evidence from Missing Federal Education Funds in Brazil.* American Economic Association, Nashville, TN, September 2011. Available: http://www.aeaweb.org

44. D. Kaufmann, A. Kraay, and M. Mastruzzi, "Governance Matters VIII: Aggregate and Individual Governance Indicators, 1996- 2008." World Bank Policy Research Working Paper 4978, World Bank. New York, NY, 2009.

45. "ITRC Fact Sheet 120: Identity Theft and Children." Identity Theft Resource Center. Washington, DC. 2015. Available: http://www.idtheftcenter.org/Fact-Sheets/fs-120.html

46. "Consumer Information: Child Identity Theft." The Federal Trade Commission Washington, DC. Available: http://www.consumer.ftc.gov/articles/0040-child-identity-theft

47. "Grand jury votes second superseding indictment charging five with conspiracy to murder overseas," US Department of Justice, US Attorney's Office, District of Minnesota. Minneapolis, MN, October 21, 2015.

48. R.G. Brody and K.A. Kiehl, "From white collar crime to red collar crime." *Journal of Financial Crime,* 201017(3), p. 351-364.

Part One

47. E. Redden, "Catch them if you can," Inside Higher Ed., September 14, 2012. Available: https://www.insidehighered.com/news/2012/09/14/international-educators-discuss-problem-fraud

48. D. Tobenkin, "Keeping it Honest: Academic Credential Fraud is Big Business," *International Educator.* National Association of International Educators. p. 32-42. January- February, 2011. Available: https://www.nafsa.org/_/File/_/ie_janfeb11_fraud.pdf

49. C. Ferraz, F. Finan, and D.B. Moreira, *Corrupting Learning: Evidence from Missing Federal Education Funds in Brazil.* American Economic Association, September 2011. Available: http://www.aeaweb.org

50. D. Kaufmann, A. Kraay, and M. Mastruzzi, "Governance Matters VIII: Aggregate and Individual Governance Indicators, 1996- 2008." World Bank Policy Research Working Paper 4978, World Bank. Washington, DC, 2009.

51. R. Klitgaaard,"International Cooperation Against Corruption," *Finance & Development.* March 2998. Available: http://www.imf.org/external/pubs/ft/fandd/1998/03/pdf/klitgaar.pdf

52. N.H. Jacoby,P. Nehemkis, and R. Eells, *Bribery and Extortion in World Business.* Trustees of Columbia University, New York, NY: Macmillian Publishing Co, Inc. ,1977.

53. J. Hallack, and M. Poisson, "Ethics and Corruption in Education: an Overview." *Journal of Education for International Development,* Volume 1, No. 1. 2005. Available: http://info.worldbank.org/etools/docs/library/242845/Hallak%20-%20 Ethics%20and%20corruption%20in%20education-%20an%20overview.pdf

54. J. Hallack and M. Poisson, "Corrupt schools, corrupt universities, What can be done?" United Nations Educational, Scientific and Cultural Organization, International Institute for Educational Planning. Paris, FR. 2007. Available: http:// unpan1.un.org/intradoc/groups/public/documents/unesco/unpan002540.pdf

55. S. P. Heyneman. "Foreign Aid to Education: Recent U.S. Initiatives- Background, Risks and Prospects," *Peabody Journal of Education,* Vol. 80., No.1., p. 107-119. Available: http://www.vanderbilt.edu/peabody/heyneman/PUBLICATIONS/ Foreign%20Aid%20to%20Education.pdf

56. W. Gustafsson, "What U.S. Foreign Aid Does for Education." The Borgen Project, Seattle, WA, January 15, 2014. Available: http://borgenproject.org/u-s-foreign-aid-education/

57. W. Gustafsson, "What U.S. Foreign Aid Does for Education." The Borgen Project, Seattle, WA, January 15, 2014. Available: http://borgenproject.org/u-s-foreign-aid-education/

58. J. Hallack and M. Poisson, "Ethics and Corruption in Education: an Overview." *Journal of Education for International Development,* Volume 1, No. 1, 2005. Available: http://info.worldbank.org/etools/docs/library/242845/Hallak%20-%20 Ethics%20and%20corruption%20in%20education-%20an%20overview.pdf

59. J. Hallack and M. Poisson, "Corrupt schools, corrupt universities, What can be done?" United Nations Educational, Scientific and Cultural Organization, International Institute for Educational Planning. Paris.2007. Available: http:// unpan1.un.org/intradoc/groups/public/documents/unesco/unpan002540.pdf

169. "Education Department Tightens Reins on More Colleges," *Inside Higher Education.* 5 January 2016. Available: https://www.insidehighered.com/ quicktakes/2016/01/05/education-department-tightens-reins-more-colleges

170. J. Jump, "Eight UK Universities on U.S. Financial Watch List," *Times Higher Education*, 16, April 2015. Available: https://www.timeshighereducation.com/news/eight-uk-universities-on-us-financial-watch-list/2019689.article

171. M. Stratford, "Cash Monitoring List Unveiled," *Inside Higher Education*, 31 March, 2015. Available: https://www.insidehighered.com/news/2015/03/31/education-department-names-most-colleges-facing-heightened-scrutiny-federal

172. "Heightened Cash Monitoring List," US Department of Education, Financial Student Aid Office, Washington, DC, June 1, 2016. Available: https://studentaid.ed.gov/sa/about/data-center/school/hcm

173. J. Marcus, " New analysis shows problematic boom in higher ed administrators," New England Center for Investigative Reporting, Boston, MA. February 6, 2014. Available: http://eye.necir.org/2014/02/06/new-analysis-shows-problematic-boom-in-higher-ed-administrators/

174. "A-133 Federal Audits," Federal Audit Clearinghouse, Washington, DC.

175. "Fraud Risk and Prevention: Campus Lesson Learned," University of Arkansas. Division of Finance and Administration, Fayetteville, AK. (n.d.). Available: http://vcfa.uark.edu/fraud-prevention/fraud-risk-and-prevention.docx

60. D. Tobenkin, "Keeping it Honest: Academic Credential Fraud is Big Business," *International Educator*. National Association of International Educators. p. 32-42. January- February, 2011. Available: https://www.nafsa.org/_/File/_/ie_janfeb11_fraud.pdf

61. "Investigative Reports," Office of the Inspector General, Department of Education and U.S. Attorney's Office, Washington, DC. April 24, 2014. Available: http://www2.ed.gov/about/offices/list/oig/invtreports/dc042014.html

62. "Investigative Reports," Office of the Inspector General, Department of Education and U.S. Attorney's Office, Washington, DC. April 24, 2014. Available: http://www2.ed.gov/about/offices/list/oig/invtreports/dc042014.html

63. "Investigative Reports," Office of the Inspector General, US Department of Education and US Attorney's Office, Washington, DC. Available: https://www2.ed.gov/about/offices/list/oig/invtreports/ca092012.pdf

64. The Center for Popular Democracy, Washington, DC, "The Tip of the Iceberg: Charter School Vulnerabilities to Waste, Fraud and Abuse," 2015. Available: http://populardemocracy.org/news/report-millions-dollars-fraud-waste-found-charter-school-sector

65. D. Tobenkin, "Keeping it Honest: Academic Credential Fraud is Big Business," *International Educator*. National Association of International Educators. p. 32-42. January- February, 2011. Available: https://www.nafsa.org/_/File/_/ie_janfeb11_fraud.pdf

66. J.F. Olson and J. Fremer, *TILSA Test Security Guidebook, Preventing, Detecting and Investigating Test Security Irregularities*, CCSSO, Washington, DC, May 2013.

67. "Investigative Reports," Office of the Inspector General, US Department of Education and US Attorney's Office, Washington, DC. April 24, 2014. Available: http://www2.ed.gov/about/offices/list/oig/invtreports/dc042014.html

68. Association of Certified Fraud Examiners (ACFE), Austin, TX, *What is Fraud?* Austin, TX, n.d. Available: http://www.acfe.com/fraud-101.aspx

69. "Investigative Reports," Office of the Inspector General, US Department of Education and US Attorney's Office, Washington, DC. April 24, 2014. Available: http://www2.ed.gov/about/offices/list/oig/invtreports/dc042014.html

70. "Investigative Reports," Office of the Inspector General, US Department of Education and US Attorney's Office, Washington, DC. April 24, 2014. Available: http://www2.ed.gov/about/offices/list/oig/invtreports/dc042014.html

71. "For Profit College Kaplan to Refund Federal Financial Aid Under Settlement with United States," US Department of Justice, U.S. Attorney's Office, Western District of Texas, January 5, 2015.

72. "Government Files Complaint Against Dallas Area-Based For-Profit Chain of Schools for False Claims," US Department of Justice, Washington, DC. August 30, 2012.

73. "SEC Announces Fraud Charges Against ITT Educational Services," US Securities and Exchange Commission, Washington, DC. May 12, 2015.

74. "Form 8-K Filing," US Securities and Exchange Commission, Washington, DC. January 27, 2014. Available: https://www.sec.gov/Archives/edgar/data/ 1066134/000129993314000113/htm_49175.htm

75. "Investigative Reports," Office of the Inspector General, US Department of Education and US Attorney's Office, Washington, DC. April 24, 2014. Available: http://www2.ed.gov/about/offices/list/oig/invtreports/dc042014.html

76. Gallup, Inc. Washington, DC. "Honesty/Ethics in the Professions," December 5-8, 2013. Available:http://www.gallup.com/poll/1654/honesty-ethics-professions.aspx and http://www.gallup.com/poll/166298/honesty-ethics-rating-clergy-slides-new-low.aspx

77. Mead, T. (2015). Longitudinal Comparison of Gallup Poll for Honesty in Professions. Unpublished Manuscript

78. Gallup, Inc. Washington, DC, "Americans Rate Nurses Highest in Ethics Professions," December 18, 2014. Available: http://www.gallup.com/poll/180260/americans-rate-nurses-highest-honesty-ethical-standards.aspx

79. R.W. Griffin and G. Moorhead, *Organizational Behavior.* Boston, MA: Houghton Mifflin, 1986.

80. P. Barnes and J. Webb, "Reducing an organization's susceptibility to occupational fraud: Factors affecting its likelihood and size," International Fraud Prevention Research Center, Nottingham Business School and Leeds Business School, UK. July 27, 2011. Available: http://www.cism.my/upload/article/201107271223530. reducing_an_organisations_susceptibility_to_fraud.pdf

81. R. Wortley, "A Classification of Techniques for Controlling Situational Precipitators of Crime," *Security Journal.* 14: p.63-82, 2001.

82. D.B. Cornish and R.V. Clarke, "Opportunities, Precipitators and Criminal Decisions: A Reply to Wortley's Critique of Situational Crime Prevention," *Crime Prevention Studies*, Vol. 16, p. 41-96, 2003.

83. R. Wortley, "A Classification of Techniques for Controlling Situational Precipitators of Crime," *Security Journal.* 14: p. 63-82, 2001.

84. M.J. Comer, *Corporate Fraud.* 3rd ed. Burlington, VT: Gower Publishing, Ltd., 1998.

85. E.W. Burgess, "The Growth of the City," in *The City: Chicago*, R.E. Part, E.W. Burgess, and R.D. Mckenzie, Eds. Chicago, IL: University of Chicago Press, 1925.

86. C.R. Shaw and H.D. McKay, *Juvenile Delinquency and Urban Areas*. Chicago, IL: University of Chicago Press, 1969.

87. S.S. Simpson, *Corporate Crime, Law, and* Social *Control*. Cambridge, UK: Cambridge University Press, 2002.

88. The Committee of Sponsoring Organizations of the Treadway Commission (COSO). "1999 analysis of cases of fraudulent financial statements investigated by the US Securities and Exchange Commission (SEC)," 1999.

89. The Institute of Internal Auditors (IIA), The American Institute of Certified Public Accountants (AICPA), and the Association of Certified Fraud Examiners (ACFE), *Managing the Business Risk of Fraud: A Practical Guide*, 2013. Available: http://acfe. gr/wp-content/uploads/2013/10/managing-business-risk.pdf

90. American Institute of Certified Public Accountants, Washington, DC. *Management Override of Internal Controls: The Achilles' Heel of Fraud Prevention*. (n.d.). Available: http://www.aicpa.org/forthepublic/auditcommitteeeffectiveness/download-abledocuments/achilles_heel.pdf

91. Association of Chief Police Officers, London, UK: "What is Fraud?" (n.d.). Available: http://www.fraud-stoppers.info/about/index.html

92. Association of Certified Fraud Examiners (ACFE), Austin, TX, " 2012 Global Fraud Study: Report to the Nations on Occupational Fraud and Abuse," 2013.

93. "Investigative Reports," Office of the Inspector General, Department of Education and U.S. Attorney's Office, Washington, DC. April 24, 2014. Available: http://www2.ed.gov/about/offices/list/oig/invreports/dc042014.html

94. D. Belkin and M. Korn, "Global Applicants Test U.S. Colleges," *The Wall Street Journal*, 30-31 May, p. A5, 2015.

180. "Fast Facts," US Department of Education, Institute of Education Sciences, The National Center for Education Statistics, Washington, DC (n.d.). Available: http://nces.ed.gov/fastfacts/display.asp?id=84

181. R. Perez-Pena, "Best, Brightest and Rejected: Elite Colleges Turn Away up to 95%," *New York Times*, 8 April, 2014. Available: http://www.nytimes.com/2014/04/09/us/led-by-stanfords-5-top-colleges-acceptance-rates-hit-new-lows.html?_r=0

182. S. Stecklow, A. Harney, and J. Park, "Students and teachers detail pervasive cheating in a program owned by test giant ACT," Reuters, 25 July, 2016. Available: http://www.reuters.com/investigates/special-report/college-cheating-act/

183. A. Hastings, "The Ugly Truth about Admissions Fraud," *HigherEdTech Decisions*, 22 August, 2016 Available: http://www.higheredtechdecisions.com/article/the_ugly_truth_about_admissions_fraud#

184. L. Rosiak and K. Watson, "Investigation: Maryland residents rip off DC schools while admins refuse to address it," The Daily Caller News Foundation, 4 July 2016. Available: http://dailycaller.com/2016/07/04/investigation-md-residents-ripping-off-dc-schools-while-admins-refuse-to-address-it/

179. Institute for International Education, Washington, DC, "IIE Releases Open Doors 2015 Data," November 16, 2015. Available: http://www.iie.org/Who-We-Are/News-and-Events/Press-Center/Press-Releases/2015/2015-11-16-Open-Doors-Data#.V8yNtzX9zIc

95. G. Maslen, "Thousands of foreign students in visa fraud racket," *University World News*. 8 August, 2014, Issue No. 330. Available: http://www.universityworldnews.com/article.php?story=20140808160700170

96. North, D. "Student Visa Fraud," Center for Immigration Studies, Washington, DC. (n.d.). Available: http://cis.org/Student-Visa-Fraud

97. Immigration and Nationality Act of 1965, (INA,§ 212(a)(6)(C)(i)).

98. D. Tobenkin, "Keeping it Honest: Academic Credential Fraud is Big Business," *International Educator.* National Association of International Educators. p. 32-42. January- February, 2011. Available: https://www.nafsa.org/_/File/_/ie_janfeb11_fraud.pdf

162. *Sham universities exploit student visas, draw scrutiny of federal investigators.* New York, NY: Fox News, January 24, 2015. Available: http://www.foxnews.com/us/2015/01/24/sham-universities-exploit-student-visas- draw-scrutiny-federal-investigators.html

163. "A Review of the Department of Homeland Security's Missions and Performance," Committee of Homeland Security and Government Affairs US Senate Committee Chair Tom Coburn 113th Congress. 15 January, 2015.

164. US Immigration and Customs Enforcement. "ICE FOIA Case Number 2015-ICFO-87685." Response to Request for Information: FOIA. September 30, 2015.

165. "A Review of the Department of Homeland Security's Missions and Performance," Committee of Homeland Security and Government Affairs US Senate Committee Chair Tom Coburn 113th Congress. 15 January, 2015.

166. "Student and Exchange Visitor Program: DHS Needs to Assess Risks and Strengthen Oversight Functions," US Government Accountability Office, Washington, DC. Report # GAO-12-572, June 18, 2012.

167. "Student and Exchange Visitor Program: DHS Needs to Take Actions to Strengthen Monitoring of Schools," US Government Accountability Office, Washington, DC. Report # GAO-12-895T, July 24, 2012.

168. "Overstay Enforcement: Additional Mechanisms for Collecting, Assessing and Sharing Data Could Strengthen DHS's Efforts by Would Have Costs," US Government Accountability Office, Washington, DC. Report # GAO-11-411, April 15, 2011.

176. R. Riley, "Ex-star principal recalls fall from grace," *USA Today* and *Detroit Free Press*, 16 December, 2015.

177. T. Baldas, "Detroit's Maserati-driving principal in Kentucky prison for bribery scheme," *USA Today* and *Detroit Free Press*, 2 September, 2016.

178. J. Mills, "Declaration of Jeffrey Mills in Support of Relator Share Award," to Superior Court of the District of Columbia, Civil Division, Phillips and Cohen, Washington, DC. Available: http://phillipsandcohen.com/2015/Declaration-of-Jeffrey-Mills.pdf

99. "Investigative Reports," Office of the Inspector General, Department of Education and U.S. Attorney's Office, Washington, DC. April 24, 2014. Available: http://www2.ed.gov/about/offices/list/oig/invtreports/dc042014.html

100. "Investigative Reports," Office of the Inspector General, US Department of Education and the US Attorney's Office, Eastern District of Michigan, March 26, 2013. Available: http://www2.ed.gov/about/offices/list/oig/invtreports/mi032013.html

101. "For Profit College Kaplan to Refund Federal Financial Aid Under Settlement with United States," US Department of Justice and the US Attorney's Office, Western District of Texas, January 5, 2015.

102. "Government Files Complaint Against Dallas Area-Based For-Profit Chain of Schools for False Claims," US Department of Justice, Washington, DC, August 30, 2012.

103. "SEC Announces Fraud Charges Against ITT Educational Services," US Securities and Exchange Commission, Washington, DC. May 12, 2015.

104. "Form 8-K Filing," US Securities and Exchange Commission, Washington, DC. January 27, 2014. Available: https://www.sec.gov/Archives/edgar/data/1066134/000129993314000113/htm_49175.htm

105. P. Barnes and J. Webb, "Reducing an organization's susceptibility to occupational fraud: Factors affecting its likelihood and size." International Fraud Prevention Research Center, Nottingham Business School and Leeds Business School, UK. July 27, 2011. Available: http://www.cism.my/upload/article/201107271223530.reducing_an_organisations_susceptibility_to_fraud.pdf

106. "HELP (The Senate Health, Education, Labor and Pensions Committee) Chairman Tom Harkin Unveils the Higher Education Affordability Act, " US Senate Washington, DC. Available: http://www.help.senate.gov/imo/media/doc/Higher%20Education%20Affordability%20Act%20Summary%20Final.pdf

107. "Written Testimony on President Obama's Plan to Make College More Affordable: A Better Bargain for the Middle Class," US Department of Education, Washington, DC, December, 2013.

108. T. Mead (2015). Risk Assessment Data Quality and Security for School and Campus Records, Unpublished Manuscript.

109. M.B. Kugler, "Public Perceptions of White Collar Crime Culpability: Bribery, Perjury and Fraud," *Law and Contemporary Problems*, Vol. 75: p. 33-59, 2012.

110. J. Kaufman, *Protecting the Veracity of our Children's Test Scores.* Dartmouth College, Hanover, NH, 2012. Available: http://www. thepresidency.org/storage/documents/Fellows_2011_-_2012_Papers/Kaufmann-_Final_Paper.pdf.

111. F. C. Fang and A. Casadevall, "Why we cheat," *Scientific American Mind.* Vol. 24 No. 2. p. 31-37. April 2013.

112. L. Filas, "Antioch teacher charged in grade tampering married to football coach," *Daily Herald,* 19, November 2011. Available: http://www.dailyherald.com/article/20111119/news/711199897/

113. H. Aris, "Yonkers School Teacher Charged with Tampering of Students' Transcripts," *Yonkers Tribune.* 29, April 2011. Available: http://www.yonkerstribune.com/2011/04/yonkers-school-teacher-charged-with-tampering-of-students-transcripts

114. D. Jones, "Philadelphia Teachers, Principal Charged in Test Cheating Scandal," *NBC Philadelphia Local News,* May 8, 2014.

115. National Association of Criminal Defense Lawyers, Washington, DC. "The Terrible Toll of America's Broken Misdemeanor Courts," April 2009. , Available: http://www.nacdl.org/public.nsf/defenseupdates/misdemeanor/$FILE/Report.pdf

116. Pew Research Center, The Pew Charitable Trusts, Washington, DC." One in 31: The Long Reach of American Corrections,"March, 2009 Available: http://www.pewtrusts.org/~/media/legacy/uploadedfiles/pcs_assets/2009/pspp1in31reportfinalweb32609pdf.pdf

117. A. Natapoff, "Why Misdemeanors Aren't So Minor,". *Slate,* 27 April 2012. Available: http://www.slate.com/articles/news_and_politics/jurisprudence/2012/04/misdemeanors_can_have_major_consequences_for_the_people_charged_.html

118. National Association of Criminal Defense Lawyers, Washington, DC. "The Terrible Toll of America's Broken Misdemeanor Courts," April 2009. , Available: http://www.nacdl.org/public.nsf/defenseupdates/misdemeanor/$FILE/Report.pdf

119. "The Economics of Higher Education," US Department of the Treasury and the US Department of Education, Washington, DC. December 2012. Available: http://www.treasury.gov/connect/blog/Documents/20121212_Economics%20of%20Higher%20Ed_vFINAL.pdf

120. M. Frenette, "An Investment of a Lifetime? The Long-term Labour Market Premiums Associated with a Post-secondary education," Analytical Studies Branch Statistics Research Paper Series, 11F0019M, no. 350. Canada. February 2014 Available: http://www.statcan.gc.ca/pub/11f0019m/11f0019m2014359-eng.htm

121. S. Saulny, R. Coolidge, and J. Phelps,"Is college worth it?" *Yahoo News.* June 27, 2014. Available: http://news.yahoo.com/blogs/power-players-abc-news/is-college-worth-it—new-documentary-explores-higher-education-costs-and-rising-student-debt-223233460.html

180. S. Ross, "Who Actually Owns Student Loan Debt?" *Investopia,* 12 August, 2016. Available: http://www.investopedia.com/articles/personal-finance/081216/who-actually-owns-student-loan-debt.asp

122. "College Aid Means Higher Tuition,"*Wall Street Journal,* Review and Outlook Section, 20 July, p. A14 , 2015.

123. Association of Certified Fraud Examiners (ACFE), Austin, TX, " 2010 Global Fraud Study: Report to the Nations on Occupational Fraud and Abuse," 2011.

124. Association of Certified Fraud Examiners (ACFE), Austin, TX, " 2012 Global Fraud Study: Report to the Nations on Occupational Fraud and Abuse," 2013.

125. J. Kaufman, "Protecting the Veracity of our Children's Test Scores," Dartmouth College, Hanover, NH, 2012. Available: http://www. thepresidency.org/storage/documents/Fellows_2011_-_2012_Papers/Kaufmann-_Final_Paper.pdf.

126. "An OIG Perspective on Improving Accountability and Integrity in ESEA Programs," US Department of Education, Office of Inspector General, Washington, DC . Report # ED-OIG/S09H0007. October, 2007.

127. "The Secretary's Eighth Report on Teacher Quality Based on Data Provided for 2008, 2009, 2010," US. Department of Education, Office of Post-Secondary Education, Washington, DC. November 2011.

128. L. Darling-Hammond and G. Sykes, (2003) "Wanted: A National Teacher Supply Policy for Education: The Right Way to Meet the Highly Qualified Teacher Challenge," *Education Policy Analysis Archives*, Vol 11, No. 33, 2003.

129. R. Weingarten, [President of American Federation of Teachers] "Unions in Public Education: Problem or solution?" Sponsored by the American Enterprise Institute,

Washington, DC. Presentation and Question and Answer Session. Participant 18, June 2014.

130. "Preparing and Credentialing the Nation's Teachers: The Secretary's Eighth Report on Teacher Quality Based on Data Provided for 2008, 2009, 2010," US Department of Education, Office of Post-Secondary Education, Washington, DC. November 2011.

131. Hart Research & Associates, Washington, DC, "It takes more than a major: employer priorities for college learning and student successs,"for the Association of American Colleges and Universities. April 10, 2013 Retrieved here: http://www. aacu.org/leap/documeNts/2013_employersurvey.pdf

132. T.J. Burant, S.M. Chubbuck, and J.L. Whip, "Reclaiming the moral in the dispositions debate," *Journal of Teacher Education*, 58 (5) p. 397-411, 2007.

133. E. Campbell, "The ethics of teaching as a moral profession," *Curriculum Inquiry*, 38 (4), p. 357-385, 2008.

134. J. Gore, J. Ladwig, T. Griffiths and W. Amosa, "Data-driven guidelines for high quality teacher education," In Proc. AARE 2007 Conference: Research Impacts: Proving or improving? Fremantle, WA, 2007.

135. National Commission on Teaching and America's Future (NCTAF), Arlington, VA, "National Commission on Teaching and America's Future," 1996.

136. "Meeting the Highly Qualified Teachers Challenge, US. Department of Education, Washington, DC. 2002.

137. P. Keith-Spiegel, B.E. Whitley, Jr., D.W. Balogh, D.V. Perkings, and A.F. Wittig, A.F. *The Ethics of Teaching: A Casebook*, 2nd ed. Mahwah, NJ: Lawrence Erlbaum, 2002.

138. T. Hutchings, "A Case for a Model Code of Educator Ethics," The National Association of State Directors of Teacher Education and Certification, Washington, DC, 2014.

139. B. Stecher and S.N. Kirby, Eds., *Organizational Improvement and Accountability, Lessons for Education from Other Sources*, Santa Monica, CA: The Rand Organization, 2004. Available: http://www.rand.org/content/dam/rand/pubs/monographs/2004/RAND_MG136.pdf)

140. W.L. Sanders and S.P Horn, "Research Findings from the Tennessee Value-Added Assessment System Database: Implications for Educational Evaluation and Research," *Journal of Personnel Evaluation in Education* 12:3, p. 247-256, 1998. Available: http://www.cgp.upenn.edu/pdf/Sanders_Horn-Research_Findings_from_TVASS.PDF

141. R. Chetty, R. Friedman, and J. Rockoff, "The Long-Term Impacts of Teachers: Teacher Value Added and Student Outcomes in Adulthood," Cambridge, MA: Harvard University, Faculty of Arts and Sciences, 2002. Available: http://obs.rc.fas.harvard.edu/chetty/value_added.html

142. J. Rumel, "Back to the Future: The In Loco Parentis Doctrine and Its Impact on Whether K-12 Schools and Teachers Owe a Fiduciary Duty to Students," *Indiana Law Review*, Vol. 46: p. 711-751, 2014. Available: http://Mckinneylaw.iu.ilr/pdf/vol46p711.pdf

143. D.J. Brewer and G.C. Hentschke, "An International Perspective on Publicly Financed, Privately Operated Schools," in *Handbook of Research on School Choice*, M. Berends, Ed. New York, NY: Routledge, 2009, pp- 227-246.

144. M. Severns and K. Glieck, "Washington DC Mayor Race," *Politico*. 9 June, 2014. Available: http://www.politico.com/story/2014/06/washington-dc-mayor-race-david-catania-muriel-bowser-107582.html#ixzz36bYijYBa)

145. L. Layton, "New Orleans Leads the Nation in Percentage of Public Charter School Enrollment," National Alliance for Public Charter Schools, Washington, DC: *Washington Post.*10 December, 2013. Available: http://www.washingtonpost.com/local/education/new-orleans-leads-nation-in-percentage-of-public-charter-school-enrollment/2013/12/10/cb9c4ca6-61d6-11e3-bf45-61f69f54fc5f_story.html)

146. "State Nonfiscal Survey of Public Elementary and Secondary Education, 1990-91 through 2012-13; Private School Universe Survey (PSS), 1995-96 through 2011-12; National Elementary and Secondary Enrollment Projection Model, 1972 through 2024; Integrated Postsecondary Education Data System (IPEDS), Fall Enrollment Survey, " US Department of Education, National Center for Education Statistics, Common Core of Data (CCD), Washington, DC. IPEDS-EF:90-99, March 2015.

147. T.G. Carroll and E. Foster, "Who will teach? Experience Matters," National Commission on Teaching for America's Future, Washington, DC, January 2010.

148. S. Headen, "Public School Classrooms Highlights Causes, Consequences and Promising Responses," Carnegie Foundation for the Advancement of Teaching,

Washington, DC. March 2014. Available: http://www.carnegiefoundation.org/news-room/press-releases/new-carnegie-report-examines-rise-in-inexperienced-teachers-in-public-schools

149. S. Headen, "Beginners in the Classroom: What the Changing Demographics of Teaching Mean for Schools, Students, and Society," Carnegie Foundation for the Advancement of Teaching, Washington, DC. 2014. Available: ttp://www.carnegiefoundation.org/sites/default/files/beginners_in_classroom.pdf

150. E. Hanushek, "The Difference is Great Teachers," *Waiting for Superman*, New York, NY: Public Affairs, 2010.

151. A. Kezar and D. Maxey, *The Changing Academic Workforce*. Trusteeship of the Association of Governing Boards of Universities and Colleges, Washington, DC, Vol 21. No. 3. May-June 2013. Available: http://agb.org/trusteeship/2013/5/changing-academic-workforce

152. J. Pfeffer, *Managing with Power: Politics and Influence in Organizations*. Boston, MA: Harvard Business School Press, 1992.

153. Association of Certified Fraud Examiners (ACFE), Austin, TX, " 2014 Global Fraud Study: Report to the Nations on Occupational Fraud and Abuse," 2015.

154. A.A. Fusco, *School Corruption: Betrayal of Children and the Public Trust*, New York, NY: iUniverse, Inc, 2005.

155. L. Segal, L. (March 2005) *Battling Corruption in America's Public Schools*, 1st ed. Cambridge, MA: Harvard University Press, 2005.

156. K. Ricks, [Meeting Associate, American Educational Research Association] Interview (September 2, 2014).

157. A.A. Fusco, *School Corruption: Betrayal of Children and the Public Trust*, New York, NY: iUniverse, Inc, 2005.

158. T. Hutchings, "A Case for a Model Code of Educator Ethics," The National Association of State Directors of Teacher Education and Certification, Washington, DC, 2014.

159. A.A. Fusco, *School Corruption: Betrayal of Children and the Public Trust*, New York, NY: iUniverse, Inc, 2005.

160. R. Fossey, "Corrupt, mismanaged and unsafe schools: Where is the Research?" *Ed Week.* 25 October 1995.

161. S.R. Barley, G.W. Meyer and D.C. Gash, "Cultures of Culture: Academics, Practitioners and the Pragmatics of Normative Control," *Administrative Science Quarterly*, Vol. 33, No. 1, p. 24-60, March 1988.

Part Two

1. J. McCandless, "U.S. Education Institutions Spend $6.6 Billion on IT in 2015," Center for Digital Education, Folsom, CA, May 22, 2015.
Available: http://www.centerdigitaled.com/higher-ed/US-Education-Institutions-Spend-66-Billion-on-IT-in-2015.html

151. M. Koba, "Education tech funding soars-but is it working in the classroom?" *Forbes,* 28 April, 2015. Available: http://fortune.com/2015/04/28/education-tech-funding-soars-but-is-it-working-in-the-classroom/

2. J.M. Silber, "Education and Training" *BMO Capital Markets.* September 2014. Available: http://www.educationindustry.org/assets/documents/KnowledgeCenterDocs/bmocm%202014%20education%20industry%20report.pdf

141. "Use of Technology in Teaching and Learning," US Department of Education, Washington, DC. (n.d.). Available: http://www.ed.gov/oii-news/use-technology-teaching-and-learning

3. G. Sinanaj, J. Muntermann, and T. Cziesla, "How Data Breaches Ruin Firm Reputation on Social Media! Insights from a Sentiment based Event Study," International Conference on Wirtschaftsinformatik, Osnabrück, Germany, March 4,2015. Available: http://www.wi2015.uni-osnabrueck.de/Files/WI2015-D-14-00293.pdf

4. D. Icove, K. Seger, and W. VonStorch, *Computer Crime: A Crimefighter's Handbook,* 1st ed. Sebastapol, CA. O'Reilly & Associates, Inc., August 1995.

5. "Class Notes," class notes for Information Security Basics, Cyber 173-W, Instructor W. Pennington, Texas A&M Engineering Extension Service, 2010.

6. "Class Notes," class notes for Information Risk Management, Cyber AWR-177-W, Instructor T. Thorston, Texas A&M Engineering Extension Service, 2012.

7. "Class Notes," class notes for Digital Forensics Basics, AWR-139-W, Instructor T. Thorston, Texas A&M Engineering Extension Service, 2011.

8. A. Acquisti, A. Friedman and R. Telang, " Is there a cost to privacy breaches? An event study," workshop on the Economics of Information Systems presented at the 27th International Conference on Information Systems, Milwaukee, WS, 2006. Available: http://www.heinz.cmu.edu/~acquisti/papers/acquisti-friedman-telang-privacy-breaches.pdf

9. L. Ponemon, "What does a data breach cost companies?" Ponemon Institute, LLC, Traverse City, MI, 2005.

10. Electronic Privacy Information Center (EPIC), Washington, DC, "Student Privacy," April 23, 2015. Available: https://epic.org/privacy/student/

11. "Top Trending Education Targets in 2015," *Surfwatch Labs.* 2015. Available: https://www.surfwatchlabs.com/?gclid=CKXqwZ_0xMUCFVKQHwodTAYAhQ

12. K. Wagstaff, and C. Sottile, "Cyberattack 101: Why hackers are going after universities," *NBC News.* 20 September 2015. Available: http://www.nbcnews.com/tech/security/universities-become-targets-hackers-n429821

13. Data Quality Campaign, Washington, DC, "State Student Data Privacy: What Happened in 2014 and What is Next? 2014 Student Privacy Bills as of August 27, 2014," August 29, 2014. Available: http://www.dataqualitycampaign.org/find-resources/state-student-data-privacy-legislation-2014/

14. "Safeguarding Student Privacy," US Department of Education, Washington, DC. Available: https://www2.ed.gov/policy/gen/guid/fpco/ferpa/safeguarding-student-privacy.pdf

15. SANS Institute, Bethesda, MA, "Information Security Managing Risk with Defense in Depth," 2003. Retrieved from: http://www.sans.org/reading-room/whitepapers/infosec/information-security-managing-risk-defense-in-depth-1224

16. S. Lineberry, "The Human Element: The Weakest Link in Information Security," *The Journal of Accountancy,* 2007. Available: http://www.journalofaccountancy.com/issues/2007/thehumanelementtheweakestlinkininformationsecurity.htm

17. T. Mead (2014, September 25). "The Educator Fraud Paradigm and Implications for Educators and Academia."Paper presented at the IAFOR North American Conference on Education 2014, Providence, RI (pg 61-82).Naka Ward, Nagoya, Aichi Japan 460-0008. Available: http://iafor.org/archives/proceedings/NACE/NACE2014_proceedings.pdf

18. E.M. Willis and P. Raines, "Technology and the changing face of teacher preparation," *Contemporary Issues in Technology and Teacher Education* [Online serial] , *1* (3), 2001 . Available: http://www.citejournal.org/vol1/iss3/currentpractice/article1.htm

143. State Educational Technology Directors Association (SETDA), Glen Burnie, MD, "National Trends Report: Enhancing Education through Technology," (n.d). Available: http://www.setda.org/c/document_library/get_file?folderId=6&name=DLFE-329.pdf

144. B. Gill, B.C. Borden and K. Hallgren, "A Conceptual Framework for Data-Driven Decision Making," Mathematica Policy Research. Princeton, NJ. Reference Number 40019.190. June 2, 2014.

19. J. Yamamoto, C. Penny, J. Leight and S. Winterton, *Technology Leadership in Teacher Education: Integrated Solutions and Experiences.* Hershey: NY. IGI Global, 2010.

142. M. Beglau, J.C. Hare, L. Foltos, K. Gann, J. James, H. Jobe, J. Knight and B. Smith, "Technology, Coaching and Community: Power Partners for Improved Professional Development in Primary and Secondary Education," *International Society for Technology in Education.* ISTE White Paper Special Conference Release. Available: http://instructionalcoach.org/images/downloads/ISTE_Whitepaper_June_Final_Edits.pdf.

20. American Association of Colleges for Teacher Education, Washington, DC, "Pk-12 educational leadership and administration," White Paper, June 2, 2014.

21. "Teachers and Technology: Making the Connection," US Office of Technology Assessment and Congressional Office of Technology Assessment. Washington, DC. GPO Rep. No. 052-003-01409-2, 1995.

22. A. Borthwick and M. Pierson, Eds. "Transforming Classroom Practice: Professional Development Strategies in Educational Technology," *International Society for Technology in Education,* 2008 Available: http://www.iste.org/docs/excerpts/PRODEV-excerpt.pdf

23. S. Goldman, K. Cole and C. Syer, *The technology/content dilemma*, US Department of Education, Research and Statistics Division Technology Conference [Online]. 1999. Available: http://www.ed.gov/rschstat/eval/tech/techconf99/whitepapers/paper4.html

24. A. Trotter, "Preparing teachers for the digital age," *Education Week on the Web* [Online]. 1999, September 23. Available: http://www.edweek.org/sreports/tc99/articles/teach.htm

25. M.L. Abbott, *States challenge grants TAGLIT data analysis: A report prepared for the Bill & Melinda Gates Foundation*, Seattle, WA. 2003. Available: http://www.gatesfoundation.org/Education/ResearchandEvaluation

26. S. Grajek, *Top Ten IT Issues, 2013: Welcome to the Connected Age*. EDUCAUSE. Washington, DC. June 3, 2013. Available: http://www.educause.edu/ero/article/top-ten-it-issues-2013-welcome-connected-age

144. Plante Moran, Southfield, MI, "The Technology Imperative: Staying Ahead of the Curve in the Classroom," (n.d.).

145. D. Palmer, 'Weak link' employees with poor cyber security training leaving banks and government vulnerable. *Computing.* [Online]. January 20, 2015. Available: http://www.computing.co.uk/ctg/news/2391093/weak-link-employees-with-poor-syber-security-training-leaving-banks-and-government-vulnerable

27. "Class Notes," class notes for Cyber Law and White Collar Crime, Cyber-AWR-168W, Instructor T. Thorston, Texas A&M Engineering Extension Service, 2011.

148. Southern Regional Education Board, Atlanta, GA, "(98T11) Technology Standards for Teachers," (1998). Available: http://dev02.cooldoginteractive.com/page/1380/98t11_technology_standards_for_teachers.html

149. The American Association of School Administrators (The School Superintendents Association), Alexandria, VA, "Technology Standards for School Administrators," 2001.

28. "Class Notes," class notes for Cyber Security Ethics, Cyber-AWR-174W, Instructor T. Thorston, Texas A&M Engineering Extension Service, 2011.

29. M. Kaiser, "Prepared Testimony on the State of Cyber security and Small Business," Intelligence and National Security Alliance. Arlington, VA. December 1, 2011. Available: http://smallbusiness.house.gov/uploadedfiles/kaiser_testimony.pdf

30. S. Wallsten, "What we are not doing when we're online," National Bureau of Economic Research. Cambridge, MA: NBER Working Paper No. 19549, October 2013. Available: http://www.nber.org/papers/w19549?utm_campaign=ntw&utm_medium=email&utm_source=ntw

31. K.J. Anderson, "Internet Use Among College Students: An Exploratory Study," *Journal of American College Health*, Vo. 50, No. 1., (n.d.). Available: http://faculty.mwsu.edu/psychology/dave.carlston/Writing%20in%20Psychology/Internet/8/i5.pdf

32. S. Jones and C. Johnson-Yale, "Professors online: The Internet's impact on college faculty," *First Monday*. Vol 10., No. 5. September 5, 2005. Available: http://www.firstmonday.org/ojs/index.php/fm/article/view/1275/1195

33. R. Rasmussen, "The College Cyber Security Tightrope: Higher Education Institution Face Greater Risks," *Security Week Network*. April 28, 2011. Available: http://www.securityweek.com/college-cyber-security-tightrope-higher-education-institutions-face-greater-risks

34. Data Quality Campaign, Washington, DC, "Teacher Data Literacy: It's About Time," February 2014. Available: http://www.dataqualitycampaign.org/wp-content/uploads/files/DQC-Data%20Literacy%20Brief.pdf

35. C.R. Jeffery, "Criminal Behavior and Learning Theory," *Criminal Law, Criminology & Police Science*, Vol 56, Issue 3, Article 4, p. 294-300, Fall 1965.

36. M. Brown, L. Trevino, L. and D. Harrison, "Ethical leadership: A social learning perspective for construct development and testing." *Organizational Behavior and Human Decision Processes*, 97(2), p. 117-134, 2005.

37. A.A. Ardichvili (University of Minnesota and Center for Ethical Business Cultures) , D.J. Jondle, and J.A. Mitchell (Center for Ethical Business Cultures), Minneapolis, MN: *Characteristics of Ethical Business Cultures*, 2008. Available: http://files.eric.ed.gov/fulltext/ED501640.pdf

38. Association of Certified Fraud Examiners (ACFE), Austin, TX, "Tone at the Top: How Management Can Prevent Fraud in the Workplace," (n.d.). Available: http://

www.acfe.com/uploadedFiles/ACFE_Website/Content/documents/tone-at-the-top-research.pdf

39. D.L. McCabe, L.K. Trevino and K.D. Butterfield, "Academic integrity in honor code and non-honor code environments," *Journal of Higher Education*, 70, p. 211-234, 1999.

40. "Improving Data Quality for Title I Standards, Assessments, and Accountability Reporting," US Department of Education, Office of Elementary and Secondary Education, Washington, DC. April 2006.

41. "State Nonfiscal Survey of Public Elementary and Secondary Education, 1990-91 through 2012-13; Private School Universe Survey (PSS), 1995-96 through 2011-12; National Elementary and Secondary Enrollment Projection Model, 1972 through 2024; Integrated Postsecondary Education Data System (IPEDS), Fall Enrollment Survey, " US Department of Education, National Center for Education Statistics, Common Core of Data (CCD), Washington, DC. IPEDS-EF:90-99, March 2015.

42. C. Fox, D. Schaffhauser, G. Fletcher and D. Levin, "Transforming Data to Information in Service of Learning," State Educational Technology Directors Association (SETDA), Washington, DC, 2013.

43. S. Grajek, *Top Ten IT Issues, 2013: Welcome to the Connected Age*. EDUCAUSE. Washington, DC. June 3, 2013. Available: http://www.educause.edu/ero/article/top-ten-it-issues-2013-welcome-connected-age

44. D. Halperin, "A Nation of Trump Universities: The Abuses of For-Profit Colleges." *The Republic Report*. 28, August 2013. Available: http://www.republicreport.org/2013/students-across-america-report-deceptions-for-profit-colleges/

45. R.P. Pena, "Federal Lawsuit Accuses For Profit Schools of Fraud." *The New York Times*. 19 February, 2014. Available: http://www.nytimes.com/2014/02/20/us/lawsuit-accuses-for-profit-schools-of-fraud.html?_r=0

46. C. Howard, "Donald Trump University Lawsuit is Lesson for All For Profit Colleges," *Forbes*. 27 August, 2013. Available: http://www.forbes.com/sites/carolinehoward/2013/08/27/donald-trump-universitys-big-lesson-for-all-for-profit-schools/

47. S. Wade, "Harvard Finds Scientist Guilty of Misconduct." *The New York Times*. 20 August, 2010. Available: http://www.nytimes.com/2010/08/21/education/21harvard.html?_r=0

48. Y. Kappes, "Former EPISD Superintendent Lorenzo Garcia gets 42 months, offers no apologies for scandal," *El Paso Times.* 5 October, 2012. Available: http://www.elpasotimes.com/episd/ci_21707413/former-episd-superintendent-lorenzo-garcia-sentenced-3-1

49. D. Yost, "Interim Report of Student Attendance Data and Accountability System." The State of Ohio, Auditor of State. Columbus, OH, October 4, 2012.

50. C.J. Willoughby, "Audit of the District of Columbia Public Schools' Graduation requirements." Government of the District of Columbia, Office of the Inspector General. Report OIG No. 06-2-25GA, Washington, DC. April 5, 2007.

51. D.K Nichols, "Letter Report: Implementation Status of Auditor Recommendations Pertaining to Audits of Agencies Under the Purview of the Committee on Finance and Revenue (FR): Special Education," Government of the District of Columbia, District of Columbia Auditor, Washington, DC, pg. 11, February 28, 2005. Available: http://dcauditor.org/sites/default/files/DCA1405.pdf

52. S. Richards, "Fraud Breeds Retractions," *The Scientist,* 1 October , 2012. Available: http://www.the-scientist.com/?articles.view/articleNo/32687/title/Fraud-Breeds-Retractions/

53. "Final Audit Report," Office of Inspector General, US Department of Education. Washington, DC. Report # ED-OIG/A07L0001, p. 3, February 2014.

146. K. Amin, "Big Data: Practical Tips for ETL Testing," *The Developer Network.* 4 June, 2014. Available: http://www.developer.comdb/big-data-practical-tips-for-etl-testing.html

147. T. Bergner and N.J. Smith, "How Can My State Benefit from an Educational Data Warehouse?" Data Quality Campaign. Washington, DC. September 2007. Available: http://www.aypf.org/documents/Publications-State_Benefits_from_Data_Warehouse.pdf

54. K. Bauman and J. Davis, "Estimated of School Enrollment by Grade in the American Community Survey, the Current Population Survey, and the Common Core Data," US Census Bureau, Washington, DC. SEHSD Working Paper 2014-7. December 31, 2013. Available: http://www.census.gov/hhes/school/files/ACS-CPS-CCD_02-18-14.pdf

55. New America's Education Policy Program, Washington, DC, "PreK-12 Financing Overview," June 29, 2015. Available: http://atlas.newamerica.org/school-finance

56. Concealed Campus, Austin, TX, "Crime on College Campuses in the U.S.," May 2009. Available: http://concealedcampus.org/campus-crime/

57. "Crime in Schools and Colleges: A Study of Offenders and Arrestees Reported via National Incident-Based Reporting System Data, " US Department of Justice, Federal Bureau of Investigations (FBI), Washington, DC. (n.d.). Available: http://fbi.gov/about-us/cjis/ucr/nibrs/crime-in-schools-and-colleges

58. "The CARD Report: Crime Analysis, Research and Development Unit. Crime in Schools and Colleges," US Department of Justice. Federal Bureau of Investigations (FBI), Washington, DC. October 2007.

59. Concealed Campus, Austin, TX, "Crime on College Campuses in the U.S.," May 2009. Available: http://concealedcampus.org/campus-crime/

60. J. New, "Final Changes to Clery Act," *Inside Higher Education*, 20 October, 2014. Available: https://www.insidehighered.com/news/2014/10/20/education-department-publishes-final-rules-campus-crime-reporting

61. M.G. Maxfield and E. Babble, *Research Methods for Criminal Justice and Criminology*, 4th ed. Belmont, CA: Thomson Wadsworth, 2005.

62. C. McCue, *Data mining and predictive analysis: Intelligence Gathering and Crime Analysis*. Waltham, MA: Butterworth-Heinemann, 2007.

63. "Preventing Violence and Promoting Safety in Higher Education Settings: Overview of a Comprehensive Approach," US Department of Education, Office of Safe and Drug Free Schools, Washington, DC. # ED-04-CO-0136. (n.d.).

64. "The CARD Report: Crime Analysis, Research and Development Unit. Crime in Schools and Colleges," US Department of Justice. Federal Bureau of Investigations (FBI), Washington, DC. October 2007.

65. N. Anderson, "55 Colleges under Title IX Investigation for their Handling of Sex Assault Claims," *The Washington Post*. 1 May, 2014.

66. United Educators Insurance, Bethedsa, MD, "Risk Research Bulletin: The Campus SaVE Act Compliance Guide," (n.d).

67. S. Sneed, [Audit Manager at Winston Salem State University]. Interview (April 23, 2015).

68. Concealed Campus, Austin, TX, "Crime on College Campuses in the U.S.," May 2009. Available: http://concealedcampus.org/campus-crime/

69. Every Town for Gun Safety, New York, NY, "School Shootings in America Since Sandy Hook," November 20, 2014. Available: http://everytown.org/article/schoolshootings/

70. "Common Fraud Schemes," U.S. Department of Justice, Federal Bureau of Investigations (FBI), Washington, DC. (n.d.) Available: http://www.fbi.gov/scams-safety/fraud

71. S. Kirchheimer, *Scam Proof Your Life*. New York, NY: AARP. Sterling Publishing, Inc, 2006.

72. R.G. Hattersley, "Top 10 Data Breaches at Educational Facilities in 2014," *Campus Safety Magazine,* 19 January 2015. Available: http://www.campussafetymagazine.com/article/top_10_data_breaches_at_educational_facilities_in_2014

73. D. Icove, K. Seger, and W. VonStorch, *Computer Crime: A Crimefighter's Handbook,* 1st ed. Sebastapol, CA. O'Reilly & Associates, Inc., August 1995.

74. R. Power, "Current and Future Danger: A CSI Primer on Computer Crime and Information Warfare,"Computer Security Institute,1995.

150. K. Amin, "Big Data: Practical Tips for ETL Testing," *The Developer Network.* 4 June, 2014. Available: http://www.developer.comdb/big-data-practical-tips-for-etl-testing.html

75. A. Acquisti, A. Friedman and R. Telang, " Is there a cost to privacy breaches? An event study," workshop on the Economics of Information Systems presented at the 27th International Conference on Information Systems, Milwaukee, WS, 2006. Available: http://www.heinz.cmu.edu/~acquisti/papers/acquisti-friedman-telang-privacy-breaches.pdf

76. L. Ponemon, "What does a data breach cost companies?" Ponemon Institute, LLC, Traverse City, MI, 2005.

77. Choicepoint, Inc., Alpharetta, GA, "2005 disclosures of U.S. data incidents," 2006. Available: http://www.privacyatchoicepoint.com/common/pdfs/Data_ Disclosures_2005.pdf, 2006.

78. M. Dresser, "Board Oks Pact to Protect UM Security Breach Victims," *The Baltimore Sun*, 23 July, 2014. Available: http://www.baltimoresun.com/news/maryland/politics/blog/bs-md-university-cyber-20140723-story.html

79. L. Ponemon, "What does a data breach cost companies?" Ponemon Institute, LLC, Traverse City, MI, 2005.

80. T. Mead (2015). Risk Assessment Data Quality and Security for School and Campus Records. Unpublished Manuscript.

81. R. M. Ingersoll and H. May, "Recruitment, Retention and Minority Teacher Shortage," Consortium for Policy Research in Education (CPRE), Philadelphia, PA: Research Report #RR-69, 2011.

82. B. Kisida and A.J. Egalite, "Education without Representation," Education Next, 16 March, 2015. Available: http://educationnext.org/education-without-representation/

152. B.D. Baker, David G. Sciarra, and D. Farrie, "Is School Funding Fair? A National Report Card," School Funding Fairness, January 2014. Available: http://www.schoolfundingfairness.org/National_Report_Card_2014.pdf)

153. US Department of Education, Institute for Education Sciences, National Center for Education Statistics. Washington, DC: NCES: 2000090, April 2000. Available: https://nces.ed.gov/surveys/frss/publications/2000090/

154. M. Broussard, "Why poor schools can't win at standardized testing, " The Atlantic 15 July 20154, Available: http://www.theatlantic.com/education/archive/2014/07/why-poor-schools-cant-win-at-standardized-testing/374287/

83. "Fast Facts," US. Department of Education, National Center for Education Statistics, Institute of Education Sciences. Washington, DC, 2015. Available: https://nces.ed.gov/fastfacts/display.asp?id=79

84. K.A.F. Knepp, "Understanding Student and Faculty Incivility in Higher Education," *The Journal of Effective Teaching,* *12*(1), p. 32-45, 2012.

85. B. Lott, "Cognitive and Behavioral Distancing," *American Psychologist.* Vo. 57, No. 2, p. 100-110, 2002. Available: http://homepage.psy.utexas.edu/homepage/class/Psy350/Spivey/pdf/8.%20%20Cognitive%20Distancing.pdf

86. "Consumer Information: Child Identity Theft," The Federal Trade Commission, Washington, DC. (n.d.). Available: http://www.consumer.ftc.gov/articles/0040-child-identity-theft

87. Data Quality Campaign, Washington, DC, "State Student Data Privacy: What Happened in 2014 and What is Next? 2014 Student Privacy Bills as of August 27, 2014," August 29, 2014. Available: http://www.dataqualitycampaign.org/find-resources/state-student-data-privacy-legislation-2014/

88. J.R. Reidenberg and J. Debelak, "Children's Education Records and Privacy: A Study of Elementary and Secondary School State Reporting Systems," Center on Law and Information Policy. New York, NY, October 28, 2009.

89. A. Liu,"Protecting Student Privacy in the Data Age," Pew Research Center, The Pew Trust, Washington, DC. December 17, 2013. Available: http://www.pewtrusts.org/en/research-and-analysis/blogs/stateline/2013/12/17/protecting-student-privacy-in-the-data-age

90. J. Templon and K.J.M. Baker, "D.C. Public Schools Website Exposed Confidential Info About Students With Disabilities," *BuzzFeedNews*, 2 February, 2015. Available: http://www.buzzfeed.com/johntemplon/dc-public-schools-website-exposed-confidential-info#.qyl15VQkM

91. "Data Disclosure Notice ," DC Office of the State Superintendent of Education, Washington, DC. March 25, 2015. Available: http://osse.dc.gov/release/data-disclosure-notice

92. M. Dresser, "Board Oks Pact to Protect UM Security Breach Victims," The Baltimore Sun, 23 July, 2014. Available: http://www.baltimoresun.com/news/maryland/politics/blog/bs-md-university-cyber-20140723-story.html

93. SANS Institute, Bethesda, MA, "Information Security Managing Risk with Defense in Depth," 2003. Retrieved from: http://www.sans.org/reading-room/whitepapers/infosec/information-security-managing-risk-defense-in-depth-1224

94. Mead, T. (2015). Data Security Risk in Education. Unpublished Manuscript

95. Gartner Inc., Stamford, CT, "Adopt an Information Classification Approach for Risk Mitigation and Regulatory Compliance, December 21, 2005. Available: http://www.gartner.com/doc/487454/adopt-information-ccclassification-approach-risk

96. V. Strauss, "Lawsuit Charges Education Department with Violating Student Privacy Rights," *The Washington Post*, 13 March 2013. Available: http://www.washingtonpost.com/blogs/answer-sheet/wp/2013/03/13/lawsuit-charges-ed-department-with-violating-student-privacy-rights/

97. Electronic Privacy Information Center (EPIC), Washington, DC, "Student Privacy," April 23, 2015. Available: https://epic.org/privacy/student/

98. Electronic Privacy Information Center (EPIC), Washington, DC, "Student Privacy," April 23, 2015. Available: https://epic.org/privacy/student/

99. K. McCarthy, "Five Colleges with Data Breaches Larger Than Sony's in 2014," *Huffington Post*. Available: http://www.huffingtonpost.com/kyle-mccarthy/five-colleges-with-data-b_b_6474800.html

100. R.G. Hattersley, "Top 10 Data Breaches at Educational Facilities in 2014," *Campus Safety Magazine*, 19 January 2015. Available: http://www.campussafetymagazine.com/article/top_10_data_breaches_at_educational_facilities_in_2014

101. "Top Trending Education Targets in 2015," *Surfwatch Labs*. 2015. Available: https://www.surfwatchlabs.com/?gclid=CKXqwZ_0xMUCFVKQHwodTAYAhQ

102. "Safeguarding Student Privacy," US Department of Education, Washington, DC (n.d.). Available: https://www2.ed.gov/policy/gen/guid/fpco/ferpa/safeguarding-student-privacy.pdf

103. Symantec Corporation, Mountain View, CA, "Internet Security Threat Report," 2015. Available: https://www.symantec.com/content/en/us/enterprise/other_resources/21347933_GA_RPT-internet-security-threat-report-volume-20-2015.pdf

104. "Top Trending Education Targets in 2015," *Surfwatch Labs*. 2015. Available: https://www.surfwatchlabs.com/?gclid=CKXqwZ_0xMUCFVKQHwodTAYAhQ

105. K. McCarthy, "Five Colleges with Data Breaches Larger Than Sony's in 2014," *Huffington Post*. Available: http://www.huffingtonpost.com/kyle-mccarthy/five-colleges-with-data-b_b_6474800.html

106. R.G. Hattersley, "Top 10 Data Breaches at Educational Facilities in 2014," *Campus Safety Magazine*, 19 January 2015. Available: http://www.campussafetymagazine.com/article/top_10_data_breaches_at_educational_facilities_in_2014

107. Symantec Corporation, Mountain View, CA, "Internet Security Threat Report," 2015. Available: https://www.symantec.com/content/en/us/enterprise/other_resources/21347933_GA_RPT-internet-security-threat-report-volume-20-2015.pdf

108. "Safeguarding Student Privacy," US Department of Education, Washington, DC (n.d.). Available: https://www2.ed.gov/policy/gen/guid/fpco/ferpa/safeguarding-student-privacy.pdf

109. Data Quality Campaign, Washington, DC, "State Student Data Privacy: What Happened in 2014 and What is Next? 2014 Student Privacy Bills as of August 27, 2014," August 29, 2014. Available: http://www.dataqualitycampaign.org/find-resources/state-student-data-privacy-legislation-2014/

110. The Family Educational Rights and Privacy Act of 1974 (FERPA) (20 U.S.C. § 1232g; 34 CFR Part 99).

111. The Fair Credit Reporting Act of 1970 , 15 U.S.C. § 1681 (FCRA).

112. The Gramm-Leach-Bliley Act (GLB Act or GLBA) or the Financial Modernization Act of 1999, Pub.L. 106–102, 113 Stat. 1338.

113. The Fair and Accurate Credit Transaction Act of 2003 (FACTA), Pub.L. 108–159.

114. The Health Insurance Portability and Accountability Act of 1996 (HIPAA; Pub.L. 104–191, 110 Stat. 1936, enacted August 21, 1996.

115. Electronic Privacy Information Center (EPIC), Washington, DC, "Student Privacy," April 23, 2015. Available: https://epic.org/privacy/student/

116. "Safeguarding Student Privacy," US Department of Education, Washington, DC (n.d.).Available:https://www2.ed.gov/policy/gen/guid/fpco/ferpa/safeguarding-student-privacy.pdf

117. J. Moran, "ERPA, Recent Changes in Federal Regulations, and State Compliance," Office of Legislative Research, Harford, CT, Report No. 2014-R-0127. May 6, 2014. Available: http://www.cga.ct.gov/2014/rpt/pdf/2014-R-0127.pdf

118. L.A. Rinehart-Thompson, "Amendments to FERPA Regulations: New Changes Attempt to Balance Safety and Privacy in Student Records, " *Journal of AHIMA*, 80, No.7, p. 56-57, July, 2009.

119. Mead, T. (2015). Privileges and Corresponding Obligations of FERPA. Unpublished Manuscript [118].

120. R. Rasmussen, "The College Cyber Security Tightrope: Higher Education Institution Face Greater Risks," *Security Week Network*, 28 April, 2011. Available: http://www.securityweek.com/college-cyber-security-tightrope-higher-education-institutions-face-greater-risks

121. Grant Thornton, Chicago, IL, "The Red Flags Rule: What Higher Education Institutions Need to Know," June 2010. Available: https://www.grantthornton.com/staticfiles/GTCom/Advisory/GRC/Red%20Flags%20materials/Red%20Flags%20Rule%20White%20Paper%20%28Higher%20Ed%29%209_21.pdf

122. "The Blue Book Volume 2- Student Eligibility," US Department of Education, Office of Federal Financial Aid, Washington, DC. January 2013. Available: http://ifap.ed.gov/bbook/attachments/2013BlueBookVol2Ch1.pdf

123. J. Smith and L. Parrish, "Do Students of Color Profit from For Profit College?" Center for Responsible Lending, Washington, DC, October 2014. Available:http://www.re-sponsiblelending.org/student-loans/research-policy/CRL-For-Profit-Univ-FINAL.pdf

124. D.E. Heller, "Does Federal Aid Drive Up College Prices?" American Council on Education, Washington, DC, 2013.

125. D. Halperin, "A Nation of Trump Universities: The Abuses of For-Profit Colleges, " *The Republic Report*. 28 August, 2013. Available: http://www.republicreport.org/2013/students-across-america-report-deceptions-for-profit-colleges/

126. College Board, Washington, DC, "Trends in Student Aid: 2013," 2013. Available: http://trends.collegeboard.org/sites/default/files/student-aid-2013-full-report.pdf

127. R. S. Brand, " Note: Student Loan Fraud: Intent to Deceive Not Required Under Section 1097(A) of the Higher Education Act. 10 ," *DePaul Business Law Journal*, 63. Fall/Winter, 1997. Available: https://litigation-essentials.lexisnexis.com/webcd/app?action=DocumentDisplay&crawlid=1&doctype=cite&docid=10+DePaul+Bus.+L.J.+63&srctype=smi&srcid=3B15&key=1428b977090f941aea4776103f3d8887

128. "For Profit Higher Education: The Failure to Safeguard the Federal Investment and Ensure Student Success, " US Senate Committee of Health, Education, Labor and Pensions, Washington, DC. July 29, 2012. Available: http://www.help.senate.gov/imo/media/for_profit_report/Contents.pdf

129. J. Smith and L. Parrish, "Do Students of Color Profit from For Profit College?" Center for Responsible Lending, Washington, DC, October 2014. Available:http://www.responsiblelending.org/student-loans/research-policy/CRL-For-Profit-Univ-FINAL.pdf

130. M.A. McGuire, "Subprime Education: For-Profit Colleges and the Problem with Title IV Federal Student Aid, " *Duke Law Journal*, Vol. 62, No. 119, p. 119- 160, 2012.

131. S. Kirchheimer, *Scam Proof Your Life*. New York, NY: AARP. Sterling Publishing, Inc, 2006.

132. J.F. Wasik, "Debt and Deceit," *Forbes*, p. 82-87, 17 August, 2015.

133. "Enrollment in Distance Education Courses, by State: Fall 2012," US Department of Education, National Center for Education Statistics, Washington, DC. Report NCES 2014-023, March 2015. Available: http://nces.ed.gov/pubs2014/2014023.pdf

134. R. Lytle, "Study: Online Education continues Growth," *U.S. News & World Report*. 11 November, 2011. Available: http://www.usnews.com/education/online-education/articles/2011/11/11/study-online-education-continues-growth

135. "Investigative Reports," Office of the Inspector General, Department of Education and U.S. Attorney's Office, Eastern District of Michigan, March 26, 2013. Available: http://www2.ed.gov/about/offices/list/oig/invtreports/mi032013.html

136. "Enrollment in Distance Education Courses, by State: Fall 2012," US Department of Education, National Center for Education Statistics, Washington, DC. Report NCES 2014-023, March 2015. Available: http://nces.ed.gov/pubs2014/2014023.pdf

137. R. Lytle, "Study: Online Education continues Growth," *U.S. News & World Report*. 11 November, 2011. Available: http://www.usnews.com/education/online-education/articles/2011/11/11/study-online-education-continues-growth

138. "Enrollment in Distance Education Courses, by State: Fall 2012," US Department of Education, National Center for Education Statistics, Washington, DC. Report NCES 2014-023, March 2015. Available: http://nces.ed.gov/pubs2014/2014023.pdf

139. Y.H. Kwak and J.B. Keleher," Risk Management for Grants Administration: A Case Study of the Department of Education, " IBM Center for The Business of Government. Washington, DC, 2015.

140. K. Tysiac,"Grant reform increases single-audit threshold, changes audit rules," *Journal of Accountancy*. December 20, 2013. Available: http://www.journalofaccountancy.com/news/2013/dec/20139321.html

Part Three

1. T. Mead, (2014, September 25). "The Educator Fraud Paradigm and Implications for Educators and Academia."Paper presented at the IAFOR North American Conference on Education 2014, Providence, RI (pg 61-82).Naka Ward, Nagoya, Aichi Japan 460-0008. Available: http://iafor.org/archives/proceedings/NACE/NACE2014_proceedings.pdf

2. E.H. Sutherland and D.R. Cressey, *Criminology*, Baltimore, MD: Lippincott, 1978.

3. D. T. Wolfe, D.T. and D.R. Hermanson, "The Fraud Diamond: Considering the Four Elements of Fraud," The CPA Journal. December 4, 2004. Available: http://www.nysscpa.org/cpajournal/2004/1204/essentials/p38.htm

4. D.R. Cressy, *Other People's Money*. Montclair, NJ: Paterson Smith,1973.

5. L. Segal, *Battling Corruption in America's Public Schools.*, 1ˢᵗ ed. Cambridge MA: Harvard University Press, March 2005.

6. A.D. Witte, and R. Witt, "Crime Causation: Economic Theories," forthcoming *Encyclopedia of Crime and Justice*. Wellesley College, NBER, and the University of Surrey. July 19, 2000 Available: https://www.surrey.ac.uk/economics/files/apaperspdf/ECON%2003-00.pdf

7. "Class Notes," class notes for Cyber Law and White Collar Crime, Cyber-AWR-168W, Instructor T. Thorston, Texas A&M Engineering Extension Service, 2011.

8. T. Mead (2014, September 25). "The Educator Fraud Paradigm and Implications for Educators and Academia."Paper presented at the IAFOR North American Conference on Education 2014, Providence, RI (pg 61-82).Naka Ward, Nagoya, Aichi Japan 460-0008. Available: http://iafor.org/archives/proceedings/NACE/NACE2014_proceedings.pdf

9. W.S. Albrecht, K. R. Howe, and M. B. Romney. *Deterring Fraud: The Internal Auditor's Perspective.* Altomonte Springs, FL: The Institute of Internal Auditors' Research Foundation, 1984.

10. S. Nichols and D. Berliner, "The Inevitable Corruption of Indicators and Educators Through High-Stakes Testing," The Great Lakes Center for Education Research and Practice, East Lansing, MI, 2005.

11. S.S. Simpson, *Corporate Crime, Law, and* Social *Control,* Cambridge, UK: Cambridge University Press, 2002.

12. E.P. Baumer and J.L. Lauritsen, "Reporting Crime to the Police, 1973-2005: A Multivariate Analysis of Long Term Trends in the National Crime Survey (NCS) and National Crime Victimization Survey (NCVS)," *Criminology,* Vo. 48, Issue 1, p. 131-185, February 2010.

13. L.F. Travis and B.D. Edwards, *Introduction to Criminal Justice.* New York, NY: Routledge, 2014.

14. Australian Federal Police, "Crime in Cyberspace: Trends. *Platypus Magazine,* 1998 June. Available: http://www.afp.gov.au/media-centre/publications/platypus/previous-editions/1998/june-1998/cyber

15. B.A. Arrigo. *The Encyclopedia of Criminal Justice Ethics.* Sage Publications, 2014.

16. Mead,T. (2015). Risk Assessment Data Quality and Security for School and Campus Records. Unpublished Manuscript.

17. C. McCue, *Data mining and predictive analysis: Intelligence Gathering and Crime Analysis.* Waltham, MA: Butterworth-Heinemann, 2007.

18. R. Riley, Institute for Fraud Prevention, Correspondence (March26, 2015).

19. "Investigative Reports," Office of the Inspector General, Department of Education and U.S. Attorney's Office, Washington, DC. April 24, 2014. Available: http://www2.ed.gov/about/offices/list/oig/invtreports/dc042014.html

20. "Investigating Student Aid Fraud: FBI Plays Supporting Role," US Department of Justice, Federal Bureau of Investigations (FBI), Washington, DC. May 27, 2014. Available: https://www.fbi.gov/news/stories/2014/may/investigating-student-aid-fraud

21. "Common Fraud Schemes," US Department of Justice, Federal Bureau of Investigations (FBI), Washington, DC. (n.d.). Available: http://www.fbi.gov/scams-safety/fraud

22. Association of Certified Fraud Examiners (ACFE), Austin, TX, " 2010 Global Fraud Study: Report to the Nations on Occupational Fraud and Abuse," 2011.

23. Association of Certified Fraud Examiners (ACFE), Austin, TX, " 2012 Global Fraud Study: Report to the Nations on Occupational Fraud and Abuse," 2013.

24. S. Kirchheimer, *Scam Proof Your Life.* New York, NY: AARP. Sterling Publishing, Inc, 2006.

25. G. Williams, "Evolutionary Hot Spots Data Mining: An Architecture for Exploring for Interesting Discoveries," PAKDD99. *Proc. Of* PAKDD99, 1999.

26. P. Chan, W. Fan, A. Prodromidis, and S. Stolfo, "Distributed Data Mining in Credit Card Fraud Detection," *IEEE Intelligent Systems* 14: p. 67-74, 1999.

27. S. Ghosh and D. Reilly, "Credit Card Fraud Detection with a Neural Network, Proceedings of the 27th Hawaii International Conference on Systems Science 3: 6210630, 1994.

28. C. Phua, V. Lee, K. Smith and R. Gayler, "A Comprehensive Survey of Data Mining-based Fraud Detection Research," Sponsored by the Australian Research Council, Baycorp Advantage and Monash University under Grant No. LP0454077, (n.d.). Available: http://arxiv.org/ftp/arxiv/papers/1009/1009.6119.pdf

134. R.G. Brody and K.A. Kiehl, "From white collar crime to red collar crime." *Journal of Financial Crime,* 17(3), p. 351-364, 2010. Available: https://www.ncbi.nlm.nih.gov/pmc/articles/PMC4235672/

135. M.D. Anderson, "When schooling meets policing," *The Atlantic,* 21 September 2015.

136. *Harvard Law Review,* Vol. 128, p. 1747-1770, 10 April 2015.

137. Dignity in Schools, Washington, DC, "A Model Code on Education and Dignity: Presenting a Human Rights Framework for Schools, October, 2013. Available: http://dignityinschools.org/our-work/model-school-code

29. United Nations Office on Drugs and Crime, Vienna, Austria, "A Manual on Monitoring and Evaluation for Alternative Development Projects," (n.d.). Available: https://www.unodc.org/documents/alternative-development/Manual_MonitoringEval.pdf

30. V. Strauss, "Report: Big Education Firms Spend Millions lobbying for pro-testing policies," *The Washington Post,* 30 March, 2015. Available: ttps://www.washingtonpost.com/blogs/answer-sheet/wp/2015/03/30/report-big-education-firms-spend-millions-lobbying-for-pro-testing-policies/

31. D.N. Figlio and L.W. Kenny, "Individual Teacher Incentives and Student Performance," *Journal of Public Economics,* 91(5-6), p. 901-14, 2007.

32. C.T. Fitz-Gibbon, *Monitoring Education.* London, UK: Continuum, 1996.

33. T. Mead (2015). Risk Assessment Data Quality and Security for School and Campus Records. Unpublished Manuscript.

34. D.H. Kamens and C.L. McNeely, "Globalization and the Growth of International Educational Testing and National Assessment," *Comparative Education Review,* Vol. 54, No. 1., p 5-25, February 2010. Available: http://www.jstor.org/stable/pdf/10.1086/648471.pdf

35. McKinsey & Company, New York, NY , "Enduring Ideas of the 7-s Framework," March 1998. Available: http://www.mckinsey.com/insights/strategy/enduring_ideas_the_7-s_framework

36. K.T. Cowan, M.C. Junge and S. Krvaric, *Federal Education Grants Management: What Administrators Need to Know School Year 2007-2008,* Washington, DC: Thompson Publishing Group, 2007.

37. Y.H. Kwak and J.B. Keleher," Risk Management for Grants Administration: A Case Study of the Department of Education, " IBM Center for The Business of Government. Washington, DC, 2015.

38. United Nations Office on Drugs and Crime, Vienna, Austria, "A Manual on Monitoring and Evaluation for Alternative Development Projects," (n.d.). Available: https://www.unodc.org/documents/alternative-development/Manual_MonitoringEval.pdf

39. "FY15 Proposed Budget Stakeholder Briefing," DC Office of the State Superintendent of Education, Washington, DC. April 22, 2014. Available: http://osse.dc.gov/sites/default/files/dc/sites/osse/publication/attachments/FY15%20udget%20Oversight%20Stakekholder%20Briefing%20PPT%20(4.22.14).pdf

40. J. Bowels, Y. Ma, A. Robbins, E. Slack, and T. Wallin, "Promising Beginnings: Evaluating External Support Organizations," Georgetown Public Policy Institute. Washington, DC. April 12, 2013.

41. U.S. Government Accountability Office, "Educational Financial Management: Weak Internal Controls Led to Instances of Fraud and Other Improper Payments," Washington, DC, Report # GAO-02-513T. April 10, 2002.

42. "FY2014 Agency Financial Report," US Department of Education, Washington, DC, November 14, 2014. Available: https://www2.ed.gov/about/reports/annual/2014report/2014-afr-2g-mgmt-assurances.pdf

43. D.H. Wrong, "The Oversocialized Conception of Man in Modern Society," *American Sociological Review*, Vol. 26, No. 2. p. 183-193, 1961.

44. R. Kumar, and V. Sharma, V. *Auditing: Principles and Practice*, Delhi, India: PHI Learning Pvt. Ltd., 2015.

45. L.W. Voma, *Fraud Risk Assessment*, Hoboken, NJ: John Wiley & Sons, Inc., 2008.

46. J. Cordeiro, A.K. Ranchordas and B. Shishkov, *Software and Data Technologies*. 4th International Conference, Springer Science and Business Media, 2009.

47. D.H. Wrong, "The Oversocialized Conception of Man in Modern Society," *American Sociological Review*, Vol. 26, No. 2. p. 183-193, 1961.

48. R.M.A. Nelissen and L.B. Mulder, "What makes a sanction "stick" The effects of financial and social sanctions on norm compliance," *Social Influence.* Vol. 8, No. 1, p. 70-80, 2012.

49. H.G. Grasmick and D.E. Green, "Legal Punishment, Social Disapproval and Internalization as Inhibitors of Illegal Behavior," *Journal of Criminal Law and Criminology*, Vo 71, Issue 3, Article 11, p. 325-335, Fall 1980. Available: http://scholarlycommons.law.northwestern.edu/cgi/viewcontent.cgi?article=6188&context=jclc

50. M.G. Maxfield and E. R. Babbie, *Research Methods for Criminal Justice and Criminology*, 4th ed. Belmont, CA: Thomson Wadsworth, 2005.

51. H.G. Grasmick and D.E. Green, "Legal Punishment, Social Disapproval and Internalization as Inhibitors of Illegal Behavior," *Journal of Criminal Law and Criminology*, Vo 71, Issue 3, Article 11, p. 325-335, Fall 1980. Available: http://scholarlycommons.law.northwestern.edu/cgi/viewcontent.cgi?article=6188&context=jclc

52. Z. Hoskins, "The Moral Permissibility of Punishment," *Internet Encyclopedia of Philosophy*, 2011. Available: http://www.iep.utm.edu/m-p-puni/

53. E. Podgor, "The Challenge of White Collar Sentencing," *Journal of Criminal Law and Criminology*, Vol. 97, Issue 3, Article 2, p. 731-760, 2007.

54. A. Natapoff, "Why Misdemeanors Aren't So Minor," *Slate*, 27 April, 2012. Available: http://www.slate.com/articles/news_and_politics/jurisprudence/2012/04/misdemeanors_can_have_major_consequences_for_the_people_charged_.html

55. National Association of Criminal Defense Lawyers, Washington, DC. "The Terrible Toll of America's Broken Misdemeanor Courts," April 2009. Available: http://www.nacdl.org/public.nsf/defenseupdates/misdemeanor/$FILE/Report.pdf

56. Pew Research Center, The Pew Charitable Trusts, Washington, DC." One in 31: The Long Reach of American Corrections," March, 2009 Available: http://www.pewtrusts.org/~/media/legacy/uploadedfiles/pcs_assets/2009/pspp1in31reportfinalweb32609pdf.pdf

57. F.S. Perri, "White Collar Crime Punishment: Too Much or Not Enough," *Fraud Magazine*, January/February 2011.

58. D. Golash, D. *The Case Against Punishment: Retribution, Crime Prevention, and the Law,* New York, NY: NYU Press, 2006.

59. R. Aviv, "The Wrong Answer," *The New Yorker,* 21 July, 2014. Available: http://www. newyorker.com/magazine/2014/07/21

60. S.E. Barkan, "Social Problems: Continuity and Change v.1.0," *Flat World Education, Inc,* 2015. Available: http://catalog.flatworldknowledge.com/bookhub/reader/ 3064?e=barkansoc_1.0-ch08_s02#barkansoc_1.0-ch00about

61. Crime Victims' Rights Act of 2004, 18 U.S.C. § 3771

62. U.S.A. Education Law. (n.d.) *Fraud.* Available: http://usedulaw.com/299-fraud. html

63. J.F. Olson and J. Fremer, *TILSA Test Security Guidebook, Preventing, Detecting and Investigating Test Security Irregularities,* CCSSO, Washington, DC, May 2013.

64. B. Jacob and S. Levitt, "Rotten Apples: An Investigation of the Prevalence and Predictors of Teacher Cheating," *The Quarterly Journal of Economics,* p. 843-877, August, 2003, and Working Paper 9413 (2002). National Bureau of Economic Research. Available: http://www.nber.org/papers/w9413

65. D. Tobenkin, "Keeping it Honest: Academic Credential Fraud is Big Business," *International Educator.* National Association of International Educators. p. 32-42. January- February, 2011. Available: https://www.nafsa.org/_/File/_/ie_janfeb11_ fraud.pdf

66. C. Beccaria, "On crimes and punishments," In R. Bellamy, Ed. (R. Davies, Translation), *On Crimes and punishments and other writings, 1-113,,* 1995. Cambridge, UK: Cambridge University Press. (Original work published 1764).

67. C.R. Jeffery, "Criminal Behavior and Learning Theory," *Criminal Law, Criminology & Police Science,* Vol 56, Issue 3, Article 4, p. 294-300, Fall 1965.

68. D. Scott, "Scandals Spur Action on Pension Forfeitures. Governing the States and Localities," *Governing.Com,* 29 February 2012. Available: http://www.governing. com/blogs/view/gov-scandals-spur-action-on-pension-forfeitures.html

69. "Federal Support for Education," U.S. Department of Education, National Center for Education Statistics, Washington, DC, June 2003. Available: http://nces.ed.gov/pubs2003/2003060d.pdf

70. Mead,T. (2015). Fraudulent Acts by Profession: A Comparative Study. Unpublished Manuscript.

71. "OIG Fraud Hotline: Fraud Prevention, "US Department of Education, Office of Inspector General, Washington, DC. Available: www2.ed.gov/about/offices/list/oig/hotline.html

72. E. Podgor, "The Challenge of White Collar Sentencing," *Journal of Criminal Law and Criminology*, Vol. 97, Issue 3, Article 2, p. 731-760, 2007.

73. F.S. Perri, "White Collar Crime Punishment: Too Much or Not Enough," *Fraud Magazine,* January/February 2011.

74. D.E. Heller, "Does Federal Aid Drive Up College Prices?" American Council on Education, Washington, DC, 2013.

75. M.A. McGuire, "Subprime Education: For Profit Colleges and the Problem with Title IV Federal Student Aid, " *Duke Law Journal,* p. 119-160, 2012. Available: http://scholarship.law.duke.edu/cgi/viewcontent.cgi?article=3355&context=dlj

76. "The Economics of Higher Education, " US. Department of the Treasury and the US Department of Education, Washington, DC, December 2012. Available: http://www.treasury.gov/connect/blog/Documents/20121212_Economics%20of%20Higher%20Ed_vFINAL.pdf

77. M. Frenette, "An Investment of a Lifetime? The Long-term Labour Market Premiums Associated with a Post-secondary education," Analytical Studies Branch, Canada, Research Paper Series, 11F0019M, no. 350, February 2014. Available: http://www.statcan.gc.ca/pub/11f0019m/11f0019m2014359-eng.htm

78. S. Saulny, R. Coolidge and J. Phelps, "Is college worth it?" *Yahoo News*, 27 June, 2014. Available: http://news.yahoo.com/blogs/power-players-abc-news/is-college-worth-it—new-documentary-explores-higher-education-costs-and-rising-student-debt-223233460.html

79. National Education Association, Washington, DC, "Myths and Facts about Educator Pay," (n.d.). Available: http:///www.nea.org/home/12661.htm

80. U. Boser and C. Straus, "Mid and Late Career Teachers Struggle with Paltry Incomes," Center for American Progress. Washington, DC, July 23, 2014.

81. T.G. Carroll and E. Foster, "Who will teach? Experience Matters," National Commission on Teaching for America's Future, Washington, DC, January, 2014

82. " Handbook of Methods," US Department of Labor Department, Bureau of Labor Statistics, Washington, DC, 2013. Available: http://www.bls.gov/opub/hom/cex/home.htm

83. E. Segran, "The Adjunct Revolt: How Poor Professors are Fighting Back," *The Atlantic.* 28 April, 2014. Available: http://www.theatlantic.com/business/archive/2014/04/the-adjunct-professor-crisis/361336/?single_page=true ov/scams-safety/fraud

84. American Federation of Teachers, "A National Survey of Part-Time Adjunct Faculty," American Academic, Vol 2, March 2010. Available: https://www.aft.org/pdfs/highered/aa_partimefaculty0310.pdf

85. Association of University Professors, Washington, DC, "The Annual Report on the Economic Status of the Profession," 2011-2012. Available: http://www.aaup.org/file/2011-12Economic-Status-Report.pdf

86. E. Segran, "The Adjunct Revolt: How Poor Professors are Fighting Back," *The Atlantic.* 28 April, 2014. Available: http://www.theatlantic.com/business/archive/2014/04/the-adjunct-professor-crisis/361336/?single_page=true ov/scams-safety/fraud

87. M.A. Eckstein, " Combating a culture of academic fraud," The International Institute for Educational Planning, The United Nations Educational, Scientific and Cultural Organization Available: http://unesdoc.unesco.org/images/0013/001330/133038e.pdf

88. B. Jacob and S. Levitt, "Rotten Apples: An Investigation of the Prevalence and Predictors of Teacher Cheating," *The Quarterly Journal of Economics*, p. 843-877, August, 2003, and Working Paper 9413 (2002). National Bureau of Economic Research. Available: http://www.nber.org/papers/w9413

89. "Atlanta Public Schools Special Investigator's Reports Vol. 1, 2 and 3," Office of the Governor Nathan Deal Special Investigators, Atlanta, GA, June 30, 2011.

90. J. Kaufman, *Protecting the Veracity of our Children's Test Scores,* Dartmouth College, Hanover, NH, 2012. Available: http://www. thepresidency.org/storage/documents/Fellows_2011_-_2012_Papers/Kaufmann-_Final_Paper.pdf.

91. C. Jerald and R. Ingersoll, "All talk, no action: putting an end to out-of-field teaching," Education Trust, Washington, DC, August, 2002..

92. B. Jacob and S. Levitt, "Rotten Apples: An Investigation of the Prevalence and Predictors of Teacher Cheating," *The Quarterly Journal of Economics,* p. 843-877, August, 2003, and Working Paper 9413 (2002). National Bureau of Economic Research. Available: http://www.nber.org/papers/w9413

93. B.A. Jacob, (December, 2002). Working Paper 9413. National Bureau of Economic Research, (December, 2002). Available: http://www.nber.org/papers/w9413

94. R. S. Brand, " Note: Student Loan Fraud: Intent to Deceive Not Required Under Section 1097(A) of the Higher Education Act. 10 ," *DePaul Business Law Journal,* 63. Fall/Winter, 1997. Available: https://litigation-essentials.lexisnexis.com/webcd/app?action=DocumentDisplay&crawlid=1&doctype=cite&docid=10+DePaul+Bus.+L.J.+63&srctype=smi&srcid=3B15&key=1428b977090f941aea4776103f3d8887

95. Gallup, Inc. Washington, DC. "Honesty/Ethics in the Professions," December 5-8, 2013. Available:http://www.gallup.com/poll/1654/honesty-ethics-professions.aspx and http://www.gallup.com/poll/166298/honesty-ethics-rating-clergy-slides-new-low.aspx

96. E.H. Sutherland and D.R. Cressey, *Criminology,* Baltimore, MD: Lippincott, 1978.

97. C.R. Jeffery, "Criminal Behavior and Learning Theory," *Criminal Law, Criminology & Police Science,* Vol 56, Issue 3, Article 4, p. 294-300, Fall 1965.

98. M. Brown, L. Trevino and D. Harrison, "Ethical leadership: A social learning perspective for construct development and testing," *Organizational Behavior and Human Decision Processes,* 97(2), p. 117-134, 2005.

99. A.A. Ardichvili (University of Minnesota and Center for Ethical Business Cultures) , D.J. Jondle, and J.A. Mitchell (Center for Ethical Business Cultures), Minneapolis, MN: *Characteristics of Ethical Business Cultures,* 2008. Available: http://files.eric.ed.gov/fulltext/ED501640.pdf

100. Association of Certified Fraud Examiners (ACFE), Austin, TX, "Tone at the Top: How Management Can Prevent Fraud in the Workplace," (n.d.). Available: http://www.acfe.com/uploadedFiles/ACFE_Website/Content/documents/tone-at-the-top-research.pdf

101. L. Trevino, G.R. Weaver, D. Gibson, and B. Toffler "Managing ethics and legal compliance: What works and what hurts," California Management Review, 41 (2), p. 131-150, 1999.

102. Association of Certified Fraud Examiners (ACFE), Austin, TX, "Tone at the Top: How Management Can Prevent Fraud in the Workplace," (n.d.). Available: http://www.acfe.com/uploadedFiles/ACFE_Website/Content/documents/tone-at-the-top-research.pdf

103. L. Segal, *Battling Corruption in America's Public Schools.*, 1st ed. Cambridge MA: Harvard University Press, March 2005.

104. D. Belkin and A. Fuller, "Accreditors of Colleges Weighing Crackdown," *The Wall Street Journal,* 27-28, June, 2015.

105. D. Belkin and A. Fuller Belkin, "Obama Targets Accreditors," *The Wall Street Journal,* p. A3, 6 November, 2015.

106. "Frequently Asked Questions: Qualifications" US Office of Personnel Management, Washington, DC (n.d.). Available: https://www.opm.gov/faqs/QA.aspx?fid=eee2a0b7-6501-42e3-ba3a-627cff1df54f&pid=8762ef37-9a4d-4582-8e5f-0b7f84a7af61

107. S. Sanders, "Report Says UNC Grade Boosting Scandal Involved Fake Classes," National Public Radio (NPR), 23 October 2014. Available: http://www.npr.org/blogs/thetwo-way/2014/10/23/358310267/report-says-unc-grade-boosting-scandal-involved-fake-classes

108. S.P. Heyneman, "Foreign Aid to Education: Recent U.S. Initiatives- Background, Risks and Prospects. Peabody Journal of Education, Vol. 80., No.1., p. 107-119, 2005. Available: http://www.vanderbilt.edu/peabody/heyneman/PUBLICATIONS/Foreign%20Aid%20to%20Education.pdf

109. M. Stratford, "U.S. Keeps Scrutiny of Risky Colleges Secret," *Inside Higher Education,* 26 March, 2015. Available: https://www.insidehighered.com/news/2015/03/26/education-dept-keeps-secret-names-colleges-found-be-risky-students-taxpayers

110. "Chapter 9: Program Reviews, Sanctions & Closeout," in *Financial Student Aid Handbook*, US Department of Education, Washington, DC. 2011-2012. Available: http://ifap.ed.gov/fsahandbook/attachments/1112FSAHbkVol2Ch9.pdf

111. "Financing education: National, state and local funding and spending for public schools in 2013," US Department of Education, Institute of Education Sciences, National Center for Education Statistics, Washington, DC, January 25, 2016. Available: http://nces.ed.gov/blogs/nces/post/financing-education-national-state-and-local-funding-and-spending-for-public-schools-in-2013

112. National Priorities Project, Northampton, MA, "Federal Budget Tipsheet: Education Spending," Available: https://www.nationalpriorities.org/guides/tipsheet-education-spending/ and "Ten Facts about K-12 Education Funding," US Department of Education, US Department of Education Budget Service and the National Center for Education Statistics. Washington, DC, 2014. Available: http://www2.ed.gov/about/overview/fed/10facts/index.html?exp

113. "Fast Facts," US Department of Education, Institute of Education Sciences, The National Center for Education Statistics, Washington, DC (n.d.). Available: http://nces.ed.gov/fastfacts/display.asp?id=84

114. P. Barnes and J. Webb, "Reducing an organization's susceptibility to occupational fraud: Factors affecting its likelihood and size," International Fraud Prevention Research Center, Nottingham Business School and Leeds Business School, UK. July 27, 2011. Available: http://www.cism.my/upload/article/201107271223530.reducing_an_organisations_susceptibility_to_fraud.pdf

115. J. Barkan, "Got Dough? How Billionaires Rule Our Schools," *Dissent Magazine*, Winter 2011. Available: http://dissentmagazine.org/article/got-dough-how-billionairs-rule-our-schools

116. A.M. Gibson, J. Wang and J.R. Slate, "Teachers Behaving Unprofessionally: Stories from Students," *Creative Commons*, 19, February 2009 and *International Journal of Educational Leadership Preparation*. Vol 4., No. 1., January- March 2009. Available: http://ijelp.expressacademic.org

117. R. Chaitt, "Removing Chronically Ineffective Teachers: Barriers and Opportunities," Center for America Progress, Washington, DC, March 2010.

118. M.A. Copland, (1999). *Problem-based learning, problem-framing ability and the principal selves of prospective school principals* (Doctoral dissertation, Stanford University, 1999). Dissertation Abstracts International, 60/08, 2750.

119. R. F Elmore, "Building a New Structure for School Leadership," The Albert Shanker Institute, Washington, DC, Winter, 2000.

120. L.S. Lumsden, "Prospects in principal preparation," ERIC Clearinghouse on Educational Management, ERIC Digest, No. 77, Eugene, OR, 1992.

121. M. McCarthy, "The evolution of educational leadership preparation programs," In J. Murphy and K. S. Louis, Eds. *Handbook of research on educational administration: A project of the American Educational Research Association,* San Francisco, CA: Jossey-Bass, 1999.

122. J. Murphy and M. Vriesenga, *Research on preparation programs in educational administration: An analysis (monograph).* Columbia, MO: University of Missouri- Columbia, University Council for Educational Administration, 2004.

123. American Association of Colleges for Teacher Education, Washington, DC, "Pk-12 educational leadership and administration," White Paper, June 2, 2014.

124. A.M. Gibson, J. Wang and J.R. Slate, "Teachers Behaving Unprofessionally: Stories from Students," *Creative Commons,* 19, February 2009 and *International Journal of Educational Leadership Preparation.* Vol 4., No. 1., January- March 2009. Available: http://ijelp.expressacademic.org

125. KMPG 2011 International Survey of Corporate Responsibility Available: https://www.kpmg.com/PT/pt/IssuesAndInsights/Documents/corporate-responsibility2011.pdf

126. Office of the Inspector General, Department of Education and U.S. Attorney's Office (April 24, 2014). Investigative Reports. Available: http://www2.ed.gov/about/offices/list/oig/invtreports/dc042014.html

127. "Investigative Reports," Office of the Inspector General, Department of Education and U.S. Attorney's Office, Washington, DC. April 24, 2014. Available: http://www2.ed.gov/about/offices/list/oig/invtreports/dc042014.html

127. C. Sanchez, "Widespread Fraud Alleged in Camden, NJ Schools," National Public Radio (NPR), 11 August, 2006. Available: http://www.npr.org/templates/story/story.php?storyId=5637480

128. J. Zubrzycki, "Former Schools Chief Sentenced to Prison," *Education Week*, 16 October, 2012. Available: http://www.edweek.org/ew/articles/2012/10/17/08jail.h32.html?tkn=ZOTFmOWWrAx%2FqtXtRvIL6wQxotZ0qYahVAcZ&print=1

129. T. Mead (2014, September 25). "The Educator Fraud Paradigm and Implications for Educators and Academia."Paper presented at the IAFOR North American Conference on Education 2014, Providence, RI (pg 61-82).Naka Ward, Nagoya, Aichi Japan 460-0008. Available: http://iafor.org/archives/proceedings/NACE/NACE2014_proceedings.pdf

130. D.B. Cornish and R.V. Clarke, "Opportunities, Precipitators and Criminal Decisions: A Reply to Wortley's Critique of Situational Crime Prevention," *Crime Prevention Studies*, Vol. 16, p. 41-96, 2003.

131. C.R. Shaw and H.D. McKay, *Juvenile Delinquency and Urban Areas,* Chicago, IL: University of Chicago Press, 1969.

132. R. J. Sampson, "Neighborhood family structure and the risk of personal victimization," In R.J. Sampson and J.M. Byrne Eds. *The Social Ecology of Crime* (p. 25-46). New York, NY: Springer-Verlag, 1986.

133. R. Wortley, "A Classification of Techniques for Controlling Situational Precipitators of Crime," *Security Journal,* 14: p. 63-82, 2001.

Part Four

1. D.H. Wrong, "The Oversocialized Conception of Man in Modern Society," *American Sociological Review,* Vol. 26, No. 2. p. 183-193, 1961.

2. H.G. Grasmick and D.E. Green, "Legal Punishment, Social Disapproval and Internalization as Inhibitors of Illegal Behavior," *Journal of Criminal Law and Criminology,* Vo 71, Issue 3, Article 11, p. 325-335, Fall 1980. Available: http://scholarlycommons.law.northwestern.edu/cgi/viewcontent.cgi?article=6188&context=jclc

1. S.P. Green and M.B. Kugler, "Public Perceptions of White Collar Crime Culpability: Bribery, Perjury, and Fraud," *Law and Contemporary Problems,* Vo. 75,

No. 33, p. 33-59. Available: http://scholarship.law.duke.edu/cgi/viewcontent. cgi?article=1667&context=lcp

2. C. Beccaria, "On crimes and punishments," In R. Bellamy, Ed. (R. Davies, Translation), *On Crimes and punishments and other writings, 1-113,*, 1995. Cambridge, UK: Cambridge University Press. (Original work published 1764).

3. R.M. Regoli and J.D. Hewitt, *Exploring Criminal Justice.* Sudbury, MA: Jones and Bartlett Publishers, Inc., 2007.

4. C.R. Jeffery, "Criminal Behavior and Learning Theory," *Criminal Law, Criminology & Police Science*, Vol 56, Issue 3, Article 4, p. 294-300, Fall 1965.

5. T. Brooks, *Punishment.* New York, NY: Routledge Books, 2012.

6. W. Rahn, B. Kroeger, and C.M. Kite, "A Framework for the Study of Public Mood," *International Society of Political Psychology.* Vol. 17, No. 1, p. 29-58, March 1996.

7. Pew Research Center, The Pew Charitable Trusts, Washington, DC, "Beyond Distrust: How Americans View Their Government," November 23, 2015.

8. R.G. Kaiser, *Act of Congress: How America's Essential Institution Works and How it Doesn't,* New York: NY: Knopf Doubleday Publishing Group, 2013.

9. M. Welch, *McCain: The Myth of a Maverick*, London, UK: Palgrave Macmillan, 2007.

10. R. Kelner and R. La Raja, "McCain-Feingold's devastating legacy," *Washington Post,* 11 April, 2014. Available: https://www.washingtonpost.com/opinions/mccain-feingolds-devastating-legacy/2014/04/11/14a528e2-c18f-11e3-bcec-b71ee10e9bc3_story.html

11. "Class Notes," class notes for Cyber Law and White Collar Crime, Cyber- AWR-168W, Instructor T. Thorston, Texas A&M Engineering Extension Service, 2011

12. J. Maues, "Banking Act of 1933, commonly called Glass-Steagall," *Federal Reserve History,* 22 November, 2013. Available: http://www.federalreservehistory.org/Events/DetailView/25

13. J.A.T. Granados and A.V.D. Roux, *Life and death during the Great Depression* Proceedings of the National Academy of Sciences. Vo. 106, No. 41., October 13,

2009, p. 17290-17295 Available: http://www.pnas.org/content/106/41/17290.full.pdf

14. A. Zibel, "Americans Borrow for Cars, Less so for Homes,". *Wall Street Journal,* 14 August, 2014. Available: http://www.wsj.com/articles/u-s-household-debt-sinks-18-billion-to-11-63-trillion-1408028756

15. "An Industry Assessment based upon Suspicious Activity Report Analysis," Financial Crimes Enforcement Network (FINCEN), Vienna, VA. November 2006. Available: https://www.fincen.gov/news_room/rp/reports/html/mortgage_fraud112006.html

16. A. Zibel, "Americans Borrow for Cars, Less so for Homes,". *Wall Street Journal,* 14 August, 2014. Available: http://www.wsj.com/articles/u-s-household-debt-sinks-18-billion-to-11-63-trillion-1408028756

17. E. Silvestrini, "Student financial aid fraud growing; feds haven't fully addressed serious vulnerability," *Tampa Tribune.* 12 September, 2015. Available: http://www.tbo.com/news/crime/student-aid-fraud-growing-feds-havent-fully-addressed-serious-vulnerability-20150912/

18. "Federal Support for Education," US Department of Education, Center for Education Statistics, Washington, DC, June 2003. Available: http://nces.ed.gov/pubs2003/2003060d.pdf

19. "Violence Against Women Act: Final Rule," *Federal Register,* Vol. 29. No. 202. Part III, US Department of Education, Washington, DC 20 October 2014. Available: https://www.gpo.gov/fdsys/pkg/FR-2014-10-20/pdf/2014-24284.pdf

20. "Taking Back the Reins: Tips for Owning your Next A-133 Audit," National Council of University Research Administrators (NCURA) *NCURA Magazine,* Vol XLVI, No. 5. October/November 2014.

21. "Education Department Updates Cash Monitoring List," *Inside Higher Education,* 14 July, 2015. Available: https://www.insidehighered.com/quicktakes/2015/07/14/education-department-updates-cash-monitoring-list

22. J. Jarvie, "Atlanta school cheating trial has teachers facing prison," *Los Angeles Times,* 6 September, 2014. Available: http://www.latimes.com/nation/la-na-cheating-trial-20140907-story.html#page=1

25. Y. Kappes, "Former EPISD Superintendent Lorenzo Garcia gets 42 months, offers no apologies for scandal," *El Paso Times*, 5 October, 2012. Available: http://www.elpasotimes.com/episd/ci_21707413/former-episd-superintendent-lorenzo-garcia-sentenced-3-1

23. K.A. Graham, M. Woodall and C. Vargas, "Charges in Culture of Cheating at Philadelphia School," *The Inquirer*, 10 May, 2014.

24. D. Jones, "Philadelphia Teachers, Principal Charged in Test Cheating Scandal," *NBC Philadelphia Local News*, 8 May, 2014.

28. C. Sanchez, "Widespread Fraud Alleged in Camden, NJ Schools," *National Public Radio (NPR)*, 11 August, 2006. Available: http://www.npr.org/templates/story/story.php?storyId=5637480

29. D. Yost, "Interim Report of Student Attendance Data and Accountability System." The State of Ohio, Auditor of State. Columbus, OH, October 4, 2012.

30. B. Bush and J.S. Richards, *"A culture of deceit in Columbus schools,"* The Columbus *Dispatch*, 28 January, 2014. Available: http://www.dispatch.com/content/stories/local/2014/01/28/1-columbus-school-audit-yost.html

31. J.S Richards and B. Bush, "FBI joins probe of schools' records," *The Columbus Dispatch*, 26 October, 2012. Available: http://www.dispatch.com/content/stories/local/2012/10/26/fbi-joins-probe-of-schools-records.html

32. K. Bellware, "Ex-Chicago Schools Chief Indicted in Bribery, Kickback Scheme," *The Huffington Post*, 8 October, 2015. Available: http://www.huffingtonpost.com/entry/barbara-byrd-bennette-indicted_5616c8fce4b0e66ad4c6fe9e

33. "St. John's University President Retires amid Embezzlement Scandal," *University Herald*, 4 May, 2013. Available: http://www.universityherald.com/articles/3184/20130504/st-john-s-university-president-retires-amid-embezzlement-scandal.htm

34. C. Dolmetsch, "Two in Columbia University Theft Get Prision Terms," *Bloomberg Business*, 24 September, 2012. Available: http://www.bloomberg.com/news/articles/2012-09-24/columbia-university-fraud-convict-gets-7-to-21-year-sentence

35. W.G. Schulz, "A Puzzle Named Bengu Sezen," *Science and Technology*, 8 August, 2011. Available: https://pubs.acs.org/cen/science/89/8932sci1.html

36. M. Miller, "Ex-PSU Professor Craig Grimes sentenced to federal prison for research grant fraud," *PennLive*, 30 November, 2012. Available: http://www.pennlive.com/midstate/index.ssf/2012/11/ex-psu_prof_craig_grimes_sente.html

37. S. Sneed, [Audit Manager at Winston Salem State University]. Interview (April 23, 2015).

38. D. Metts, [Director, Office of Internal Audit and Director, Internal Audit Committee at Tennessee Technological University]. Interview (April 23, 2015).

39. "Internal Audit," Winston Salem State University, Winston Salem, NC. (n.d.). Available: https://www.wssu.edu/administration/internal-audit/documents/hotline-policy-procedures.pdf

40. T. Mead (2014, February 27). Discouraging Cheating with Detection, Deterrence and Investigative Systems: Three Systems Compared New York, Atlanta, Georgia and Washington, DC. Paper presented at the International Center on Academic Integrity Conference 2014, Jacksonville, Florida. Available: http://www.academicintegrity.org/icai/assets/ICAI_2014_Tonya_Mead.pdf

41. "The False Claims Act: A Primer," US Department of Justice, Washington, DC, April 22, 2011. Available: http://www.justice.gov/sites/default/files/civil/legacy/2011/04/22/C-FRAUDS_FCA_Primer.pdf

42. Mead, T. (2015). Risk Assessment Data Quality and Security for School and Campus Records. Unpublished Manuscript.

43. The Federal False Claims Act, Financial Aid Fraud of 2000(20 U.S.C. § 1097(a).

44. R. S. Brand, " Note: Student Loan Fraud: Intent to Deceive Not Required Under Section 1097(A) of the Higher Education Act. 10 ," *DePaul Business Law Journal*, 63. Fall/Winter, 1997. Available: https://litigation-essentials.lexisnexis.com/webcd/app?action=DocumentDisplay&crawlid=1&doctype=cite&docid=10+DePaul+Bus.+L.J.+63&srctype=smi&srcid=3B15&key=1428b977090f941aea4776103f3d8887

45. Wallin & Klarich, Tustin, CA, "Consequences of Filing a Fraudulent Claim for Student Financial Aid," July 1, 2014. Available: https://www.wklaw.com/fraudulent-claim-for-student-financial-aid/

46. McKinsey & Company, New York, NY , "Enduring Ideas of the 7-s Framework," March 1998. Available: http://www.mckinsey.com/insights/strategy/ enduring_ideas_the_7-s_framework

47. R.W. Griffin and G. Moorhead, *Organizational Behavior.* Boston, MA: Houghton Mifflin, 1986.

48. A. McNeal, "The Role of the Board in Fraud Risk Management," *Director Notes.* The Conference New York, NY, 2011. Available: https://www.conference-board.org/ retrievefile.cfm?filename=TCB-DN-V3N21-111.pdf&type=subsite

49. Mead,T. (2015). Risk Assessment Data Quality and Security for School and Campus Records. Unpublished Manuscript.

50. D. Belkin and A. Fuller, "Accreditors of Colleges Weighing Crackdown," *The Wall Street Journal,* 27-28, June, 2015.

51. C.R. Jeffery, "Criminal Behavior and Learning Theory," *Criminal Law, Criminology & Police Science*, Vol 56, Issue 3, Article 4, p. 294-300, Fall 1965.

52. L. Trevino, G.R. Weaver, D. Gibson, and B. Toffler "Managing ethics and legal compliance: What works and what hurts," California Management Review, 41 (2), p. 131-150, 1999.

53. M. Brown, L. Trevino, L. and D. Harrison, "Ethical leadership: A social learning perspective for construct development and testing." *Organizational Behavior and Human Decision Processes*, 97(2), p. 117-134, 2005.

54. A.A. Ardichvili (University of Minnesota and Center for Ethical Business Cultures) , D.J. Jondle, and J.A. Mitchell (Center for Ethical Business Cultures), Minneapolis, MN: *Characteristics of Ethical Business Cultures*, 2008. Available: http:// files.eric.ed.gov/fulltext/ED501640.pdf

55. Association of Certified Fraud Examiners (ACFE), Austin, TX, "Tone at the Top: How Management Can Prevent Fraud in the Workplace," (n.d.). Available: http:// www.acfe.com/uploadedFiles/ACFE_Website/Content/documents/tone-at-the-top-research.pdf

56. H.L. Packer, *The Limits of the Criminal Sanction.* Stanford, CA: Stanford University Press, 1968.

57. F. Zimring and G. Hawkins, *Deterrence: The Legal Threat in Crime Control,* Chicago, IL: University of Chicago Press, 1973.

58. J. Andenaes, *Punishment and Deterrence,* Ann Arbor, MI: University of Michigan Press, 1974.

59. D.L. McCabe, L.K. Trevino and K.D. Butterfield, "Academic integrity in honor code and non-honor code environments," *Journal of Higher Education,* 70, p. 211-234, 1999.

60. "Educational Financial Management: Weak Internal Controls Led to Instances of Fraud and Other Improper Payments," US Government Accountability Office, Washington, DC. Report # GAO-02-513T , April 10, 2002.

61. "Test Security Leading Practices," US Government Accountability Office, Washington, DC. Report # GAO-13-495, May 16, 2013.

62. "Improving Data Quality for Title I Standards, Assessments, and Accountability Reporting," US Department of Education, Office of Elementary and Secondary Education, Washington, DC, April 2006.

63. "An OIG Perspective on Improving Accountability and Integrity in ESEA Programs," US Department of Education, Office of Inspector General, Washington, DC, Report # ED-OIG/S09H0007, October 2007.

64. "Final Management Information Report Fraud in Title I- Funded Tutoring Programs," US Department of Education, Office of Inspector General, Washington, DC, Control #X42N0001, . October 2013. Available: http://www2.ed.gov/about/offices/list/oig/auditreports/fy2013/x42n0001.pdf

65. "FY2014 Agency Financial Report," US Department of Education, Washington, DC, November 14, 2014. Available: https://www2.ed.gov/about/reports/annual/2014report/2014-afr-2g-mgmt-assurances.pdf

66. "Investigative Reports," Office of the Inspector General, Department of Education and U.S. Attorney's Office, Washington, DC. April 24, 2014. Available: http://www2.ed.gov/about/offices/list/oig/invtreports/dc042014.html

67. "OIG Fraud Hotline: Fraud Prevention, "US Department of Education, Office of Inspector General, Washington, DC. Available: www2.ed.gov/about/offices/list/oig/hotline.html

68. R. Wortley, "A Classification of Techniques for Controlling Situational Precipitators of Crime," *Security Journal.* 14: p. 63-82, 2001.

69. J.E. Murphy, "Using Incentives in Your Compliance and Ethics Program," Society of Corporate Compliance and Ethics, Minneapolis, MN, 2011.

70. T. Mead (2015). Classification Table of White Collar Crime Prevention in Education. Unpublished Manuscript.

70. T. Mead (2015). Classification Table of White Collar Crime Prevention in Education. Unpublished Manuscript.

71. "Guidelines Manual," US Sentencing Commission, Washington, DC, 2004.

72. "The New Sentencing Guideline for Fraud Cases. U.S. Sentencing Commission Amendments (took effect November 1, 2015)," *Rdeliason.com* 4 January, 2016. Available: https://rdeliason.com/2015/05/04/the-new-sentensing-guideline-for-fraud-cases/

73. T. Mead (2015). Risk Assessment Data Quality and Security for School and Campus Records. Unpublished Manuscript.

74. "Class Notes," class notes for Cyber Law and White Collar Crime, Cyber- 168W, Instructor T. Thorston, Texas A&M Engineering Extension Service, 2011.

75. "Class Notes," class notes for Information Security for Everyone, Cyber AWR-175W, Instructor T. Thorston, Texas A&M Engineering Extension Service, 2011.

76. "Class Notes," class notes for Information Risk Management, Cyber AWR-177W, Instructor T. Thorston, Texas A&M Engineering Extension Service, 2012.

77. "Sample Framework for a Fraud Control Policy," Information Systems Audit and Control Association, Rolling Meadows, IL (n.d.). Available: http://www.isaca.org/chapters2/Western-Michigan/events/Documents/Fraud%20Risk%20Assessment_Handouts.pdf

78. Association of Governing Boards and United Educators, Washington, DC and Chevy Chase, MD, "The State of Enterprise Risk Management at Colleges and Universities Today," 2009.

79. Applied Risk Management, LLC, Stoneham, MA, "Campus Violence Prevention and Response: Best Practices for Massachusetts Higher Education," for the Massachusetts Department of Higher Education, June 2008.

80. Mead,T. (2015). Risk Assessment Data Quality and Security for School and Campus Records. Unpublished Manuscript.

81. The Committee of Sponsoring Organizations of the Treadway Commission (COSO). "1999 analysis of cases of fraudulent financial statements investigated by the US Securities and Exchange Commission (SEC)," 1999.

82. Mead,T. (2015). Risk Assessment Data Quality and Security for School and Campus Records. Unpublished Manuscript.

83. D.S. Nagin, "Deterrence in the Twenty-First Century," The Center for Evidence-Based Crime Policy, George Mason University, Fairfax, VA. May 17, 2013. Available: http://cebcp.org/wp-content/CRIM760/Nagin-2013.pdf

84. L. Segal, *Battling Corruption in America's Public Schools.*, 1ˢᵗ ed. Cambridge MA: Harvard University Press, March 2005.

85. Mead,T. (2015). Risk Assessment Data Quality and Security for School and Campus Records. Unpublished Manuscript.

86. T. Mead (2015). Link Analysis for Test Integrity and Exam Security. Unpublished Manuscript.

87. United Nations Office on Drugs and Crime, Vienna, Austria, "A Manual on Monitoring and Evaluation for Alternative Development Projects," (n.d.). Available: https://www.unodc.org/documents/alternative-development/Manual_MonitoringEval.pdf

88. H.F. Ladd, "Now is the time to experiment with inspections for school accountability," *The Brown Center Chalkboard.* Brookings Institution, Washington, DC, 26 May, 2016. Available: http://www.brookings.edu/blogs/brown-center-chalkboard/posts/2016/05/26-inspections-school-accountability-ladd

89. E. Barnett and C. Weems, "Program Review Essentials and Top 10 Compliance Findings," Session 33, *2015 FSA Training Conference for Financial Aid Professionals,* December 1-5, 2015, Las Vegas, NV.

90. "Program Review Guide," US Department of Education, Washington, DC, 2009. Available: http://www.ifap.ed.gov/programrevguide/attachments/2009Program ReviewGuide.pdf

91. "Ten Facts about K-12 Education Funding," US Department of Education, US Department of Education Budget Service and the National Center for Education Statistics. Washington, DC, 2014. Available: http://www2.ed.gov/about/overview/ fed/10facts/index.html?exp

92. "FY2014 Agency Financial Report," US Department of Education, Washington, DC, November 14, 2014. Available: https://www2.ed.gov/about/reports/ annual/2014report/2014-afr-2g-mgmt-assurances.pdf

93. "Semiannual Report No. 32. Corrective Action Plan Resolutions," US Department of Education, Washington, DC, May 2005.

94. "A-133 Federal Audit Reports (2010, 2013, and 2014)" Federal Audit Clearing House, Washington, DC. Available: https://harvester.census.gov/facdissem/ Main.aspx

95. "FY2014 Agency Financial Report," US Department of Education, Washington, DC, November 14, 2014. Available: https://www2.ed.gov/about/reports/ annual/2014report/2014-afr-2g-mgmt-assurances.pdf

96. "The Blue Book Volume 2- Student Eligibility," US Department of Education, Office of Federal Financial Aid, Washington, DC, January 2013. Available:http:// ifap.ed.gov/bbook/attachments/2013BlueBookVol2Ch1.pdf

97. "State Nonfiscal Survey of Public Elementary and Secondary Education, 1990-91 through 2012-13; Private School Universe Survey (PSS), 1995-96 through 2011-12; National Elementary and Secondary Enrollment Projection Model, 1972 through 2024; Integrated Postsecondary Education Data System (IPEDS), Fall Enrollment Survey, " US Department of Education, National Center for Education Statistics, Common Core of Data (CCD), Washington, DC. IPEDS-EF:90-99, March 2015.

98. C. Ronez, "Whistleblowing Policy," *Risk Management Demystified*, 12 January, 2016. Available:https://riskmanagementdemystified.com/2016/01/12/whistleblowing-policy-how-to-get-it-right-to-have-an-effective-tool-for-fraud-prevention-and-detection-in-your-organization/

99. Ethics Resource Center, Arlington, VA, "Inside the Mind of a Whistleblower," 2012.

100. "Semiannual Report No. 32. Corrective Action Plan Resolutions," US Department of Education, Washington, DC, May 2005.

101. Association of Certified Fraud Examiners (ACFE), Austin, TX, "Tone at the Top: How Management Can Prevent Fraud in the Workplace," (n.d.). Available: http://www.acfe.com/uploadedFiles/ACFE_Website/Content/documents/tone-at-the-top-research.pdf

102. American Society for Quality, Service Quality Division, Milwaukee, WI, "Body of Knowledge," September 18, 2009. Available: http://asq.org/service/body-of-knowledge/tools-corrective-preventive-action

103. Class Notes," class notes for Information Security Basics, Cyber 173-W, Instructor W. Pennington, Texas A&M Engineering Extension Service, 2010.

104. E.D. Zwicky, S. Cooper, and D. B. Chapman, D.B. *Building Internet Firewalls,* 2nd ed. Sebastopol, CA: O'Reilly & Associates, 2000.

105. SANS Institute, Bethesda, MA, "Information Security Managing Risk with Defense in Depth," 2003. Retrieved from: http://www.sans.org/reading-room/whitepapers/infosec/information-security-managing-risk-defense-in-depth-1224

106. Mead,T. (2015). Risk Assessment Data Quality and Security for School and Campus Records. Unpublished Manuscript. Adapted from US Census Overview of Data Disclosure Policies; https://www.census.gov/srd/papers/pdf/rr92-09.pdf and http://fpg.unc.edu/sites/fpg.unc.edu/files/resources/reports-and-policy-briefs/DaSyDeidentificationGlossary.pdf

107. "Overview of Data Disclosure Policies," US Census, Washington, DC, (n.d.) Available: https://www.census.gov/srd/papers/pdf/rr92-09.pdf

108. "Data De-identification Glossary," Frank Porter Graham Child Development Institute, The University of North Carolina- Chapel Hill, Chapel Hill, NC. (n.d.). Available: http://fpg.unc.edu/sites/fpg.unc.edu/files/resources/reports-and-policy-briefs/DaSyDeidentificationGlossary.pdf

109. Class Notes," class notes for Information Security Basics, Cyber 173-W, Instructor W. Pennington, Texas A&M Engineering Extension Service, 2010.

110. "Children's Educational Records and Privacy," Fordham Center on Law and Information Policy, New York, NY, October 28, 2009.

111. Data Quality Campaign, Washington, DC, "Supporting Data Use While Protecting the Privacy, Security and Confidentiality of Student Information: A Primer for State Policymakers," January 15, 2012. Available: http://dataquality campaign.org/resource/supporting-data-use-protecting-privacy-security-confidentiality-student-information-primer-state-policy-makers/

112. P.F. Drucker, *The Philosophy and Practice of Management.* New York, NY: Harper & Row, 1954.

113. R. Riley, [Institute for Fraud Prevention] Correspondence (March 26, 2015)

114. S. Klepper, and D.S. Nagin, "The Deterrent Effect of Perceived Certainty and Severity of Punishment," *Criminology,* Vol. 27, Issue 4, p. 721-746, November 1989

115. K.R. Williams and R. Hawkins, "Deterrence Theory and Non Legal Sanctions." in *Encyclopedia of Criminological Theory,* F. T. Cullen and P. Wilcox Eds, Thousand Oaks, CA: Sage Publications, 2010.

116. M. Torny, *Crime and Justice, Volume 42: Crime and Justice in America: 1975-2025,* Chicago, IL: University Chicago Press, 2013.

117. McKinsey & Company, New York, NY, "Enduring Ideas of the 7-s Framework," March 1998. Available: http://www.mckinsey.com/insights/strategy/enduring_ideas_the_7-s_framework

118. H.M. Trice and J. Beyer, *The cultures of work organizations,* Englewood Cliffs, NJ: Prentice Hall, 1993.

119. Association of Certified Fraud Examiners (ACFE), Austin, TX, " 2014 Global Fraud Study: Report to the Nations on Occupational Fraud and Abuse," 2015.

120. L. Segal, *Battling Corruption in America's Public Schools.,* 1st ed. Cambridge MA: Harvard University Press, March 2005.

121. I.G. Sarason and B.R. Sarason, *Abnormal Psychology: The Problem of Maladaptive Behavior,* 11th ed. Upper Saddle River, NJ: Prentice Hall, 2005.

122. R. Tedlow, *Denial: Why Business Leaders Fail to Look Facts in the Face—and What to Do About It,* New York, NY: Penguin Random House, 2010.

123. L. Berkowitz, *Aggression: Its Causes, Consequences, and Control,* Philadelphia, PA: Temple University Press, 1993.

124. D.D. Van Fleet and RW. Griffin, "Dysfunctional Organization Culture: The Role of Leadership in Motivating Dysfunctional Work Behaviors," *Journal of Managerial Psychology,* Vol. 21, Issue 8, p. 698- 708, 2006.

125. J. Kerr and J.W. Slocum, "Managing corporate culture through reward systems," *Academy of Management Executives,* Vol, 19, No. 4, p. 130-138, 2005. .

126. C.R. Jeffery, "Criminal Behavior and Learning Theory," *Criminal Law, Criminology & Police Science,* Vol 56, Issue 3, Article 4, p. 294-300, Fall 1965.

127. D.D. Van Fleet and RW. Griffin, "Dysfunctional Organization Culture: The Role of Leadership in Motivating Dysfunctional Work Behaviors," *Journal of Managerial Psychology,* Vol. 21, Issue 8, p. 698- 708, 2006.

128. Mead,T. (2015). Shared Values and Organizational Culture Alignment Checklist. Unpublished Manuscript.

129 "Internal Audit," University of Louisiana Office of Internal Audits and Ethics Liaison," Louisville, KY. (n.d.) Available: https://internalaudit.nsula.edu/fraud-awareness/

130. C.R. Jeffery, "Criminal Behavior and Learning Theory," *Criminal Law, Criminology & Police Science,* Vol 56, Issue 3, Article 4, p. 294-300, Fall 1965.

131. I. Onwudiwe, J. Odo, and E. Onyeozili, "Deterrence Theory," in *Encyclopedia of Prisons & Correctional Facilities,* M. Bosworth, Ed. Thousand Oaks, CA: SAGE Publications, Inc, p. 234-238, pp. 234- 238. Doi: http:// dx.doi.org/10.4135/9781412952514.n91

132. L.J. Fennelly, *Handbook of Loss Prevention and Crime Prevention,* Burlington, MA: Elsevier Butterworth-Heinemann, 2005.

133. Z. Hoskins, "The Moral Permissibility of Punishment," *Internet Encyclopedia of Philosophy,* 2011. Available: http://www.iep.utm.edu/m-p-puni/

134. C. Ronez, "Whistleblowing Policy," *Risk Management Demystified*, 12 January, 2016. Available: https://riskmanagementdemystified.com/2016/01/12/whistleblowing-policy-how-to-get-it-right-to-have-an-effective-tool-for-fraud-prevention-and-detection-in-your-organization/

135. E. Campbell, "The ethics of teaching as a moral profession," *Curriculum Inquiry*, 38 (4), p. 357-385, 2008.

136. Association of Certified Fraud Examiners- ACFE, Austin, Texas.

137. Ethics Resource Center, Arlington, VA, "Inside the Mind of a Whistleblower," 2012.

138. The Center for Audit Quality, Washington, DC, "The Fraud Resistant Organization," November 17, 2014. Available: http://www.thecaq.org/docs/anti-fraud-collaboration-report/the-fraud-resistant-organization.pdf?sfvrsn=4

139. W.S. Albrecht, K. R. Howe, and M. B. Romney. *Deterring Fraud: The Internal Auditor's Perspective*. Altomonte Springs, FL: The Institute of Internal Auditors' Research Foundation, 1984.

Appendices
A. Heightened Cash Management Report, Federal Student Aid. U.S. Department of Education, Available: https://studentaid.ed.gov/sa/about/data-center/school/hcm.

B. Staffing Changes in U.S. Colleges and Universities, The New England Center for Investigative Reporting, February 6, 2014.

C. Federal Audit Clearinghouse, US Office of Management and Budget, Available: https://harvester.census.gov/facweb/

Contact email: tonya@ishareknowledge.com

ABOUT THE AUTHOR

Photo Courtesy: Jason
Dixon Photography

Tonya J. Mead, Certified Fraud Examiner, Private Investigator, MBA, MA is also a School Psychologist and Certified Regular K-12 Administrator. She is the president of Shared Knowledge, LLC a private investigations firm in Virginia and District of Columbia http:// ishareknowledge.com

She is a recipient of the 2013 Cafritz Award for Excellence in Government Service and Public Leadership in recognition for her work in designing and managing an investigative program to transform the perceptions of the public school systems in the District of Columbia.